Latin America and the Glob

Latin America and the Global Economy

Export Trade and the Threat of Protection

Edited by

Ronald Fischer

First published 2001 by
PALGRAVE
Houndmills, Basingstoke, Hampshire RG21 6XS and
175 Fifth Avenue, New York, N. Y. 10010
Companies and representatives throughout the world

PALGRAVE is the new global academic imprint of
St. Martin's Press LLC Scholarly and Reference Division and
Palgrave Publishers Ltd (formerly Macmillan Press Ltd).

ISBN 0–333–77458–2

This book is printed on paper suitable for recycling and
made from fully managed and sustained forest sources.

A catalogue record for this book is available
from the British Library.

Library of Congress Cataloging-in-Publication Data
Latin America and the global economy : export trade and the threat of
protection / edited by Ronald D. Fischer.
        p. cm.
Includes bibliographical references and index.
ISBN 0–333–77458–2
        1. Nontariff trade barriers—Latin America. 2. Protectionism—Latin
America. I. Fischer, Ronald D.

HF1430 .L38 2000
382'.7—dc21

                                                00–031127

10   9   8   7   6   5   4   3   2   1
10   09 08 07 06 05 04 03 02 01

Printed and bound in Great Britain by
Antony Rowe Ltd, Chippenham, Wiltshire

Contents

List of Figures and Tables

Figures

Tables

Preface

As tariffs and quota barriers have come down in the developed world, developing countries face new forms of protectionism. These barriers to trade may be even more insidious than traditional barriers because they hide behind customs procedures, standards and regulations, or consist of threats to apply protectionist legislation such as anti-dumping regulations. Even though it is difficult to find quantitative statistics on these measures, they are known to have a large negative impact on international trade. There are few studies of the impact of these measures, and those devoted to their effects on developing countries are even fewer. This book attempts to respond to these issues by providing both theoretical papers that help to analyze the effects of the new forms of protection and a set of case studies that help appreciate their importance for a small open developing economy.

This book is the result of the joint work and discussion of the members of the Centro de Economía Aplicada (CEA) of the Departamento de Ingeniería Industrial of the Universidad de Chile. The objective of CEA is to apply economic theory to real-life problems, in particular to the problems that have slowed the development of Latin American countries. This project was supported by a grant from the Andrew W. Mellon Foundation, to whose generosity we are grateful. As is usual, the authors of the different articles are responsible for their own opinions.

RONALD FISCHER

This book is dedicated to Danielle

Notes on the Contributors

All chapters of this book were written while the authors were affiliated to the Centro de Economía Aplicada (CEA) of the Departamento de Ingeniería Industrial of the Universidad de Chile.

Eduardo Engel is Full Professor and Director of CEA. He has been Visiting Professor at Harvard University, MIT and Stanford University. He has published in *American Economic Review, Econometrica, Quarterly Journal of Economics, Review of Economic Studies* and other journals. He has consulted for the International Monetary Fund, the World Bank and other multilateral agencies.

Gabriel Fierro who is currently vice-dean of students in the Facultad de Ciencias Físicas y Matemáticas of the Universidad de Chile, has written and consulted on energy and environmental management and economics.

Ronald Fischer has taught at the University of Virginia and is Associate Professor at CEA. He has written extensively on new forms of protection and international trade, and has published in *American Economic Review, Quarterly Journal of Economics,* the *Journal of International Economics* and other journals. He has consulted for the World Bank, the Inter–American Development Bank and other multilateral agencies.

Jorge Friedman is currently an economics consultant and teaches at the Universidad de Santiago. He has specialized in development and tax evasion issues and is a regular consultant for the World Bank and national organizations.

Patricio Meller is Full Professor at CEA. He is along time member of CIEPLAN. He has been director of both CIEPLAN and the Departamento de Ingeniería Industrial of the Universidad de Chile. He is a specialist in International Trade and Latin American Economics and has written numerous books on these subjects, including *Western Hemisphere Trade Integration: A Canadian–Latin American Dialogue* (co-editor R. G. Lipsey) (1997), and a history of the Chilean economy published in 1996.

Alejandra Mizala is an Associate Professor at CEA. She specializes in labor economics and has published in *Economic Development and Cultural Change, World Development,* the *Journal of Human Resources,* the *Review of Income and Wealth* among others. She has consulted for the World Bank, the Inter–American Development Bank and for the Chilean Ministry of Education and other national and international organizations.

Raúl O'Ryan is an Associate Professor at CEA. He specializes in environmental economics and has published in the *Journal of Environmental Economics and Management, Environmental and Resource Economics, World Development* and other journals. He has worked on the design of environmental standards for contaminants in mining and in urban pollution and has done extensive consulting for various national and international organizations.

Pilar Romaguera is Associate Professor at CEA. She is a specialist in labor economics and is currently doing research for the World Bank and for the Chilean government. She has published in *Economic Development and Cultural Change, Applied Economics,* the *Journal of Human Resources* and other journals.

Pablo Serra is an Associate Professor at CEA. He has been a visiting professor at the University of Virginia, and has written extensively in trade and in energy economics for *Energy Economics, Quarterly Journal of Economics, International Economic Review, World Development* and other journals. He is a member of the Chilean Antitrust Commission and has consulted for the World Bank, the Inter-American Development Bank and other multilateral agencies.

Andrés Ulloa is currently pursuing his PhD at the Agricultural and Resource Economics Department, University of Maryland.

1
Introduction

Ronald Fischer[*]

1 The new protectionism and Latin America

Latin American countries are liberalizing their trade, following a long period in which the preferred path to development was based on import substitution. Along the way, these countries have discovered that the rules of international trade are not as transparent as they appear in textbooks. There are multifarious mechanisms, denoted collectively as The New Faces of Protectionism, which prevent Latin American countries from gaining secure access to foreign markets, despite the fact that they face low tariffs for most of their exports.

Between 1945 and 1970, trade among developed countries was progressively liberalized, largely through multilateral agreements to reduce tariffs. The success of these agreements was so complete that developed countries have set near-zero tariffs on the majority of the products they import, especially from other developed countries. In fact, average tariffs in these countries have come down from 40 per cent in 1947 to 4 per cent in 1994 (Staiger 1995). This experience stands in contrast to that of Latin American countries which, encouraged by ECLAC (Economic Commission for Latin America and the Caribbean), embarked on a heterodox development strategy based on import substitution and did not involve themselves in the negotiations to liberalize trade. The shift in economic focus which began in Chile during the mid-1970s led to a reassessment of trade in Latin America. By that time, however, the liberalizing thrust in developed countries had declined, and the impediments to trade which are the subject of this book became relevant.

* This article received support from FONDECYT Project 1950513.

The new protectionism differs from classical forms of protectionism such as tariffs and quotas. It consists of measures such as minimum quality standards, ecological dumping allegations, threats of anti-dumping and anti-subsidy measures, phytosanitary restrictions and technical barriers to trade. In view of the growing importance of these forms of protection, we must develop new tools of analysis in order to understand their effects and to limit the damage to the trade of countries engaged in the trade liberalization process. The purpose of this book is to analyze these new forms of protection from two points of view: first, via theoretical studies of contingent protection and of the protectionist use of minimum quality standards; and, second, through five case studies of sectors affected by such measures in a small open country. The case studies refer to the Chilean economy, but the lessons are applicable to the other Latin American which have followed the trend towards openness and exports.

There are good reasons to believe that the new forms of protection may seriously affect the development of a small open economy's exports. As an example, in recent years the Chilean economy has been affected by measures which include:

1 new law governing the recycling of packaging materials (the Töpfer Law in Germany) making it prohibitive to export fresh fruit packed in wooden boxes. The consequence was a significant increase in the costs of fruit exports and the bankruptcy of firms involved in box manufacture.

2 An unilateral ban on Chilean fruit exports to the United States, because of the discovery of two grapes supposedly contaminated with cyanide.

3 Allegations of dumping and phytosanitary problems in fishmeal exports to Mexico, a country with which Chile had recently signed a free trade agreement.

4 A dumping allegation affecting salmon exports to the United States; salmon being one of the biggest growth industries of recent years.

5 Difficulties in exporting wooden moldings to Canada because the standards of that country require them to be made of a single piece of wood; whereas in Chile moldings are assembled out of shorter pieces.

The new protectionism has led to the most recent multilateral negotiating rounds concentrating less on lowering tariffs and more on reducing these new trade barriers. This was already evident in the Tokyo

Round of the GATT (General Agreement on Tariffs and Trade) which ended in 1979, which was the first round that attempted to make progress in this field. However, eliminating non-tariff barriers has proved to be considerably more difficult than expected. Unlike the simple goal of lowering tariffs, today's negotiators face a host of protectionist tools which are difficult to classify and quantify.

1.1 Standards with protectionist effects

From their beginnings in 1947, the initial GATT agreements established that standards and norms should not be used with a protectionist intent.[1] The original GATT agreements proved unable to prevent the use of protectionist standards, since they lacked effective mechanisms to ascertain whether a country was breaking the rules. Furthermore, it was argued that the setting of standards was the prerogative of each country, and that to restrict their use infringed on national sovereignty.

In some cases – for example trade restrictions based on the use of standards (quality, phytosanitary, environmental and technical standards) – it is difficult to distinguish between legitimate domestic policy decisions and those that conceal protectionist aims. Is it acceptable, for example, for the United States to impose a measure that supposedly protects dolphins, but which puts foreign competitors in the tuna market at a disadvantage? Is it legitimate for the United States to criticize Japan's competition policy and accuse it of being protectionist? Given that such measures enjoy support both from the import substituting firms as well as from organized interest groups (environmentalists, for example), it is politically difficult for governments to avoid using them. The GATT Uruguay Round tried to establish rules to regulate this protectionist behavior, going beyond those established in previous rounds. Membership in the new World Trade Organization (WTO), GATT's successor, is open only to countries that are signatories of the expanded GATT agreed in the Uruguay Round and a series of additional requirements.[2] However, the effectiveness of the new agreements will only be known when jurisprudence is accumulated under the new rules. The examples that follow show the universal use of standards in protection.

1.1.1 The case of hormones in meat

In 1989 the European Union (EU) banned the sale of meat and side-products produced with natural or synthetic hormones. On the basis of GATT rules, the United States alleged that there was no internationally recognized scientific evidence to show that treatment with growth hormones is harmful. In response to the exclusion of exports worth an estimated US\$ 97 million, the US imposed tariffs equivalent to this amount on products coming from the European Union, and tried, unsuccessfully, to get a WTO panel to resolve the case (National Research Council 1995). Recently, the WTO panel ruled in favor of the US, allowing the US to suspend concessions (i.e. raise tariffs) on US\$ 117MM of imports from the European Union.

1.1.2   The case of automobile efficiency standards (CAFE)

In 1975 the US introduced legislation designed to increase car fuel efficiency, the CAFE (Corporate Average Fuel Efficiency Standards), setting minimum standards of fuel economy for automobiles. CAFE penalized car companies whose average fleet (i.e. cars sold in a year) fell below a certain standard. The efficiency standard, currently 27.5 miles per gallon, implies that a vehicle manufacturer has to pay a US\$ 50 fine for each mile per gallon under the standard, on each vehicle sold.[3] This type of standard penalizes foreign manufacturers specializing in luxury vehicles, whose average efficiency is worse than the norm. On the other hand, North American manufacturers can compensate for the high fuel consumption of their expensive cars with sales of small cars, thereby increasing average efficiency. The EEC (European Economic Community) filed a complaint with a GATT arbitration panel. The EEC argued that a tax based on the fuel efficiency of each automobile model or, alternatively, a gas tax was the best way of increasing efficiency. The US, for its part, argued on formal grounds that the measures were not discriminatory and that, in any case, they were within their rights according to GATT Article XX (dealing with the conservation of natural resources). The panel found in favor of the EEC but only on the basis of a technicality. It recommended that the US make the necessary changes to avoid discriminating between automobiles produced by the same company but it accepted the United States' argument regarding the use of averages, which was the fundamental point in discussion.

1.1.3   Argentine meat and hoof-and-mouth disease

Over the last two decades Chile has managed to eradicate a series of agricultural plagues, such as hoof-and-mouth disease and the fruit fly, and this has enabled Chilean agricultural products to be exported to countries which impose strict sanitary standards. In most cases, the elimination of plagues has been beneficial for the country, but there are some cases where the attempt to exterminate a plague may be interpreted as a protectionist measure. Consider the eradication of hoof-and-mouth disease, to which Chile has devoted significant resources, mainly due to the fact that hoof-and-mouth disease was endemic in Argentina.[4] The declared aim of the policy was to eliminate hoof-and-mouth disease to allow Chile to export beef. However, during the long period in which this policy has been in force, Chile has exported only small amounts of meat. This is understandable, for Chile is a country which has no comparative advantages in beef production. However, the policy managed to reduce meat imports from Argentina, as it prevented imports of cattle on the hoof due to phytosanitary restrictions. Only in recent years has it been possible to import vacuum-wrapped off-the-bone beef from Argentina, and this has given rise to numerous complaints from Chilean beef producers. Thus, the effort to eliminate hoof-and-mouth disease can also be seen as a mechanism for suppressing imports of Argentine beef. Furthermore, Chile has recently introduced a non-standard method for grading meat, causing Argentinian (and US) beef producers to complain that it represents a technical barrier to trade.[5]

1.2 Contingent protection

Contingent protection is another difficult problem that has been discussed in the GATT-WTO negotiating rounds. The distinguishing feature about anti-subsidy and anti-dumping measures (as well as similar measures such as safeguard clauses imposed when imports grow too fast) is that they threaten exports even when not in force; hence the term contingent protection. The effect of contingent protection is due to the implicit threat of punishment, unless the foreign exporter behaves more "cooperatively" with the domestic industry. The mere existence of anti-dumping measures changes the environment faced by an exporting firm, as it is threatened with the possibility of punishment if the importing country decides to carry out an investigation, which in general occurs at the petition of domestic competitors. One of the big achievements of the Tokyo Round was to establish codes which set rules for the design of national anti-subsidy (countervailing duties) and anti-dumping legislation. However, attempts to restrict the abuse of contingent protection by bringing it under a GATT (WTO) jurisdiction code have not been completely satisfactory (Marceau 1994), despite the fact that the recent Uruguay Round managed to limit abuses in the administration of the codes in some countries. For example, until the Uruguay Round, the United States used a series of administrative laws which biased the results in favor of declaring dumping (Boltuck and Litan 1991). After this negotiating round, the US agreed to modify its rules to reduce such biases. However, following complaints by the traditional users of anti-dumping legislation, it was decided to weaken the new standards by introducing exceptions as well as other changes which reproduce the protectionist characteristics of traditional US antidumping legislation (Palmeter 1995)

1.2.1 The use of anti-dumping legislation

Anti-dumping measures are especially appropriate for protectionist purposes. By *dumping* we mean price discrimination between countries or, alternatively, the practice of selling in export markets at a price below cost. The difference between the two prices[6] is known as the margin of dumping, and when this margin is positive the foreign firm is said to be engaged in dumping. From a theoretical point of view, anti-dumping regulation is redundant. Indeed, on paper, its goal is to prevent predatory competition from abroad, which does not require a special law but only the extension of national anti-monopoly legislation to cover competition with foreign countries. However, as many authors have insisted (Prusa and Hansen 1993; Staiger and Wolak 1994), the more elastic nature of anti-dumping legislation makes it possible to exercise protectionism in sectors facing greater international competition due to the tariff reductions arising from multilateral agreements.

In the period 1980–88, the US, the main user of these measures, instigated 411 anti-dumping actions, of which 147 resulted in a favorable outcome, 108 were withdrawn by their proponents, while the remainder were rejected.[7] According to the WTO anti-dumping code, after initiating an investigation, three circumstances have to be demonstrated before dumping can be punished. Firstly, it has to be shown that dumping is actually taking place, i.e. that there is price discrimination between countries.[8] After showing the existence of a positive dumping margin, the regulator has to show that the industry has suffered *material damage*,[9] in other words, a substantial damage. Finally, it must be shown that dumping is responsible for the damage. If these conditions are fulfilled, the code authorizes the importing country to impose a surcharge high enough to eliminate the margin of dumping. Alternatively, the exporter can make a commitment to raise its prices (known as a price undertaking).

In the US, in order to avoid political pressures the procedure to determine whether dumping or material damage is occurring is administrative.[10] However, the US Congress has modified the administrative procedures and introduced a bias towards declaring the existence of dumping even when this does not exist. In addition to the protectionist effects of punishment, mere investigation has a significant effect on exporters. Staiger and Wolak (1994) have suggested that this is due not only to the fact that the legislation allows retroactive measures, but that in addition the investigative process itself has protectionist effects, and this is one of the reasons for their existence. This is the type of reaction that gives rise to the theory of Contingent Protection (Fischer 1987; Fischer 1992; Reitzes 1993; Prusa 1994).

2 Theoretical aspects

This book is divided into two parts. The theoretical section of this book explores both forms of protection: those based on the threat of future punishment and those based on the use of quality standards or norms. The second section begins with an overview of the reforms in trade policy in Latin America, their effects and the threat posed by the new forms of protection. The main body of the second section treats five case studies of the effects of these new forms of protection in Chile.

2.1 Contingent protection

Chapter 2 carries out a theoretical analysis of contingent protection in a simplified setting designed to highlight the main features of this type of protection. Two firms, one in the exporting country and another in the importing country, compete in the importing country's market. The competition faced by the domestic firm lowers its profit. Contingent protection is a mechanism which threatens sanctions whose probability depends on the observable behavior of the foreign firm. This signal might be the margin of dumping or the extent of market penetration by the foreign firm. A higher value of the signal increases the likelihood of punishment. For example, a bigger margin of dumping makes both detection and punishment of the foreign firm more likely. Moreover, the sanction on the foreign firm may depend on the value of the signal. In general, the observed value of the signal depends on the actions of the two firms. Hence, the domestic firm might choose to modify its behavior so as to increase the probability of a punishment for the foreign rival. The setup is that of a dynamic game, as both firms realize that their present actions affect the likelihood of a future sanction on the foreign firm (anti-dumping measure, anti-subsidy tariff, etc.). The chapter describes the firms' strategic reactions under contingent protection and shows that the effects depend on the type of competition between the firms as well as on the type of punishment. In the case of dumping, the foreign firm tries to reduce the likelihood of punishment, and this means lowering the margin of dumping, i.e., lowering prices in its own market and trying to raise prices in the foreign market. This implies that under quantity competition, the foreign firm reduces exports. The domestic firm, meanwhile, will try to raise the probability of a punishment by increasing its sales, which will tend to raise the margin of dumping. The end result is that in the first period, i.e., prior to the possible punishment, total sales are higher and imports are lower. In this particular example, for small punishments, consumers in both countries benefit from AD legislation during the first period. The results of this model correspond quite well to the observed behavior of the salmon industry in Chile, which was recently threatened by a dumping investigation in the United States. In this case, the reactions of the Chilean firms have been as follows:

1 Attempts to raise the price in the export market (price undertaking), a strategy that often leads to a suspension of the investigation.
2 Lowering the price in other markets so as to reduce the margin of dumping.
3 Cutting back exports and directing surpluses towards alternative markets.
4 Lobbying to try to influence the results of the investigation.[11]

The preliminary determination in the case of Chilean salmon exports has found that two out of five firms are dumping, with margins of 2.9 per cent and 5.6 per cent respectively.

2.2 Protection and standards

In Chapter 3, Ronald Fischer and Pablo Serra examine the use of quality standards as protectionist measures. The authors consider two different models of standards. In the first model, quality enhancements reduce a negative externality: for example, the standards governing the pollutants produced by automobiles. It is assumed that the quality enhancement does not affect directly the utility perceived by consumers.[12] To underline the importance of standards as barriers to trade, note that three of the case studies that follow document protection based on standards. Unlike most other protectionist measures, standards serve, in principle, to correct for externalities. Accordingly, there is a theoretical justification for their use. However, it is difficult to distinguish a protectionist standard from one that is set at the level that corrects an externality. There are two reasons why a country might impose a protectionist standard. In the first place, it may serve to raise relative costs for foreign producers, thereby enabling rents to be transferred to national firms. Secondly, it is easier to raise standards if the costs can be transferred to foreign producers.[13]

It follows, therefore, that it is natural to define a protectionist standard as one that is higher than the standard the country would impose if all firms were domestic. On the basis of this definition, it is shown that the quality standard chosen by a social planner maximizing domestic social welfare is always protectionist. This chapter suggests that the relative size of the domestic and foreign markets will influence the definition of the standard that is eventually imposed. When the foreign competitor's own market is small, the domestic producer knows that a high standard is needed to eliminate the foreign firm from its only important market. In this case the costs of eliminating the foreign firm are high, and the domestic firm may prefer not to press for a minimum quality standard that excludes the foreign firm. The reason is that the profits under monopoly may be less than under duopoly, due to the high cost of the standards needed to eliminate foreign imports. On the other hand, if the foreign market is large, the costs of raising quality in order to adapt to the domestic standard are high for the foreign firm. Hence the foreign firm may abandon its export market even when the standard required of exports is relatively low. In this case, the domestic firm lobbies for the lowest standard that excludes imports.[14] The chapter also analyzes the standard desired by the social planner which, it is shown, may be higher or lower than the standard desired by the domestic firm.

The second model analyzes the case where standards are used to reduce an informational asymmetry: consumers do not know the quality of the goods they consume. In this case, standards are required in order to exclude units of the good whose value to consumers is less than the cost of production. Using a simple specification in which a higher quality of a good indicates that the useful component of the good is a larger fraction of each unit sold, the authors show that consumers would prefer lower standards than those preferred by producers. A social welfare maximizing planner would set a standard that is excessively lax from the point of view of both foreign and domestic firms. Firms would prefer the planner to restrict the amount of goods closer to the monopoly quantity. In this case, the planner is not protectionist, since it harms domestic firms. The situation is different when the average quality of imports is lower than that of domestic production (for all minimum standards) and consumers cannot identify foreign goods. In that case, a welfare maximizing planner would choose a higher standard that favors domestic firms at the expense of foreign firms: i.e. it would be a protectionist standard. However, this source of protectionism (which is due to the unobservability of the country of origin of the goods) can be readily eradicated by requiring labels on the goods that indicate the country of origin of the goods, a universal procedure. Hence, in this model, the only explanation for a protectionist standard is due to the pressure of domestic producers at the expense of domestic welfare.

3   The new protectionism in practice

What are the practical effects of the new forms of protectionism? The second part of the book presents a series of case studies that examine the effects on different sectors. An introductory section provides a description of the changes in the approach to trade in Latin America in the last decade.

3.1   Latin American trade regime: reforms and perceptions

In this section, Ronald Fischer and Patricio Meller (Chapter 4) examine Latin American countries and the effects of the reforms that have taken place recently. In general, these countries have changed from the inward-oriented economic attitude sponsored by the United Nations Economic Commission for Latin America (ECLAC), towards an outward-looking perspective that is part of the "Washington Consensus". The chapter details the changes in the level of tariffs and in quantitative restrictions, showing that there is a clear divide between the 1980s and the 1990s, with recent tariff structures that are flatter and lower. The authors document an explosion of Free Trade Agreements (FTAs) within Latin America. Even if these agreements are not always effective and are riddled with excluded goods and services, they represent a change in perceptions that indicates a willingness to trade with neighbors that did not exist previously.[15] The effect has been a doubling in the rate of growth of exports in the last decade, coupled with an especially high growth rate in intra-LA trade. Cross-border investments have also become common. Nevertheless, the amounts exported by these countries are small. Even a country with low, uniform tariffs and few other forms of protection, such as Chile, did not get to export one thousand dollars of exports per capita, a quarter of the corresponding value for OECD countries.

A worrying trend for the area is the growth in the new forms of protection as traditional trade barriers are lowered. A survey of the major Latin American countries and their trade partners shows an increase in the use of sophisticated methods such as the use of standards, certification procedures and anti-dumping and anti-subsidy measures against other countries in Latin America. Moreover, there is a willingness to fall back on administrative protection with measures that are cumbersome and protectionist. Even countries that are members of a customs union, such as MERCOSUR, can indulge in costly trade wars using these instruments. Developed countries have also stepped up their use of these measures and they appear less enthusiastic in their support of free trade. It would be ironic if, when LA countries finally start to believe in the benefits of free trade, the developed countries were to close the door on their imports.

3.2 Poisoned grapes, mad cows and protectionism

In Chapter 5, Eduardo Engel examines the different reactions of importing countries in two occasions where imported products were suspected of being contaminated and hence presented a potential health risk. His aim is to put forward a new definition of a protectionist measure via two case studies. Engel proposes defining as protectionist any measure that reduces world welfare.

Firstly, Engel studies the well-known case of a shipment of Chilean grapes in which two grapes were found to be contaminated with a non-lethal dose of cyanide on arrival in the United States. As a consequence, the Food and Drug Administration (FDA) banned the entry of all Chilean fruit exports to the US. The losses to Chilean agriculture were estimated at US$ 300 million. Subsequent investigations have shown that the grapes must have been contaminated on arrival in the US. Despite many attempts to obtain compensation, the US government has refused. Engel contrasts this response to the case of "mad cows". The countries of the European Union (EU) tried to prevent British beef entering the rest of the continent, fearing it might be contaminated with bovine encephalopathy (mad cow disease), a disease which was suspected of being transmissible to human beings. Despite a real health risk, in contrast to the Chilean case, the EU offered to compensate the United Kingdom for up to 70 per cent of the costs of destroying the contaminated herds. Notwithstanding this fairly generous compensation, the United Kingdom boycotted EU meetings and prevented important decisions being taken until the other countries in the EU accepted a limited culling plan rather than the original proposal. The comparison between the two cases enables Engel to compare different definitions of a protectionist standard. If one considers world welfare, the ban on British beef is not protectionist. In the case of the Chilean grapes, it is difficult to believe that the embargo maximized global welfare, which means that it might have a protectionist component. Engel concludes, firstly, that incentives are required so that regulators in the importing country internalize the cost of their decisions on the exporting country; and, secondly, that speedy consultation procedures need to be set up to prevent worsening the problems caused by import bans on phytosanitary grounds. Engel's analysis is important because the Chilean case highlights that food exporting developing countries are vulnerable to unilateral embargoes at any time. Hence the multilateral trading organizations must establish clear rules for the exclusion of products and create compensation mechanisms and rapid response procedures.

3.3   Trade and the environment: mining

Chapter 6, by Raúl O'Ryan and Andrés Ulloa, examines the effects of allegations of environmental dumping on Chile's mining industry (mainly copper). Environmental dumping is defined as the ability of firms to set lower prices when looser environmental standards in the country reduce production costs relative to other countries. The chapter begins with a detailed exposition of the arguments for and against the use of trade measures to correct environmental externalities in exporting countries. Next, it analyzes the validity of the arguments for setting up a new type of trade impediment to punish environmental dumping. The authors conclude that unless the externality spills over to other countries, it is difficult to justify the use of environmental production standards. They also argue that optimal environmental standards depend on the specific location, for it is not a matter of indifference whether a mine contaminates an inhabited, agricultural area or an uninhabited desert. However, they note that the effect of the threats of environmental dumping on Chilean mining do not depend on the fairness of the arguments, since Chile cannot influence the internal decisions of consumer countries. In response to the potential threat, the state mining company is implementing a decontamination plan which will invest more than US$ 1 billion between 1997 and 2000 in sulfuric acid plants, tailing treatments, filters and other items. Private mining companies, for their part, have already installed low-pollution technology. The effect of all these investments is that within a few years, Chile will produce twice as much copper as in 1994 with less pollution.

However, environmental threats to Chile's copper exports persist: the possibly unsustainable use of subterranean waters in fossil beds by mines in Northern Chile could form the basis for new arguments to restrict the entry of Chilean copper. Worse still, new ISO 14,000 environmental standards regulating the entire life cycle of the final product could restrict exports to markets which traditionally have not used environmental arguments to restrict imports, such as those in Asia. Under the new norms, all components of the final product have to have been produced under ISO 14,000 standards. This will force Asian countries wishing to export to countries implementing ISO 14,000 standards to impose the standards on their own inputs. Finally, the study also considers the possibility that copper may be declared a health risk in uses such as roofing, water pipes, and others.

3.4 Trade and the environment: forestry

Chapter 7 studies the effects of environmental considerations on the development and trade in one of Chile's most dynamic growth sectors in the last twenty years: the forestry sector. Without forgetting the issues of pollution already covered in the case of mining, it concentrates on a different issue, namely, the fact that environmental activism has fundamentalist aspects that make it ignore scientific considerations, in its desire to stop the exploitation of native forests. The authors believe that in some cases environmentalist motives have been hijacked by protectionist interests. They point out that cellulose producers in Scandinavian countries have developed clean technologies and then have joined lobbies against cellulose imports from less-clean producers, usually from developing countries. In an effort to contain these threats, developing-country firms have had to adopt standards that are higher than those that are efficient (even if environmental effects are included), raising costs and making them less competitive.

The authors argue that even though effective environmental protection of forests is fairly new in Chile, most of the industrial raw materials for the forestry industry originates in plantations grown in highly eroded non-forested lands. Moreover, plantations reduce the pressure on native forests. Hence, rather than being harmful, this plantations have a favorable effect on the environment. The threats of environmental protection have had the perverse effect of lowering the investment in plantations and reducing the interest of large corporations in investigating sustainable use of native forests. The authors show that the arguments about the disappearance of native forests in Chile are misguided on average (though there may be localized problems), since the native biomass is growing at least at a rate four times higher than the rate of extraction. The costs of the protectionist threats facing Chilean exporters are large, and, according to the authors, they do not even achieve the effect that is sought, namely, the protection of native forests.

3.5   Protection and labor standards

In Chapter 8, Alejandra Mizala and Pilar Romaguera examine the possibility that differences in labor standards be used as threats to trade. To this end, they consider whether Chile should modify its labor standards in the event of being invited to join NAFTA (North American Free Trade Agreement), given the possibility that the changes have an efficiency cost. After a comparative review of labor legislation, the authors find that at the formal level, Chilean labor legislation is on a par with that of the United States and Canada, so is not necessary to introduce significant modifications. However, they warn that, under the side agreements on labor required in NAFTA, countries need to ensure compliance with their own labor laws. Mizala and Romaguera argue that Chile lags behind in compliance: there are sectors where supervision of labor legislation is precarious. This is especially serious, given the context of these agreements, in the export sector. This chapter examines the problems in four major Chilean export sectors: forestry, mining, salmon production, and fruit. The first conclusion is that there are enormous differences in compliance with the norms between firms and subcontractors, for which reason the authors propose legislation be modified to make firms responsible for the labor problems (especially safety) of their contractors. Secondly, they find that the sectors with the biggest problems are those that are furthest away from population centers and least accessible, hence poorly supervised: forestry camps and salmon farm rafts, for example. The authors point out that this is an area where Chilean unions have made alliances with their counterparts in Canada and United States, so that negotiators in these countries sometimes have information on labor legislation infringements which their Chilean counterparts themselves do not know about.

3.6   Investment risk and Latin American multinationals

In Chapter 9 Jorge Friedman looks at foreign direct investment carried out by Chilean firms, and the problems they have faced. The chapter's first contribution is to show the surprising importance of Chilean foreign investment, which as a percentage of national product exceeds that of several developed countries. The chapter analyzes the reasons why Chilean capital has been almost wholly invested in neighboring countries. According to Friedman, early liberalization and privatization in the Chilean economy provided Chilean entrepreneurs with know-how concerning the operation of Latin American economies in the process of liberalization. This know-how gave them a comparative advantage compared with entrepreneurs in countries in the initial stages of liberalization, and also with respect to foreign firms ignorant of the particular characteristics of the region's economies. Much of Chilean investment has been directed at the electrical sector, where regulatory systems similar to Chile's have been adopted in Argentina and Peru. This system of electricity regulation is more modern than those established in most developed countries (apart from the United Kingdom), which has given Chilean electrical companies an additional advantage in competing for electrical companies undergoing privatization. Other sectors that have received significant investment are supermarket chains, forestry products, private pension funds, banks, wine makers, and health insurance companies. Friedman notes that Chilean investors have chosen to ally themselves with developed country firms, so as to have stronger support in the face of nationalistic threats. These threats are one of the most important problems facing Chilean investments in neighboring countries, and it has become a threat to their expansion. Friedman examines a series of instances where various threats such as the possibility of changes in the rules of the game, discrimination against foreign investors, violation of agreements, and direct attacks on Chilean staff in foreign firms have tended to slow the pace of investment. These threats have a negative effect on the external investments of Chile (a country without great influence in the region), and are equivalent to the effect of contingent protection on trade.

4 Final comments

The papers collected in this volume suggest that the new forms of protectionism may be even more effective in distorting trade than traditional measures such as tariffs and quotas. As this is an emerging issue, the technocrats in charge of developing country's negotiations do not have experience in these issues and, needless to say, the new protectionism is not taught in international trade courses. However, they involve issues that need to be understood in order to reach sustainable international agreements and in order to design responses that anticipate these new threats to trade. There is, as yet, no general theoretical framework that would allow us to determine what are the desirable results of international negotiation on these subjects and that would allow us to compare it to potentially achievable results in trade treaties or multilateral negotiations. This book is an attempt at analyzing these issues by combining a theoretical framework with the experience of cases in which these new forms of protection are important for developing countries.

Notes

1 Notwithstanding this restriction, the initial round of GATT in 1947 established that norms and regulations could be used to "order" a market, a loophole which allowed the infamous marketing orders which have prevented, for example, the entry of Chilean grapes during harves periods in the United States.

2 These include: the Technical Barriers to Trade Agreement (TBT, the Standards Code), which disciplines the abuse of technical regulations related, even indirectly, to trade; the Sanitary and Phytosanitary Agreement, which controls the use of sanitary and phytosanitary measures that affect trade; and finally, the Anti-dumping and Countervailing Subsidy Codes, which constrain national laws dealing with dumping and export subsidies.

3 For example, if company A had an average efficiency of 25 miles per gallon, it would pay a sum of US$ 125 (2.5 × US$ 50) per vehicle sold. If the average efficiency was above the standard it would not pay a tax, nor would it earn a reward.

4 Argentina shares several thousand kilometers of thinly populated frontier with Chile. Periodically smuggled cattle infect Chilean herds. When this happens all cattle in a large neighborhood must be destroyed in order to contain the disease.

5 Despite the protectionist consequences, the elimination of hoof-and-mouth disease has probably generated unintended positive externalities for Chile. Importing countries are more willing to relax their phytosanitary requirements given that Chile has managed to eliminate an endemic disease of a neighboring country, thereby increasing their confidence in phytosanitary mechanisms in Chile.

6 For example, between the domestic and the export price.

7 In most of the cases that were withdrawn, the accused firms reached an agreement with domestic firms to raise their prices, i.e. they agreed to be less competitive.

8 In general the margin of dumping is positive if export prices are lower than prices in the country of origin. Another possibility is to compare prices with those in other export markets or with a constructed cost figure.

9 "Harm that is not inconsequential, immaterial or unimportant", Trade Agreements Act, 1979, an uncommonly vague definition.

10 In the EU, the process is less administrative, and for that very reason more subject to pressures. The procedure in Chile is similar to the European one.

11 The Chilean salmon exporters association hired a lobby group headed by Robert Dole, Republican presidential candidate in 1996.

12 As in the case of car emission standards. This is an important restriction of the model that avoids quality issues that are usually analyzed in the Industrial Organization literature on standards.

13 This argument arose from an observation by Eduardo Engel.

14 The model assumes that producing under two different quality standards has a high cost, or alternatively, that there is an important fixed cost attached to each variety. In both cases, only one standard is actually produced. Fischer and Serra (in press) treat the more complex case in which both standards can be produced simultaneously.

15 As is well known, FTAs do not imply an unambiguous trend towards multi-lateral free trade.

References

Boltuck, R. and R. E. Litan (1991). *Down in the Dumps: Administration of the Unfair Trade Laws.* Washington, DC: The Brookings Institution.

Fischer, R. D. (1987), "Essays in Game Theory and International Economics", Ph.D. thesis, University of Pennsylvania.

Fischer, R. D. (1992). "Endogenous probability of protection and firm behavior", *Journal of International Economics,* 32, 149–63.

Fischer, R. D. and P. Serra (in press). "Standards and Protection", *Journal of International Economics.*

Marceau G. (1994). *Antidumping and Antitrust Issues in Free Trade Areas,* Clarendon Press: Oxford, Oxford UK.

National Research Council (1995). *Standards, Conformity Assessment and Trade.* Washington, DC: National Academy Press.

Palmeter, D. N. (1995). "United States implementation of the Uruguay Round antidumping code", *Journal of World Trade,* 29(3), 39–81.

Prusa, T. (1994). "Pricing behavior in the presence of antidumping law", *Journal of International Integration,* 9(2), 260–89.

Prusa, T. J. and W. L. Hansen (1993, Winter). "Does administrative protection protect?", *Cato Review of Business and Government: Regulation,* 35–43.

Reitzes, J. D. (1993). "Antidumping policy", *International Economic Review,* 34, 745–63.

Staiger, R. W. (1995). "International rules and institutions for cooperative trade policy", in G. M. Grossman and K. Rogoff (eds), *Handbook of International Economics,* Vol.3, chapter 29, pp. 1495–551. North-Holland.

Staiger, R. W. and F. A. Wolak (1994). "Measuring industry-specific protection: antidumping in the United States", *Brookings Papers in Economic Activity,* 51–118.

Part I
Theory

2
Contingent Protection

Ronald Fischer[*]

1 Introduction

The aim of this chapter is to summarize the results of the theory of contingent (or potential) protection. This theory studies protection mechanisms that are activated when certain variables alert a public agency about a real or assumed violation of the rules of international trade. In the case of dumping, the signal in question is the margin of dumping; in the case of countervailing duties, it is the detection of subsidies. These protection mechanisms have gained increasing importance in international trade, and so far multilateral agencies have been incapable of restricting their use. International trade theory has been intensely concerned with investigating the effects of protectionism on countries' welfare. Typically, trade restrictions are modeled in a deterministic way: a tariff, a quota, discriminatory phytosanitary standards, etc. Consequently, multilateral agencies have made significant efforts to reduce this type of impediment to trade. Signatories to the Uruguay Round agreements and previous GATT Rounds, for example, are required to lower tariffs, limit quotas, restrict discriminatory standards and establish rules to ensure compliance with agreements. Given the limitations imposed by such accords, countries have sought new forms of protectionism which, while they may violate the spirit, do not violate the letter of the agreements. In an attempt to escape from these restraints, developed countries have developed new forms of protection that are not contemplated in the agreements. As an example, consider voluntary export restraints, which replace import quotas and are

* This article received support from FONDECYT Grant No. 1950513. I am grateful for the numerous suggestions made by Alexander Galetovic.

"voluntary", so appear not to violate the letter of the agreements. Another case is the use of non-discriminatory phytosanitary (or quality) standards, which have often been introduced with the aim of protecting producers rather than users, by raising the costs to foreign firms competing with domestic production (see Fischer and Serra, in this book).

Contingent protection is a second form of this phenomenon. Contingent protection occurs when a country's exports face a probability of being sanctioned, and includes measures against export subsidies, as well as anti-dumping measures and the like; moreover the category may be expanded so as to include measures related to standards, in cases where there is uncertainty about the mechanism by which standards are verified.[1] The issue of contingent protection is specially interesting when it is endogenous, i.e. when it is the actions of the agents involved that determine the probability of sanctions. This type of protection is important because protectionist effects are induced even before the sanction is imposed. In the case of contingent protection, foreign agents modify their normal strategies out of fear of sanction, while domestic agents are motivated by a desire for the competition to be sanctioned. For this very reason their action is not detected by multilateral mechanisms, which are suitable for calling into question actually observed protectionism, but are fairly ineffective against threats of sanctions.[2] However, it is clear that when investors evaluate projects, or when they have to decide which markets are more attractive, the risk of sanction has a significant effect on their decision. Furthermore, it should not be forgotten that frequently the magnitude of the sanction is also uncertain, thereby adding a further risk. This means that contingent protection might be a more effective protection device than an equivalent deterministic protection measure (in expected protection value).[3]

Firms that fear being accused of dumping use other instruments apart from their strategic action variables (quantities, prices, investment, etc.), and hire lawyers and lobbying services, and attempt to influence public opinion. This behavior has been analyzed by Das (1990). In the Das model, exporting and importing firms make lobbying efforts that determine the likelihood of a quota. Firms try to alter the political market in their favor, as this allows them to obtain or mitigate protection measures. However, in the Das model the market behavior of firms does not change unless a sanction is imposed. In the present model, firms' action variables (prices, quantities, or even quality) are managed as a strategic game between national and foreign firms. As an example, foreign firms may raise their prices, or else divert exports to other markets so as to reduce the probability of sanction. Meanwhile, national firms seeking an investigation make great efforts to convince the monitoring agencies that their situation is unsustainable, by cutting output, profits or employment. This strategic game occurs before the sanction is imposed and so corresponds to contingent protection. Such reactions were observed in the recent United States' anti-dumping accusation against Chilean salmon producers. Two of the reactions that were considered by the Chilean Salmon Exporters Association were to raise prices in the USA (so as to reduce the margin of dumping) and to divert exports from the United States towards other markets (also reducing the margin of dumping).

Anti-dumping legislation is the classic form of contingent protection. Under the Antidumping Code of WTO, the procedure is for an agency (or several agencies) in the importing country to decide whether three criteria are met: (i) the selling price in the importing country is below the price in the country of origin or in other markets; (ii) the imports are causing, or threaten to cause, material injury to the industry that competes with the imports;[4] and (iii) that the harm is caused by imports. For our purposes, these criteria will be referred to as *signals*. What is important in these signals is that it is the firms themselves, through their actions (by lowering or raising prices or quantities), that determine the value of the signal, and hence the probability of a sanction in the future. The effects of contingent protection consist of changes in the firms' behavior, in which they try to manipulate the signals to increase (if they compete with imports) or reduce (if they are exporters) the likelihood that the foreign firms' behavior will be sanctioned. The theoretical literature on contingent protection is not abundant, and it has largely stressed the static aspects of anti-dumping measures (Viner 1923; Finger 1987), without considering the effects that concern us in this chapter. The work of Bhagwati and Srinivasan (1976) was the first to present a model considering non-deterministic protection measures. Moreover, in their model the probability of protection is not exogenous, but depends on the actions of the exporting country. In its simplest version, it is a two-period model of trade between two countries. One of the two countries faces the possibility of a sanction – in this case the imposition of a quota – that depends on its level of exports. In this model, the level of imports is the signal for contingent protection. Bhagwati and Srinivasan (1976) show that the possibility of a future quota reduces present exports. A problem in their model is that the country imposing the restrictions is entirely passive, and there is no strategic interaction between the different economic agents. Subsequent developments studied models of imperfect competition where there are economic rents that can be transferred by appropriate policy. This makes it possible to analyze the strategic reactions of the firms, which makes the models more realistic and emphasizes new aspects of contingent protection. There have only been a few papers on this subject, including Fischer (1987, 1992), Reitzes (1993), Prusa (1994). The empirical literature is at an even earlier stage, presumably for lack of data. Prusa (1996) analyzes data from the USA and shows that the mere filing of a dumping complaint with the government is sufficient to change the behavior of the firms involved.

2   The signal in the theory of contingent protection

This section defines and exemplifies the concept of a signal. In general, any variable on which the authority in the importing country bases a decision to impose a trade restriction measure will be understood as a signal.

It is assumed that a country has one or more official agencies responsible for monitoring the values of signals that are affected by imports. However, monitoring is only carried out at the request of local producers. Examples of signals include the margin of dumping (in the case of anti-dumping legislation), profitability and employment in the import-competing industry and the existence of subsidies in the exporting country.

International trade legislation, and in particular multilateral trade agreements such as the WTO (or its predecessor GATT, the General Agreement on Trade and Tariffs) establish the types of variables on which it is legal to act, and the procedures to be followed for obtaining redress. To be brief, we define a WTO-acceptable signal if the WTO and other trade agreements, accept it as a variable that can be used to justify imposing a trade restriction. These variables include: the margin of dumping, a sudden expansion of imports, subsidies to sectoral exports and phytosanitary restrictions. There are other variables which, according to the WTO, do not justify the introduction of trade restrictions without compensation; for example, excessively rapid market penetration by the imported product, the environmental effects of productive processes, or labor laws in the country of origin. However, this second group of variables has been used to deny preferences in the framework of free trade agreements going beyond the scope of the WTO, as documented in later chapters.

It is important to state that as the monitoring agency only observes conduct through imperfect observations of the signal, at times it will impose a sanction when no violation exists, or else will not do so when in fact there is one. From the contingent protection standpoint, what matters is that signals are observed imperfectly, and that the probability of a signal exceeding the *de minimis* value is a random variable.[5] The intensity with which signals are monitored is uncertain, but depends on the pressure exerted by lobbies acting for the import-competing industry and for the foreign producers.[6] Countries usually exhibit a bias towards their own producers, who have advantages in presenting evidence in their favor.[7] Furthermore, in many countries the anti-dumping legislation contains procedural rules that add an additional bias towards finding a positive margin of dumping (Boltuck and Litan 1991).

In some cases the conjunction of two signals is required to impose a sanction on exports from the investigated countries. In the case of dumping, the WTO establishes a set of rules (the AD Code) for the working of anti-dumping regulations in signatory countries. The rules state that not only does a country need to prove a positive margin of dumping, but it must also show the existence of material injury in the sector and that this damage is caused by dumping. The intensity of protectionist measures depends on the value(s) the signal(s) take. In the USA, the surcharge imposed on goods convicted of dumping is equal to the margin of dumping, whereas in Europe it is the lesser of the margin of dumping and the rate that would eliminate the material injury. In what follows, we analyze the signals used in the most important types of contingent protection. It is necessary to define some notation. Lower-case variables correspond to the country importing the good in question. Variables marked with an asterisk (*) relate to the exports of the foreign country. Finally, upper-case variables correspond to the domestic market of the foreign country; for example p is the price of the good that competes with imports, p^* is the price of the imported good and P represents its price in the foreign market. Prices are denoted by p, quantities by q and costs by c. Percentage change is denoted by a circumflex accent on the variable ($\wedge$).

2.1 Dumping

In most countries, trade legislation penalizes dumping, when detected by a positive value of either of two signals. Firstly, dumping exists when there is price discrimination between countries, i.e. when the price in the exporting country, or in some other country to which it exports, is higher than in the importing country.[8] The second criterion is based on comparing the costs of the foreign firm to its export prices. The second criterion is more arbitrary, as it requires the reconstruction of the costs of the exporting firm.[9] The margin of dumping is defined as $P - p^*$, under the definition based on observed prices, or as $P_c - p^*$, where P_c is the constructed price in the case where the margin of dumping is determined on the basis of costs. The anti-dumping code establishes that the penalty may not be greater than the margin of dumping. Often the exporter is allowed to make an undertaking to keep prices high, which enables him to avoid the countervailing duty to which the importing country is entitled.[10]

As mentioned above, the determination of a positive margin of dumping is not a sufficient condition to impose countervailing duties; the rules require that material injury is being caused to local producers by imports. This criterion depends on variables such as profits, market share, employment trends and capacity utilization.[11] In this chapter we follow Prusa (1996) by considering domestic industry profits as the most important criterion for damage. It is clear that these variables can be manipulated both by domestic firms and by exporters, and this generates a dynamic strategic game.

2.2 Safeguard measures

Safeguard measures can be imposed for a limited time when there is a rapid expansion of imports, or for other reasons that justify a country temporarily abandoning its WTO obligations (while offering compensation, such as the opportunity to raise tariffs against home country exports, to the countries affected by the measure). In this case, the signal can be defined as the market penetration of imports $q^*/(q + q^*)$ or, better still, as the change in this variable between two periods. Safeguard measures normally consist of tariff surcharges, and even allow countries to abandon their WTO commitments. Here the application of safeguard measures needs to be justified by another signal, this time an indication of *serious* injury to the industry. The latter criterion is theoretically stricter than the criterion of material injury. As the existence of serious injury is harder to prove, safeguard measures are becoming uncommon (Prusa 1996).[12]

2.3 Export subsidies

Export subsidies are prohibited in multilateral trade agreements. In principle one should distinguish between domestic subsidies and export subsidies. The first normally do not generate direct distortions in international trade, whereas export subsidies distort. However, there are big problems in discriminating between the two types of subsidy, because, for example, a domestic production subsidy may unduly favor exporting firms.[13] The US takes into account the specificity of the subsidy to test whether it is aimed at the export sector. As in the case of dumping allegations, it is necessary to satisfy a criterion of material injury, and the countervailing duty may not be greater than the subsidy.

3 The general model

This section presents a general model of contingent protection based on Prusa (1994), in which agents interact strategically. A reference framework is presented that accommodates various signals corresponding to different types of contingent protection. The model considered has two periods: in the first, an agency monitors one or more imperfect signals of the variable it is interested in (the margin of dumping, export subsides, etc.), and in the event of proceeding, it sanctions in the second period. The sanction may be a fine on the foreign firm, a customs surcharge or the imposition of an import quota. In general, foreign firms try to avoid the sanction by changing the value of their strategic variables.[14] For example, in the case of dumping they will try to reduce the margin of dumping.[15] Local firms will try to force a sanction, altering their behavioral variables so as to raise the probability of sanction. For example, they may try to lower their profits (or make losses) to be able to show that imports are causing material injury.

We will assume that the firms have strategic variables which we represent by the vectors z and z^* respectively. These variables may be quantities, prices or other things. The values of the variables chosen by the firms generate a signal which is observed by the monitoring agency, which sanctions if necessary. We recall that in some cases penalization requires the conjunction of two conditions: for example, dumping signals and material injury. The first condition determines the level of the sanction, while the second condition is required for its implementation, in accordance with the WTO Dumping Code. We define two signals for these cases: the detection of the margin of dumping – or export subsidy – as one signal, and the detection of material injury as the second. The real values of these variables will be designated by $\bar{s}_1(z, z^*)$ and $\bar{s}_2(z, z^*)$ respectively. However, the monitoring agency does not observe the real value of the signals but observes them with an error. In the case of dumping, if the observed value of the signal $\bar{s}_1$ is $s_1 > 0$, the monitoring agency indicates that it has determined a margin of dumping of s_1. More formally, the observed values of the signals can be written as:

$$
\begin{aligned}
s_1(z_1, z_1^*) &= \bar{s}_1(z_1, z_1^*) + \epsilon, & \epsilon \sim F \\
s_2(z_1, z_1^*) &= \bar{s}_2(z_1, z_1^*) + \mu, & \mu \sim G
\end{aligned}
\tag{2.1}
$$

The variable ϵ has a distribution F. The first signal corresponds to the detection of dumping, whereas the second corresponds to detection of material injury. The random variable μ is distributed according to G. The existence of these random variables is due to the inability to observe the real value of the variables. We assume that a positive observed value of a variable leads the agency to infer the existence of an infringement. Hence, the likelihood that the monitoring agency determines the existence of material injury, given that the real value of the signal is $\bar{s}_2$, is given by:

$$\rho(z_1, z_1^*) \equiv \int_{-\bar{s}_2}^{\infty} dG(z) \tag{2.2}$$

In the specific case of dumping, the level of sanction, if there is one, depends on the value of s_1, because whether there is a punishment or not depends on s_2.[16] Often, as in the United States, the value of different signals is determined by different government departments. Elsewhere, for example in the European Union and in Chile, the same agency monitors both signals.

4   The second period

During the second period, firms already know whether the monitoring agencies have determined a sanction. If the previous period's observations do not lead to penalization (i.e. s_1 or $s_2 < 0$), the situation for the firms is equivalent to a standard duopoly with a one-period horizon. In this case firms' profits are given by:

$$\Pi_2(\tilde{z}_2, \tilde{z}_2^*), \qquad \Pi_2^*(\tilde{z}_2, \tilde{z}_2^*) \tag{2.3}$$

respectively. Profits are assumed to be concave in the variables z_i. If the monitoring agencies decide that the foreign firm should be sanctioned (s_1 and $s_2 > 0$), the profits of the firms reflect the sanction, which in turn depends on the value of s_1, the signal that determines its value:

$$\Pi_2(z_2, z_2^*, s_1(z_1, z_1^*)) \tag{2.4}$$

A similar expression holds for for Π_2^*, corresponding to the foreign firm. We define the difference in profits with and without penalty as:

$$\Delta(z_1, z_1^*) = \Pi_2(z_2, z_2^*, s_1(z_1, z_1^*)) - \Pi_2(\tilde{z}_2, \tilde{z}_2^*) \tag{2.5}$$

with an equivalent expression for the foreign firm. This difference depends only on first period values for the variables, as firms are assumed to maximize during the second period.[17] To find the expected value of the firms' (z_1, z_1^*) choices, we observe that for each outcome of the random variable ϵ, there is an observed signal $s_1(z_1, z_1^*)$. Assuming that material injury has been observed ($s_2 > 0$), the value of $s_1 > 0$ determines the sanction and hence the value of $\Delta(z_1, z_1^*)$. Taking the expected value of all possible realizations of ϵ, we have that the difference in expected profits, conditional on material damage being observed, as a result of the firms choosing the values (z_1, z_1^*) for their strategic variables, can be written as:

$$E\Delta(z_1, z_1^*) = \int_{s_1+\epsilon>0} \Delta(z_1, z_1^*)dF \tag{2.6}$$

A similar expression holds for $E\Delta^*(z_1, z_1^*)$. Normally, we assume that $E\Delta(z_1, z_1^*) > 0$ and that $E\Delta^*(z_1, z_1^*) < 0$, i.e. the sanction favors the local firm and hurts the foreign one.[18]

4.1 The first period

In the first period the firms maximize profits over the two-period horizon, i.e. as the sum of first-period profits plus the expected value of profits in the second. The possibility of a sanction in the second period, which depends on the joint actions of the firm and its rivals, is built into the first period decisions of the firm. Denoting the inter-temporal discount factor by δ, the profits of the domestic firm can be written as:

$$E\Pi(z_1, z_1^*) = \Pi_1(z_1, z_1^*) + \delta(1 - \rho(z_1, z_1^*))\Pi_2(\tilde{z}_2, \tilde{z}_2^*)$$
$$+ \delta\rho(z_1, z_1^*)\left\{\int_{s_1+\epsilon>0} \Pi_2(z_2, z_2^*, s_1(z_1, z_1^*))dF\right\} \tag{2.7}$$
$$= \Pi_1(z_1, z_1^*) + \delta\left\{\Pi_2(\tilde{z}_2, \tilde{z}_2^*) + \rho(z_1, z_1^*)E\Delta(z_1, z_1^*)\right\}$$

The first term on the right-hand side represents first-period profits. The second term in brackets corresponds to the (discounted) profits in the second period in the event of no sanction. The last term corresponds to the change in profits resulting from the sanction, multiplied by the probability that a sanction is applied. A similar expression holds for the foreign firm. Maximizing expression (2.7) and its foreign equivalent with respect to the first-period variables, and noting that second period profits when there is no penalty do not depend on first period variables, the first-order conditions are:[19]

$$0 = \frac{\partial E\,\Pi}{\partial z_1} = \frac{\partial \Pi_1}{\partial z_1} + \delta \left\{ \rho'(z_1, z_1^*) \frac{\partial s_2}{\partial z_1} E\Delta(z_1, z_1^*) \right.$$

$$\left. + \rho(z_1, z_1^*) \frac{\partial (E\Delta(z_1, z_1^*))}{\partial z_1} \right\}$$

$$0 = \frac{\partial E\,\Pi^*}{\partial z_1^*} = \frac{\partial \Pi_1^*}{\partial z_1^*} + \delta \left\{ \rho'(z_1, z_1^*) \frac{\partial s_2}{\partial z_1^*} E\Delta^*(z_1, z_1^*) \right. \tag{2.8}$$

$$\left. + \rho(z_1, z_1^*) \frac{\partial (E\Delta^*(z_1, z_1^*))}{\partial z_1^*} \right\}$$

The second term in brackets in each of equations (2.8) is defined as the *strategic effect*, and we will denote it by S and S^* respectively. The strategic effect corresponds to the change in first-period actions caused by the probability of sanction in the second period. It has two components: the first term in brackets represents the effect of a marginal increase in the firm's first-period variables (z_1 for the domestic firm) on the probability of sanction, whereas the second term represents the effect of the change in the variable on profits, given that there is a sanction. These expressions will be used to study the different types of effects of contingent protection. It will be seen that the effects depend on two factors:

- The type of competition between the firms: i.e. in terms of prices or quantities.
- The sign of the strategic effect.

Figure 2.1 represents the strategic effect of contingent protection on the behavior of the firms during the first period of the model. The figure shows the shifts in the reaction functions in the case where each firm has one strategic variable, which are strategic substitutes, and where the strategic effects are positive for the local firm and negative for the foreign one. This will occur in the case of anti-dumping measures, if the firms compete on quantities and the sanction is an import surcharge. In this situation the foreign firm reduces its market share whereas the domestic firm increases its share, and (in differential terms) total quantity increases in the first period.[20]

The explanation for this result is intuitive: the foreign firm cuts its sales in the local market in order to raise prices, narrow the margin of dumping and hence lower the probability of a sanction. The national firm, for its part, boosts sales in order to bring prices down and increase the margin of dumping, so as to raise the probability of an import

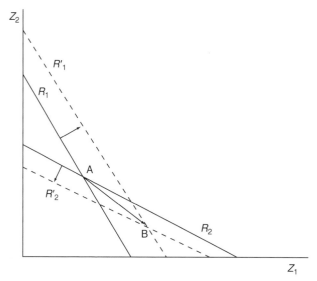

Figure 2.1   The strategic variables are substitutes (Case 1)

surcharge thereby protecting it from foreign competition. The result (for small penalties) is an increase in total sales, which means that potential protection may have an unexpected first-period effect: the price of the product falls compared to a model where there is no potential protection. This is the case discussed by Fischer (1987, 1992) and Reitzes (1993).

Safeguard measures in response to market penetration by imports, usually consist of import surcharges. Such measures can give rise to situations like those described in Figure 2.2. As mentioned above, in this case the signal is import penetration measured by $q_1^*/(q_1^* + q_1)$. In the first period the foreign firm tends to cut back its sales in order to reduce its market share and make a sanction less likely. The local firm, meanwhile, tries to increase the foreign firm's market penetration by cutting its own sales, thus raising the probability of a sanction. The net effect is reflected in a shift of the reaction functions to the dotted lines in Figure 2.2, with the equilibrium moving from A to B. The final result is a reduction in total market sales with a rise in prices that may increase the profits of both firms. As in the previous example, it is noteworthy that import penetration can go up as a result of contingent protection.

If the "sanction" resulting from market penetration favors both the national firm and the foreign one, the shift in the reaction functions shown in Figure 2.2 may occur in the opposite direction. This can

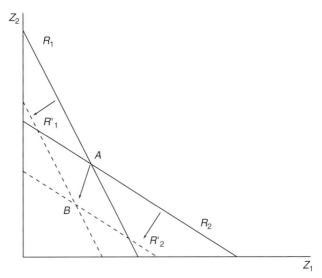

Figure 2.2   The strategic variables are substitutes (Case 2)

happen when the punishment for dumping favors the cartelization of the market, or in the case of voluntary export restraints, as mentioned before. In this case both firms want the signal to be detected, so the reaction curves of the two firms shift out. In general, it is not possible to say which of the two (or whether both) firms sell more in the new equilibrium. However, due to the stability conditions of the equilibrium (Tirole 1987), in this case total sales are greater and prices are lower in the new equilibrium. Hence we would have the apparently perverse result that anti-dumping legislation increases the margin of dumping, reflecting the fact that in this case dumping is not sanctioned but rewarded instead.

Figure 2.3 shows the case where the goods are strategically complementary, as would occur under price competition between the firms.[21] We consider the case of dumping sanctioned by an import surcharge. This benefits the domestic firm and hurts its foreign rival, so the former will try to increase the margin of dumping by lowering prices, while the second will try to reduce it by raising them. The new reaction functions are shown as the dotted lines in Figure 2.3. The movement from the previous equilibrium at *A* to the new equilibrium at *B* shows that the domestic firm's price falls, while the effect on the foreign firm's price is ambiguous and so is the effect on the margin of dumping. However, the change in relative domestic prices induced by the threat of

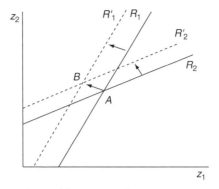

Figure 2.3 The strategic variables are complements

a sanction implies that the domestic firm becomes more competitive and increases its market share. It is interesting to verify these predictions being borne out in reality. In the case of anti-dumping legislation in the USA, Prusa (1996) has documented the effects induced by the filing of an anti-dumping accusation. Much of the effect expected by the sector seeking protection is obtained by the mere presentation of a complaint. As predicted by our model, an accusation – regardless of its merits – lowers the exports of the foreign firm. (see Figure 2.1) or else may lead it to raise its prices (see Figure 2.2).[22] In cases where the accusation is rejected, the reduction in exports from the accused countries may be as much as 10 to 20 per cent.

A more specific example is the recent case of anti-dumping accusations in the USA against Chilean salmon producers. Even before US producers filed their complaint, the Chilean Association of Salmon Producers was studying reactions such as raising prices in the USA (in order to reduce the margin of dumping) and diverting exports from the USA to other markets (reducing the margin of dumping by cutting supply to the USA).

5 Welfare

In this section we examine the social welfare effects of introducing contingent protection. We follow Reitzes (1993) and examine the welfare effects in the first period, as this is where the strategic component is important.[23] We also study the special case where each firm controls a single strategic variable. First, we consider welfare in the importing country. Marginal costs, c, are constant and equal for domestic and foreign firms; we assume quantity competition in order to simplify the results. If the goods are homogeneous, welfare can be expressed as gross consumer surplus less national production costs, less the price paid to exporters:

$$W_1 = \int_0^{q_1(z_1, z_1^*) + q_1^*(z_1, z_1^*)} p(q)dq + (p_1 - c)q_1 - p_1(q_1 + q_1^*) \qquad (2.9)$$

In order to consider the effect of introducing a small penalty, we will use the following device. Holding constant both detection technology and the size of the fine, the strategic effects S and S^* will be multiplied by a parameter λ and the change in welfare due to contingent protection will be evaluated in the neighborhood of $\lambda = 0$ (see Appendix). In this way, the small parameter λ can be interpreted either as a small detection capacity or a minuscule penalty. Differentiating with respect to this parameter, we have:

$$\begin{aligned}\frac{dW_1}{d\lambda} &= -p'\left(\frac{dq_1}{d\lambda}(q_1 + q_1^*) + q_1^*\frac{dq_1^*}{d\lambda}\right) \\ &= -p'(q_1 + q_1^*)\left(\frac{dq_1}{d\lambda} + \Phi\frac{dq_1^*}{d\lambda}\right)\end{aligned} \qquad (2.10)$$

where we have used the fact that if $\lambda = 0$, the firms behave as if there was no protection, and the foreign firm market share is denoted $\Phi \equiv q_1^*/(q_1 + q_1^*)$.[24] Note that the expression for the change in welfare (2.10), has the same sign as the term in brackets. In some cases the interpretation of the term in brackets is straightforward: if the protectionist measure reduces the sales of both firms in the local market, social welfare is reduced, as the increase in profits of the local firm does not compensate for the decrease in consumer surplus, especially given that a fraction of the now larger profits are exported. In other cases such as anti-dumping legislation shown in Figure 2.1, social welfare increases only if imports do not account for a significant share of the domestic market. The intuition is that an increase in domestic sales has two effects: it raises the profits of the domestic firm, and it offsets the drop in sales of the foreign firm. If total sales in the domestic market remain constant or increase, the effect is clearly positive, because the profits of the local producer go up while consumer surplus does not decline. When the increase in sales by the domestic firm does not offset the drop in imports, the sign of the effect depends on whether the rise in profits of the domestic firm compensates for the reduction in consumer surplus, which happens unless there is a large degree of import penetration. Now consider welfare in the exporting country. Let Q_1 be the sales in the foreign market during the first period. In the foreign country, welfare includes a component that corresponds to the profits earned in the export market:

$$W_1^* = \int_0^{Q_1(z_1, z_1^*)} p_1^*(Q_1)dQ_1 + (p_1 - c_1^*)q_1^* + (p_1^* - c_1^*)Q_1 - p_1^*Q_1 \quad (2.11)$$

The effect of a small amount of contingent protection on the welfare of the exporting country is:

$$\begin{aligned}
\frac{dW_1^*}{d\lambda} &= p_1^* \frac{dQ_1}{d\lambda} + p_1' q_1^* \frac{dq_1}{d\lambda} - p_1^{*\prime} \frac{dQ_1}{d\lambda} Q_1 - p_1^* \frac{dQ_1}{d\lambda} \\
&= p_1' q_1 \frac{dq_1}{d\lambda} - p_1^{*\prime} Q_1 \frac{dQ_1}{d\lambda}
\end{aligned} \quad (2.12)$$

In the case illustrated in Figure 2.1, social welfare in the foreign country increases if exports are small relative to the foreign firm's domestic market. The threat of contingent protection redirects the sales of the foreign firm towards its own market (in order to reduce the margin of dumping), which benefits local consumers. On the other hand, the decrease in exports reduces the foreign firm's profits. However, the first effect is more important than the second, unless sales abroad are very important relative to national sales, and this depends on the relative size of the two domestic markets. It is interesting to see that in this model the introduction of contingent protection – anti-dumping legislation – may benefit both the exporting country (by making its domestic firm become less of a monopoly) and the importing country. The opposite result (as regards the importing country) occurs when the probability of a protectionist measure is determined by import penetration. In that case sales in the importing country fall, as both the exporter and the domestic producer want to reduce their sales.

6 Conclusions

Contingent protection has become one of the main mechanisms by which countries violate the spirit of multilateral free trade agreements. Given that contingent protection represents only a potential threat of sanction, it is difficult to prove that a country is using such measures with protectionist aims, despite the fact that the main effects of contingent protection occur before the sanction is implemented. As one would expect, the threat of such measures causes foreign firms to alter their behavior in order to reduce the likelihood of a subsequent penalty. Local firms, meanwhile, take advantage of the fact that penalization favors them and act so as to raise the probability of a sanction. The effects considered in this chapter are quite important, as is shown by Prusa (1996).

The general framework described in this chapter makes it possible to analyze various specific forms of contingent protection under imperfect competition. To recapitulate, a signal is a variable observed by the monitoring agency whose value depends at least partly on the actions of domestic and foreign firms. When the value of the signal exceeds a limiting value, the exporting firm receives a sanction. The fact that the monitoring agency's observations are subject to error, generates a probability distribution over sanctions. The firms try to modify the probability of sanction by altering the variables under their control, namely, quantities or prices. The direction of the strategic effects depends both on the type of sanction and on whether the strategic variables are (strategic) complements or substitutes. For example, in the case of competition on quantities, with a sanction that favors the local firm at the expense of the foreign one (for example, a surcharge if dumping is observed), the effect on behavior in the first period is to increase sales by the national firm and to redirect foreign firm's sales towards its own market, raising sales in all markets.

Contingent protection affects social welfare in both importing and exporting countries. Changes in welfare also depend on the type of penalty and on the form of competition. Normally, the effect of contingent protection is to reduce welfare in both countries, but there are cases where both countries benefit from contingent protection: this can happen with anti-dumping legislation, since total sales in the local market rise due to the domestic firm's efforts to lower prices in order to get a penalty imposed on the exporting firm. In this case, in its effort to reduce the probability of a penalty, the foreign firm boosts sales in its own country, thereby benefiting its consumers.

Perhaps the most important conclusion of this chapter is that potential protection measures, which are difficult for multilateral agencies to control, have important strategic effects. These have been studied by Prusa (1996), who shows that their importance should be measured not only by the number of cases where an accusation is upheld and penalization imposed, nor by the number of cases in which foreign firms agree to raise their prices so as not to compete so strongly with domestic firms. Instead it is necessary to study the effect caused by the threat of potential sanctions on firms' behavior and on trade flows.

Appendix

In this Appendix we describe the methods used in the case of small penalties ($E\Delta$) or small probabilities of sanction (ρ).

Suppose we consider a fixed penalty function $E\Delta(z_1, z_1^*)$ which is a function of the first-period action variables z_1, z_1^*. To obtain a small sanction, we multiply the sanction $E\Delta$ by a small real number $\lambda > 0$. The new strategic effect for the domestic firm (as a function of λ) can be written as:

$$ES(\lambda) = \delta\left\{ \rho'(z_1, z_1^*)\frac{\partial s_2}{\partial z_1}\lambda E\Delta(z_1, z_1^*) + \rho(z_1, z_1^*)\frac{\partial(\lambda E\Delta(z_1, z_1^*))}{\partial z_1} \right\}$$

i.e. $ES(\lambda) = \lambda ES$. Differentiating with respect to λ and evaluating at $\lambda = 0$, we obtain expression (2.10). A similar analysis leads to (2.12), the change in welfare in the foreign country in response to a small penalty.

We can carry out an analogous procedure for the case where the probability of sanction is small. Assume a fixed sanction function $\rho(z1, z1^*)$, which is multiplied by a real number $\lambda > 0$. Following the above procedure we obtain $ES(\lambda) = \lambda ES$ and we recover (2.10). In this case, however, the result is not as general as in the previous case, since the probability detection function can converge to zero nonlinearly, requiring a complex proof to show that the result continues to hold when this happens.

Notes

1   As an example, the USA has accused South Korea of using standards that have not been publicized. In the case of processed agricultural products and medical equipment, Korea is accused of using unclear and non-transparent standards (National Research Council 1995). Chilean exports of fish meal and fruit to Mexico have been held back due to supposed phytosanitary problems.

2   Multilateral organizations use sets of principles (the *Codes*) which define acceptable legislation for contingent protection in an attempt to restrain their use.

3   "...the prospect of protection, as it is institutionalized in the policy in the policy-making process and rules of administrative protection, may induce real changes in economic activity regardless of whether the barriers have in fact been imposed. Firms that compete with imports, and exporting firms, may be able to manage the possibility of protection under the existing rules by modifying their decisions on foreign investment, protection, employment, exports investments and other things... Thus the simple absence of trade barriers in certain areas is not sufficient to ensure, as is typically assumed in international trade theory, that both the conduct of firms and international trade are free from distortion arising from trade policy" (Leidy, 1995).

4   Imports cause serious injury when they are the main cause of the industry's problems. Imports cause material injury when they are one of the factors affecting the industry.

5   The minimum value of the signal that allows the importing country to punish the exporter.

6   Fischer and Mirman (1994) study the strategic behavior of firms that experiment to decide the intensity of dumping control.

7   See Helpman (1995) for the modern theory of the political economy of such lobbies and their interactions. For our purposes, the tariff values that appear in his article should be reinterpreted as the intensity of monitoring in different sectors.

8   The number of cases presented by Australia, the EEC, USA and Canada between 1980 and 1989, is about 900.

9   For further details see Boltuck and Litan (1991).

10   Ethier (1998) makes the interesting claim that contingent protection is usually associated to compensations of this type.

11   From an economist's point of view this criterion makes little sense. Imports always harm domestic competition, even if they do not affect the quantities sold by the local industry, because the sale price always falls.

12   The number of cases formally registered up to 1985 was more than 120. There are other cases of informal safeguard measures such as voluntary export restrains, delay in customs processes, etc.

13   Between 1979 and 1989, 300 petitions to impose countervailing duties due to subsidies were presented in the United States.

14   There are times when the punishment permits collusion between the firms, such that both prefer it, in which case the domestic firm will try to get sanctioned. See Krishna (1989) and Harris (1985) for an analysis of the cartelizing effect of a quota.

15   In response to a dumping accusation by the US salmon industry, Chilean producers have studied the possibility of cutting prices in some markets in Europe to reduce the margin of dumping.

16   In expression (2.2) there is an abuse of notation, as ρ is a function of $s_2(z_1, z_2^*)$, with $\rho' > 0$.

17   This means we study subgame perfect equilibria.

18   Sometimes this does not happen, such as when the "sanction" facilitates collusion between the firms, as occurs with minimal customs values and price undertakings. A similar case is voluntary export restraints analyzed in Harris (1985) and Krishna (1989), as mentioned before. Ethier (1998) claims that these "compensations" are an essential component of this type of protection.

19   The second-order conditions guaranteeing the stability of the equilibrium are quite complex and we will assume they are fulfilled. Prusa (1994) examines a case where this does not occur.

20   This requires fulfilment of the usual conditions for the Nash equilibrium to be unique.

21   In the case of imperfect substitutability.

22   Prusa (1994) argues that the effect exists even when the accusation is rejected in the preliminary stage.

23   Fischer (1992) studies an example that considers welfare in the two periods. In general, welfare in two periods depends on the type of sanction. If the sanction is a fine that does not distort the firms' behavior, the important effects on welfare are confined to the first period. If the sanction introduces a significant distortion, the analysis is more complex and goes beyond the scope of this chapter.

24   At $\lambda = 0$ the standard first-order conditions $p_1 - c_1 + p'_i q_1 = 0$ under no protection are satisfied. Hence, from the envelope theorem, $d\Pi_1/d\lambda = p'_1 q_1 (dq^*_1/d\lambda)$.

References

Bhagwati, J. N. and T. N. Srinivasan (1976). "Optimal trade policy and compensation under endogenous uncertainty: The phenomenon of market disruption", *Journal of International Economics*, 6, 317–36.

Boltuck, R. and R. E. Litan (1991). *Down in the Dumps: Administration of the Unfair Trade Laws*. Washington, DC: The Brookings Institution.

Das, S. (1990). "Foreign lobbying and the political economy of protection", *Japan and the World Economy*, 2.

Ethier, W. J. (1998, September). "The International commercial system", *Essays in International Finance 210*, Princeton University Department of Economics, Princeton, NJ.

Finger, M. J. (1987). "Antidumping and antisubsidy measures", in M. J. Finger and A. Olechowski (eds), *The Uruguay Round: A Handbook for Multilateral Trade Negotiations*. Washington, DC: The World Bank.

Fischer, R. D. (1987). "Essays in Game Theory and International Economics", Ph. D. thesis, University of Pennsylvania.

Fischer, R. D. (1992). "Endogenous probability of protection and firm behavior", *Journal of International Economics*, 32, 149–63.

Fischer, R. D. and L. J. Mirman (1994). "Learning about enforcement: A model of dumping", *Journal of Economic Integration*, 9(2).

Harris, R. (1985). "Why voluntary exports restraints are 'voluntary'", *Canadian Journal of Economics*, XVIII, 799–809.

Helpman, E. (1995, October). "Politics and trade policy", *Technical Report 5309*, National Bureau of Economic Research.

Krishna, K. (1989). "Trade barriers as facilitating practices", *Canadian Journal of Economics*, 26, 251–70.

Leidy, M. D. (1995). "Trade policy and indirect rent seeking: A synthesis of recent work". Cited in D. Rodrick, "Political Economy of Trade Policy", in G. Grossman and K. Rogoff (eds), *Handbook of International Economics, Volume III*. North-Holland, 1995.

National Research Council (1995). *Standards, Conformity Assessment and Trade*. Washington, DC: National Academy Press.

Prusa, T. (1994). "Pricing behavior in the presence of antidumping law", *Journal of International Integration*, 9(2), 260–89.

Prusa, T. J. (1996). "The trade effects of US antidumping actions", *Technical Report 5440*, National Bureau of Economic Research.

Reitzes, J. D. (1993). "Antidumping policy", *International Economic Review*, 34, 745–63.

Tirole, J. (1987). *The Theory of Industrial Organization*. Cambridge, MA: MIT Press.

Viner, J. (1923). *Dumping: A Problem in International Trade*. Chicago, IL: University of Chicago Press.

3
Minimum Standards: A New Source of Protection

*Ronald Fischer and Pablo Serra**

1 Introduction

The purpose of this chapter is to derive conditions under which the use of minimum standards (MS) harms foreign exporters,[1] a topic of increasing relevance as technical trade barriers replace tariffs as one of the tools of choice of protection. The National Research Council (1995) remarks that although the extent and costs of traditional forms of protection have been extensively documented, little effort has been made to analyze and measure the effects of technical barriers to trade. This is particularly true in the case of standards, despite evidence suggesting that these are important trade barriers and that their use as a protectionist device may be on the rise.

As norms and standards usually apply to both national and foreign production, they differ from classical forms of protectionism, which openly discriminate against imports. However, MS may hide protectionist intentions and it is even possible that protection is the only goal of a non-discriminatory standard. An example of this type of standards is *marketing orders*,[2] which, as Bockstael (1984) points out, are usually applied to features which are visible to consumers. Bockstael argues that MS may be a recurrent form of protection, since the rents they generate are politically more palatable than traditional trade barriers. Since MS are often imposed in response to pressures from local producers seeking protection against competition from imports, consumers usually do not benefit from them. But even when standards raise welfare in the country, they usually reduce the profits of foreign firms, so they

* We are grateful for comments by Alex Galetovic. Ronald Fischer gratefully acknowledges support from FONDECYT, Project 1950513.

can be considered barriers to trade under certain definitions of a protectionist standard.

Unfortunately, there is no generally agreed definition among economists of what constitutes a technical trade barrier. Hillman (1991) defines a technical barrier to trade as any government action that discriminates against exports. However, Chambers and Pick (1994) point out that standards applying to both local and foreign producers can still be biased against exports. Engel (Chapter 5) proposes a definition whereby a measure is protectionist if it differs from what a world social welfare-maximizing planner would choose.

Fischer and Serra (in press) adapt Engel's definition to the case of externalities: a protectionist standard is one that exceeds the standard a welfare-maximizing government would set if all producers were domestic. In the presence of externalities the MS that maximizes local welfare is likely to result in lower profits for the foreign firm than the MS that maximizes a welfare function that includes profits from foreign firms. Hence the MS chosen by a welfare-maximizing local social planner (LSP) is likely to hurt foreign firms.

While our previous definition captures the idea of improving social welfare at the expense of foreigners, this concept of what it means to be *protectionist* differs from the common understanding that protection should help domestic producers; this is not necessarily the case under our definition. A better name for standards covered by the previous definition is that of *beggar-thy-neighbor standards*, while reserving the name of *protectionist standards* for those beggar-thy-neighbor standards that have the additional effect of transferring rents to domestic producers.

The General Agreement on Trade and Tariffs (GATT), established in 1947, allows the use of standards to protect human, animal and vegetable life (article XX (b)) or to *order a market* (article XI, 2 (b)), as long as such measures do not discriminate or act as a form of protection. Hence the GATT distinguishes between two types of standards. Examples belonging to the first group are the European Union ban on meat and meat products derived from animals treated with growth hormones, or the limits many countries impose on the sulfite content of wine. The second group includes the US prohibition on the sale of fruits and vegetables that do not satisfy certain quality requirements (or *marketing orders*), or the Chilean requirement that meat sold in their country must conform to *standard cuts*. This chapter considers both types of standards.

Since the Agreement was established, there have been suspicions that standards have been used as indirect forms of protection. The GATT

Uruguay Round created a new entity that supersedes GATT, the World Trade Organization (WTO), which is charged with supervising the international trade system. Membership is open only to members of GATT that have accepted all of the Uruguay Round agreements, including an Agreement on Technical Barriers to Trade, a Code of Good Practice (for the preparation, adoption and application of standards) and an Agreement on the Application of Sanitary and Phytosanitary Measures. The new agreements establish that standards must be based on scientific evidence and that in order to harmonize standards, countries should base their own standards on international norms and recommendations if these exist.[3]

In order to formalize the use of MS as a protectionist tool we present two models, one corresponding to each type of standard. In the first model, the existence of a negative consumption externality justifies the imposition of a standard. Otherwise the negative externality would unduly affect people's welfare. The second model considers a good of heterogeneous, unobservable quality. In this case, if consumers were unable to determine the country of origin of the goods, and if the average quality of foreign goods were lower than the average quality of domestic good, the information asymmetry could result in a welfare loss.

In the first model, a higher value for the standard corresponds to a reduction in the negative externality which is a by-product of consuming the good. In order to simplify the analysis, we assume that the MS has no direct effect on individual consumer welfare. One example of this type of MS is the requirement that automobiles have a catalytic converter in order to reduce emissions. Other examples of standards that reduce negative consumption externalities without having a direct impact on consumer utility are requirements that aerosols and refrigeration equipment do not contain CFCs, in order to protect the ozone layer, as well as standards on biodegradable detergents and rules relating to the recycling of bottles and packaging materials.

In this model, a homogeneous good is produced by two firms, one domestic and one foreign. The foreign firm exports and produces for its own national market, but the domestic firm does not export to the foreign country.[4] It is assumed to be prohibitively expensive for a firm, due to development costs, to produce more than one standard. Hence an increase in the MS demanded by the domestic country, over and above the worldwide standard, compels the foreign firm to choose between raising its standard and, therefore, the costs of its entire production or, alternatively, abandoning exports and concentrating on its own market.

We assume that the LSP considers the welfare of domestic society at large. Hence its objective function includes, apart from reducing the negative externality (improving the environment), the possibility of shifting rents towards the domestic producer via a minimum standard that drives out the foreign firm. There are two factors that point in the other direction, i.e. towards reducing the level of the standard. First, the exclusion of foreign competition increases the market power of the local firm; and second, a new standard raises the domestic firm's production costs. The analysis of our model shows that when the relative size of the foreign market exceeds a certain value, the planner chooses to exclude the foreign firm; on the other hand, if the relative size of the foreign market falls short of this threshold, the planner imposes a standard that allows imports. We also show that the MS preferred by the planner is always higher when one of the firms is foreign than when all production is domestic. Moreover, raising the standard reduces the profits of the foreign producer. Hence the planner always adopts a beggar-thy-neighbor standard.

Since higher standards increase the production cost for both firms, the local firm benefits only if the effect on the foreign firm is relatively greater than the effect on itself. This occurs when exports represent a small fraction of the foreign firm's sales, i.e. when the foreign firm's own market is relatively large. On the other hand, if exports are a large fraction of the foreign firm's sales, the standard required to exclude the foreign firm is extremely high, and the domestic firm may prefer a duopoly with a lower MS. Hence even when the MS set by the LSP excludes the foreign firm from the local market, the local firm could still be hurt. Moreover, when the MS does not exclude the foreign firm, the MS always hurts the local firm compared to the situation with no MS. Hence, although the MS chosen by the LSP always damages the foreign firm, it does not necessarily benefit the local firm. In this case the main purpose of the MS is protecting local consumers.

The second model analyzes the use of MS in the presence of information asymmetries. We consider a good of heterogenous quality which cannot be observed by buyers beforehand. The local market is supplied by numerous local and foreign producers under competition. We simplify the analysis by assuming capacity to be fixed (i.e. this is a short-term analysis), and that existing demand will ensure full utilization of existing capacity. Quality differences are a side-effect of the production process: an example would be a fruit producer who, at the time of the harvest, finds himself with a fixed output of heterogeneous quality. The producer cannot alter the quality of the crop, but may harvest only the fruit that meets the quality standard. Quality is modeled so that a unit of inferior quality is equivalent to a fraction of a unit of the best quality. This formalization of quality is a natural extension of the definitions that appear in Ronnen (1991) and Boom (1995), where the per-unit benefit produced by a good of quality b is b. Each consumer demands a large amount of the good, so that only average quality matters to consumers. In this context, any quality standard lowers consumer welfare, as it excludes a fraction of production, thereby reducing total supply and raising prices.

The quality standard that maximizes social welfare if all producers are domestic is one that excludes all goods that generate lower utility than their production cost. If consumers can identify the country of origin of the products they buy, the MS that maximizes domestic welfare is lower than the standard that maximizes welfare if all firms were domestic. The intuition runs as follows: raising the quality standard benefits producers and hurts consumers. When the country imports a fraction of its consumption, the incentives to raise standards are lower than for the autarkic economy, because foreign profits are not included in domestic welfare. Hence the LSP sets a standard that is lower than the one desired by domestic and foreign firms. This is a case of a beggar-thy-neighbor standard, but it can hardly be called protectionist as it also hurts local producers. The winners with the MS set by the LSP are local consumers. Producers, both local and foreign, prefer a higher standard under which supply is closer to the monopolistic solution.

The alternative case occurs when consumers cannot determine whether the good is imported or manufactured domestically. We assume that domestic production has higher average quality at any minimum quality level and that the average difference in quality falls as the standard is raised. In this case, the standard that maximizes domestic welfare can be a protectionist beggar-thy neighbor standard, i.e. it could simultaneously increase domestic firms' profits and reduce foreign firms' profits relative to the MS chosen when the two firms are domestic.

Note that it is the unobservability of the country of origin of the goods that reduces domestic welfare. There is a simple solution to this problem. By requiring labels that indicate the origin of the goods (a universal procedure) a country eliminates the asymmetry of information motive for protection. Thus, a protectionist standard can only be explained as the result of pressures exerted by local producers at the expense of domestic welfare.

A series of articles have studied product quality standards as a trade barrier (Bredhal, Schmitz and Hillman 1987; Bockstael 1984;

Chambers and Weiss 1992). In general, the literature analyzing the use of standards for strategic purposes has concentrated on environmental *production* standards (Barret 1994; Kennedy 1994).[5] These authors use rent-transfer arguments similar to those of Brander and Spencer (1985) to show that countries have an incentive to lower their environmental standards so as to reduce production costs and become more competitive in foreign markets. As in Brander and Spencer, the simultaneous use of standards as a strategic trade instrument has negative consequences for the two countries. However, unlike the articles cited, in our two cases the country's social planner could *raise* standards. The explanation is due to the fact that in those papers, firms compete in a third market, while in this article the firms compete in the importing country.

Boom (1995) develops a duopoly model with vertical product differentiation, where each firm is localized in one country. Each firm can produce a single quality, for which reason the quality standard imposed by any one country alters the decisions of both firms. In that paper, as in all the literature on vertical differentiation, it is assumed that quality increases the utility of consumption. The author shows that if a country raises its minimum quality standards (MS), consumers benefit by an increase in quality and a reduction in prices, provided both firms continue supplying both markets. Boom suggests that the MS can be used as a technical barrier to trade, but she does not develop this possibility further.

The rest of this paper develops the ideas contained in this introduction. Section 2 presents various examples of protectionist MS. The next section describes the model of standards designed to protect against externalities. Section 4 examines the case in which standards are designed to organize markets, i.e. where standards are designed to correct information asymmetries. The final section presents the conclusions of this study.

2 Examples of protectionist MS

In this section we describe a series of examples that show the use of non-discriminatory standards as trade barriers. The European Union has prohibited beef imports from animals treated with growth hormones, i.e. mainly from the US. According to the National Research Council, a US government agency, this restriction is an unwarranted restriction of trade because there are no scientific arguments supporting prohibition (National Research Council 1995).

Bredahl, Schmitz and Hillman (1987) analyze the marketing order imposed on imports of Mexican tomatoes into the US in 1968–69.[6] In that season, the marketing board decreed that green tomatoes (not vine-ripened), typically produced in Florida, should have a diameter of 2–9/32" or greater, while vine-ripened tomatoes, usually produced in Mexico, should have a minimum diameter of 2–17/32". The authors estimate that imports declined by 1,120 cwt., and that tomato prices rose from US$ 14.16/cwt. to US$ 17.62/cwt. The requirement was eliminated after consumer groups lobbied against it, partly because they were unhappy with the higher tomato prices, but also because Mexican tomatoes were of a higher quality.

The newly proposed Chilean alcohol legislation's a good example of a standard designed to prevent imports. The present law is openly discriminatory against foreign imports, setting a 25 per cent alcohol tax on pisco (a traditional chilean distilled alcohol which represents 84 per cent of domestic liquor consumption) and a 70 per cent alcohol tax on whisky, which is imported and represents 5 per cent of consumption.[7] This tax was in open violation of the WTO treaties, since if liquors are taxed because they contain a dangerous substance (alcohol), the tax should be on the alcohol content, not on the type of liquor.[8] Given a European threat of an accusation in an WTO panel, the Chilean government is currently introducing a new alcohol law. The new legislation imposes an *ad valorem* tax on alcohol that sets differentiated rates according to the alcohol content, as shown in Table 3.1.

There are two reasons why the proposed legislation continues to discriminate against imports. First, an *ad valorem* tax sets a higher tax on more expensive liquors, hurting imports. Such a tax contradicts the fact that it is the total alcohol content and not its value that should be

Table 3.1 Alcoholic content and *ad valorem* taxes in the proposed legislation

Alcohol content (%)	tax (%)
Less than 35	27
35–36	31
36–37	35
37–38	39
38–39	43
More than 39	47

Source: *El Diario*, 28 September 1998, special supplement.

taxed, hence, specific taxes are appropriate. Second, 80 per cent of pisco consumption has an alcohol content of 30°, and the second most important variety has 35°. Whisky, on the other hand, is normally sold for export at 40° or more, hence subject to the highest tax rate of 47 per cent (see Table 3.1). Since the Chilean market is small, it is unlikely that exporters would be willing to change their alcohol graduations in order to pay the lower alcohol taxes.[9] Hence, the Chilean alcohol tax implicitly discriminates against whisky imports. Recognizing this fact, the European Union has called for a WTO panel,[10] and again the appeals panel ruled against Chile.

Another interesting example from Chile relates to beef. In the late 1970s, Chile implemented a policy to eradicate foot-and-mouth disease in order to enable meat producers to export to developed countries, which impose strict phytosanitary requirements. Chile has no comparative advantage in meat production and shares a two and a half thousand mile border with Argentina, a country with a huge comparative advantage in meat production, but which suffered from endemic foot-and-mouth (at that time). This was an expensive policy. Animals smuggled from Argentina often caused localized epidemics and the slaughter of affected cattle, with the Chilean government paying an indemnization to farmers. This policy was pursued for almost 15 years, without leading to the promised exports. More importantly for Chilean meat producers, the policy limited imports from Argentina. By the early 1990s, however, Argentine exporters had developed vacuum packaging off-the-bone, which eliminated the possibility of contagion from Argentine meat and led to soaring imports from Argentina. Moreover, Argentina started its own policy of eradication of foot-and-mouth disease. Coincidentally, Chile introduced a *sui generis* system for grading meat quality which was incompatible with the one used by Argentina and other important meat exporters such as the US. The US and Argentina argue that they use internationally accepted systems and that the cost of setting a special grading system in order to export to such a small market, raises prices and hence protects local producers.

2.1 Harmonization of standards

When standards are analyzed as a tool of protection, it is possible to explain the difficulties in getting countries to harmonize their standards. The problem is further complicated because it is common for products to be subject to multiple MS, each corresponding to different product characteristics. When the various MS differ from country to country, exporters are at a disadvantage because they have to attain

Table 3.2   Residue standards for fruit pesticides and fungicides in different countries

Product	USA	Germany	France	Holland	United Kingdom
		Standards for apples			
Malathion	8	0.5	0.5	0.5	0.5
Permethrin	0.05	1	1	1	1
Phosmet	10	2	2	1	10
Bromopropylat	NR	2	2	2	0.5
Captan	25	3	3	15	3
Iprodione	NR	10	10	10	10
		Standards for grapes			
Malathion	8	0.5	0.5	0.5	0.5
Permethrin	NR	1	1	1	1
Phosmet	10	0.01	NR	NR	NR
Bromopropylat	NR	2	2	2	5
Captan	50	3	3	2	3
Iprodione	60	10	10	10	10

Note: NR: Not recorded, i.e. fruit not accepted if residues are measurable.
Source: Data compiled from Prochile by C. Holuigue.

the highest level in each of the different dimensions if they wish to preserve flexibility in their exports. In fact, an exporter wishing to reallocate its production between different markets according to the demand it faces, has to satisfy the strictest level in each category. Alternatively, the exporter could allocate production to a single country, so as to satisfy only that country's standards. However, the impossibility of reallocating exports is costly, as it prevents arbitrage between export markets.

As an example, let us consider the case of fruit exporters. Pesticide residues are regulated by norms that vary between countries.[11] Table 3.2 shows a selection of residue standards for fruit pesticides and fungicides in different countries. However, the figures in the table do not necessarily imply that the non-harmonization of standards has a protectionist aim. There are alternative explanations: for example, different risk perceptions in different countries, or there may be lobbying against the raising of standards for pesticides produced and used in the particular country. Notwithstanding these considerations, the evidence suggests that norm-setting includes protectionist objectives.

3 A model of consumption externality

The model considers a two-country world.[12] There is a homogeneous good produced by two firms, one national and one foreign. The foreign firm produces for its own local market and for export. The domestic firm does not export to the foreign country, owing to high transport costs, or for other reasons. Firms compete on quantities; they have identical costs and constant returns to scale. We further assume that the standard has no effect on demand for the good, as probably occurs with many environmental standards.

The domestic country does not impose explicit trade restrictions, which in principle implies that the *ex-ante* behavior of the two firms corresponds to that of a symmetric duopoly. More formally the domestic firm solves:

$$\max_{\{q_1\}} \Pi(q_1; q_2; \tau) = p(q_1 + q_2)q_1 - c(\tau)q_1 \tag{3.1}$$

where Π are the profits of the domestic firm, p is the domestic inverse demand function, q_1 and q_2 are the domestic firm's sales and domestic imports respectively. The parameter $\tau \in \mathcal{R}^+$ represents the level of the MS in the home market (H). We use $c(\tau)$ to denote (constant) unit production costs at standard level τ. Unit production costs rise with the standard (i.e. it is more expensive to produce at a higher standard) and c is convex in the standard, i.e. raising the standard becomes increasingly costly. Given that unit costs are an increasing function of the standard, and that the standard does not alter the demand for the good (the effects of the standard are reflected only in the level of the externality), firms will always produce at the lowest allowed standard.[13] Likewise, the inverse demand curves have a negative slope. These conditions can be expressed as:

$$c' \geq 0, c'' > 0, \ p' < 0 \tag{3.2}$$

Starred variables correspond to the foreign country. We assume that the foreign country has an optimal minimum standard which is fixed and lower than the standard in the domestic country. Without loss of generality, the foreign standard is set at zero. In proposition 4 we show that the foreign standard is always lower than the domestic standard, so the assumption implies no restriction. Hence, when the foreign firm exports, it solves:

$$\max_{\{q_2, q^*\}} \Pi^*(q_2, q^*; q_1; \tau) = p(q_1 + q_2)q_2 + p^*(q^*)q^* - c(\tau)(q_2 + q^*) \tag{3.3}$$

where Π^* represents its profits, p^* the inverse demand function in the foreign-country market and q^* are its sales in that market. If the foreign firm prefers not to export it solves:

$$\max_{\{q^*\}} \Pi^*(q^*; \tau) = p^*(q^*)q^* - c(0)q^* \qquad (3.4)$$

Therefore, assuming constant marginal utility of income, and that there are no costs involved in verifying whether or not the good complies with the MS, social welfare in H can be expressed as gross consumer surplus plus the effect of the negative consumption externality, minus the cost of local production and minus the cost of imports.

$$W^d(q_1, q_2, \tau) = \int_0^q p(s)ds + L(q, \tau) - c(\tau)q_1 - p(q)q_2 \qquad (3.5)$$

where $q \equiv q_1 + q_2$ is total consumption in H and $L(q, \tau) < 0$ is the loss associated with the externality. When the MS keeps imports out, social welfare is equal to gross consumer surplus, plus the negative externality and minus the cost of local production:

$$W^m(q_1, \tau) = \int_0^{q_1} p(s)ds + L(q_1, \tau) - c(\tau)q_1 \qquad (3.6)$$

A rise in the domestic MS lowers the incentive for the foreign firm to export. To demonstrate this result formally, we need to impose a technical condition on the concavity of the demand functions, thereby guaranteeing the stability of the Cournot equilibrium in H. This condition will be used in the subsequent development.

Condition 1 $p''q_i + p' < 0$, $p^{*''}q^* + p^{*'} < 0$.

Proposition 1 *If condition 1 is fulfilled*
  1 The foreign firm's profits from exports fall as the MS is raised in H.
  2 Under monopoly, the domestic firm's profits fall as the MS is raised.

Proof: See Appendix.

If there is no MS in country H, the foreign firm will always export. As we have assumed there is no MS in the foreign country, returns from exports fall as the MS is raised in country H, because the foreign firm has to comply with the requirement both for its own domestic production, and for the export market. When the foreign firm does not export, its profits do not depend on the minimum standard ruling in H. There

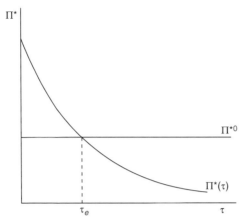

Figure 3.1 Profits of the foreign firm as a function of the standard

is, therefore, an MS τ_e in H which leaves the foreign firm indifferent between exporting and producing solely for its own market with no standard.[14] This minimum standard τ_e is the solution to:

$$(p^*(q^*(0)) - c(0))q^*(0) = (p^*(q^*(\tau_e)) - c(\tau_e))q^*(\tau_e) + (p(q(\tau_e)) \\ - c(\tau_e))q_2(\tau_e) \tag{3.7}$$

We use $q^*(\tau)$, $q(\tau)$, $q_1(\tau)$ and $q_2(\tau)$ to denote production levels when the MS is τ. Figure 3.1 shows how to find the standard which leaves the foreign firm indifferent between exporting and not doing so. In the figure, we use Π^{*0} to denote the profit that the foreign firm obtains in its own market when $\tau = 0$, see (3.4), and $\Pi^*(\tau)$ denotes its profits when it operates in both markets, under minimum standard τ, see (3.3). Then τ_e is where $\Pi^{*0} = \Pi^*(\tau)$.

We now consider the problem facing the domestic firm which has to decide whether to press for the lowest MS that drives the foreign firm away from the local market, or whether it is preferable to maintain a duopoly with no standard. So as not to complicate the exposition, we assume the foreign firm does not export when $\tau = \tau_e$. Figure 3.2 shows the domestic firm's profit under monopoly and duopoly as functions of the standard τ (the superscript d indicates duopoly and m indicates monopoly.) The curve drawn in bold shows profits earned by the domestic firm at each minimum standard. The jump in profits that occurs when standard τ_e is reached, is the result of a change in regime from duopoly to monopoly. This happens when the foreign firm decides not to export, due to the fact that the MS in country H is very high. Note

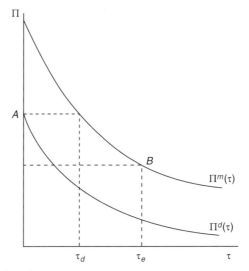

Figure 3.2 Profits of the domestic firm under monopoly and duopoly

that the only standards that are relevant to the domestic firm's decisions are the null standard (corresponding to point A) if the firm prefers a duopoly, and the standard τ_e (corresponding to point B) when it prefers a monopoly, as can be seen in Figure 3.2.

3.1 Minimum standards and relative market sizes

The relative size of the foreign market is one of the main factors that determines the MS that is preferred by the domestic firm. This is the relevant variable in our model, given that the strategic situation arises because the foreign producer has an alternative to exporting, namely its own domestic market. We use γ to denote the size of the foreign market. We assume that a larger country is equivalent to γ replications of the base country.[15] Since the domestic market remains unchanged, γ also represents the relative size of the foreign market in terms of the domestic market. We assume that the demand function can be written as $q^*(p^*; \gamma) = \gamma q^*(p^*)$. Hence, $dp^*/d\gamma > 0$ and $d^2 p^*/d\gamma dq^* = -(p^{*\prime} + q^* p^{*\prime\prime})/\gamma$, which is positive by condition 1. The main result of this section is to demonstrate that the exclusion standard τ_e diminishes with the relative size of the foreign market. The explanation of this result is simple: as the size of the foreign market increases, so does the cost to the foreign firm of producing at the standards required in the export market. This leads the foreign firm to cease exporting and revert to its domestic standard of zero.

Proposition 2 *Assume condition 1 is satisfied, then the MS which excludes the foreign firm from the domestic market falls as the size of the foreign market rises, i.e., $d\tau_e/d\gamma < 0$.*

Proof: Totally differentiating both terms of the exclusion condition (3.7) with respect to γ, and using the Envelope Theorem, we obtain:

$$
\begin{aligned}
q^*(0)\frac{dp^*}{d\gamma}\big|_{p^*(q^*(0))} &- q^*(\tau_e)\frac{dp^*}{d\gamma}\big|_{p^*(q^*(\tau_e))} \\
&= (p'q_2(\tau_e)\frac{dq_1}{d\tau} - c'(\tau_e)(q_2(\tau_e) + q^*(\tau_e)))\frac{d\tau_e}{d\gamma}
\end{aligned}
\tag{3.8}
$$

but since $q^*(0) > q^*(\tau_e)$ and $d^2p^*/d\gamma dq^* > 0$, the LHS of (3.8) is positive, which implies that the proposition is valid if the term in brackets in (3.8) is negative. Using equation (3.27) in the Appendix, the bracketed term in (3.8) is negative if:

$$
\frac{p'q_2}{2p''q_1 + 3p'} - (q_2 + q^*) < 0
$$

which is true, since $p''q_1 + p' < 0$, by condition 1. Note that the proposition implies there is a one-to-one relation between the two variables γ and τ_e.

Q.E.D.

The next step is to study the relation between the relative size of the foreign market and the domestic firm's incentives to exclude the foreign competitor. If the aim is to drive out the foreign firm and maintain a monopoly, the domestic firm needs to produce at standard level τ_e. If, on the other hand, the domestic firm prefers to accommodate to the entry of imports it will prefer no minimum standard ($\tau = 0$). The difference between profits under the two alternatives is:

$$
\Delta\Pi = \Pi^m(\tau_e) - \Pi^d(0).
\tag{3.9}
$$

As unit costs are constant, a change in the size of the foreign market does not alter sales in the domestic market when the domestic market has no MS. Therefore:

$$
\frac{d\Delta\Pi}{d\gamma} = \left(\frac{d\Pi^m}{d\tau_e}\right)\left(\frac{d\tau_e}{d\gamma}\right)
\tag{3.10}
$$

It was shown above that $d\tau_e/d\gamma < 0$. In addition:

$$\frac{d\Pi^m}{d\tau_e} = (p'(q_1)q_1 - p(q_1) - c(\tau))\left(\frac{dq_1}{d\tau_e}\right) - c'(\tau)q_1 = -c'(\tau)q_1 \leq 0 \quad (3.11)$$

Therefore, the greater the size of the foreign market, the greater the incentives to exclude the foreign firm. The explanation of this result is that the MS that makes it possible to exclude the foreign firm falls as the relative size of the foreign market grows. We can show that $\Delta\Pi$ as a function of γ intersects the abscissa. Indeed, when there is no demand in the foreign country ($\gamma = 0$), in order to exclude the foreign firm the MS has to be set so that the foreign firm (and by symmetry, the local firm) makes zero profits. Hence, the local firm prefers to allow imports, i.e. $\Delta\Pi(\gamma = 0) < 0$. On the contrary, when the relative size of the foreign country is very large (γ tends to infinity), any MS, however low, is enough to keep imports out. Thus, it always suits the local firm to exclude the foreign competitor, i.e. $\Delta\Pi(\gamma = \infty) > 0$. By continuity, there exists γ_d such that $\Delta\Pi(\gamma_d) = 0$

Hence, γ_d is the smallest relative foreign market size such that the domestic firm benefits from excluding the foreign firm by means of a minimum standard. Associated with this relative size, there is a standard $\tau_d \equiv \tau_e(\gamma_d)$ which keeps the foreign firm out. If the foreign market is larger than γ_d, keeping the foreign firm out is profitable, because the MS needed to do so is low. If the foreign market size is below γ_d, it is too

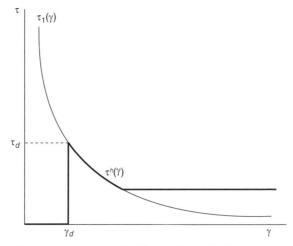

Figure 3.3 Minimum standard desired by the domestic firm

expensive to produce at a standard that would cause exclusion, so the domestic firm prefers a duopoly with no MS.

The curve in bold $\tau^h(\gamma)$ in Figure 3.3 indicates the minimum standard desired by the local firm for each foreign market size. The MS is $\tau = 0$ for relative sizes below γ_d. When this size is attained, the desired standard jumps to τ_d. Therefore, once γ_d is exceeded, any further increase in the size of the foreign market reduces the standard desired by the domestic firm according to the function $\tau_e(\gamma)$.

3.2 Social welfare and relative size of the foreign market

In this section we consider the existence of a consumption externality, such that the functional relation between standard and welfare depends on the externality $L(\tau, q)$. We consider an externality of the type $L(\tau, q) = (b(\tau) - d)q$, with $d > b(\tau) > 0$, $b' > 0$, $b'' < 0$. In other words, we assume that consumption produces a negative externality, which rises proportionately with consumption per individual. The magnitude of the externality declines when the standard of the product is increased, but at a diminishing marginal rate.

Figure 3.4 shows social welfare under both monopoly and duopoly for different standards, where τ_c denotes the MS for which the country's welfare is maximized when there are imports, and τ_a the MS that maximizes the country's welfare when there are no imports. In the first case, the social optimum is attained under duopoly, so the LSP will not want to exclude the foreign firm. In the second configuration, the optimum is reached under monopoly, and the planner would prefer there to be no imports, in order to attain the social optimum.

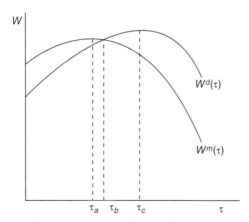

Figure 3.4 Social welfare as a function of standard

To obtain Figure 3.4 we require, first, that with no standard ($\tau = 0$) there is a strong negative externality, so the higher consumption under duopoly is worse than the lower level of consumption under monopoly. Second, as the standard increases, consumption falls at an increasing rate. This condition is likely to hold when the cost of meeting higher standards increases with the standard, as we have assumed. The third condition is that the marginal effect on net welfare of an increase in quality falls as quality increases. Finally, at some level, standards need to make production socially unprofitable. In the Appendix we show that these conditions are sufficient for welfare functions to have the configurations shown in Figure 3.4.

Given welfare functions similar to those in Figure 3.4, the standards which maximize social welfare for different relative market sizes are shown in Figure 3.5, which is derived from the following result:

Proposition 3 *If the welfare functions have the shape of those shown in Figure 3.4, the functional relation between foreign market size and the minimum standards chosen by the LSP, is given by:*

1 If $\gamma < \gamma_c$ the standard is positive but allows imports in.

2 If $\gamma \in [\gamma_c, \gamma_b]$, the minimum standard falls along the curve $\tau_e(\gamma)$ under duopoly.

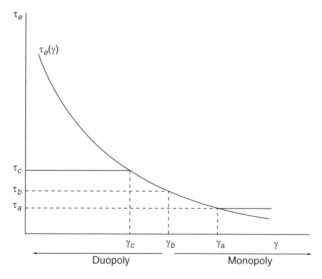

Figure 3.5 Minimum standard desired by the planner; the externality case

3 If $\gamma \in [\gamma_b, \gamma_a]$, the minimum standard moves along the curve $\tau_e(\gamma)$ under monopoly.

4 If $\gamma > \gamma_a$, the standard is positive and constant (lower than the standard under duopoly), and does not allow imports.[16]

where γ_c, γ_b and γ_a are the values that satisfy $\tau_c = \tau(\gamma_c), \tau_b = \tau(\gamma_b)$ and $\tau_a = \tau(\gamma_a)$, respectively.

Proof: Let us assume that the planner is constrained to use an MS equal to $\tau_e(\gamma)$ for each γ. We define $\Delta W(\gamma) \equiv W^m(\gamma) - W^d(\gamma)$. We know that when γ tends to infinity $\Delta W(\gamma)$ is positive. On the other hand, when γ tends to zero, keeping out the foreign competitor turns out to be very costly, so $\Delta W(\gamma)$ is negative. As well as this, we have:

$$\frac{d\Delta W}{d\gamma} > 0$$

so $\Delta W(\gamma)$ crosses the abscissa, i.e. there exists a γ_b such that $\Delta W(\gamma_b) = 0$.

In the segment $\gamma \in [0, \gamma_c]$, a duopoly with MS equal to τ_e is socially preferable to a monopoly with the same minimum standard. The social welfare-maximizing MS when imports are excluded is τ_a, a lower standard than that needed to exclude the foreign producer, τ_e. Under duopoly, the optimum MS is τ_c, so this is ultimately what the planner chooses.

In the segment $\gamma \in [\gamma_c, \gamma_b]$ a duopoly with minimum standard τ_e is preferable to a monopoly under this standard. The LSP would prefer a duopoly with an even higher standard, but that is not feasible for this range of γ, because the foreign producer would choose not to export. Nor is a monopoly possible with an MS below τ_e, so the social optimum is a duopoly under standard τ_e.

In the segment $\gamma \in [\gamma_b, \gamma_a]$, a monopoly under MS τ_e is socially preferable to a duopoly with that standard.

The LSP would prefer an even lower minimum standard under monopoly, τ_a, but this would attract imports, which the LSP wants to avoid, so the planner chooses τ_e.

Finally, when $\gamma \in [\gamma_a, \infty]$, the LSP can choose a minimum standard τ_a to maximize welfare under monopoly, without fear of eliciting imports.

Q.E.D.

The planner tries to balance three effects: the negative effect of the externality, the positive effect of competition on consumers and the negative effect of rent transfers abroad. It is clear that under duopoly the planner chooses a higher MS than under monopoly. Under duopoly the volume of production is greater, and with it, the magnitude of the externality, so a more demanding standard is needed. Secondly, under duopoly, part of the costs of a higher MS is absorbed by the foreign producer. If, starting from a low level, we increase the size of the foreign market, the initial standard will not allow the duopoly to be sustained, so the planner lowers it and chooses the highest standard compatible with duopoly, i.e. $\tau_e(\gamma)$. As the size of the foreign market is increased, the MS needs to be continuously lowered, which raises the firms' rents. Eventually a point is reached where the planner prefers to exclude the foreign producer, as the benefits from profits transferred to the local producer are greater than the losses caused by eliminating foreign competition. In this segment, the LSP chooses the lowest standard that eliminates the foreign producer.

If we compare the standards desired by the domestic firm with those that maximize social welfare, it can be seen that when $\gamma \in [0, \gamma_d]$, the standard desired by the LSP is positive and therefore greater than what the firm would choose. If $\gamma_d < \gamma_c$, there is a discontinuity in the standard preferred by the firm, which leads it to desire higher than socially-optimum standards at γ_d, which fall along the curve $\tau_e(\gamma)$ until γ_c[17] This can be seen by superimposing Figures 3.3 and 3.5. It is important to note that in the segment $[\gamma_c, \gamma_b]$, the standard preferred by the LSP and the firm are nearly identical, although the standard desired by the firm is marginally higher, so as to exclude imports. When the foreign market is bigger than γ_a, the social planner sets a constant standard the one desired by the domestic firm.[18]

3.3   A protectionist standard

Recall that we have defined a MS as protectionist if it is higher than the one the LSP would have chosen if all firms are domestic. To appreciate the scope of our definition, let us compare the standards that result from maximizing social welfare when both firms are domestic, with the corresponding standards when one of the firms is foreign.

Proposition 4 *If condition 1 is satisfied, the standard chosen by the LSP is protectionist.*

Proof: Consider welfare under duopoly when one of the firms is foreign:

$$W^d = \int_0^{2q_1} p(s)ds - p(2q_1)q_1 - c(\tau)q_1 + 2q_1(b(\tau) - d)$$

If we now consider welfare when both firms are domestic, we have:

$$W^D = \int_0^{2q_1} p(s)ds - 2c(\tau)q_1 + 2q_1(b(\tau) - d)$$

The difference $W^D - W^d = (p - c)q_1$ satisfies:

$$\frac{d(W^D - W^d)}{d\tau} = -c'(\tau)q_1 + (p + 2p'q_1 - c)\frac{dq_1}{d\tau} = p'\frac{dq_1}{d\tau} - c'(\tau)q_1$$

where we have used the envelope theorem. This last term is negative given the expression for $dq_1/d\tau$ derived in the Appendix and condition 1. This means that the marginal benefit of a rise in MS is greater under a duopoly where one firm is a foreign exporter than in the case where both firms are local, so the MS used in the former case will always be higher.

$$\textbf{Q.E.D.}$$

This result reflects the fact that when part of the costs of a higher standard can be charged to the foreign firm, the planner demands higher standards than if the two firms are domestic. Proposition 4 also implies that when the foreign country sets the optimal minimum standard (without facing the threat of imports), it will always set a lower standard than the home country, confirming that our earlier assumption on the relative level of standards in the two countries was innocuous.

4   A model of standards and information asymmetries

The second model examines information asymmetries as the reason for minimum standards. The specification is biased towards the introduction of standards even without protectionist intent. In this case, as opposed to the preceding model, we show that a planner is not protectionist by our definition, unless consumers cannot identify foreign goods of lower average quality. In this model the quality of the good is heterogenous, and it is normalized to the interval $[0,1]$. Capacity is fixed, as we are considering a short-term analysis. As a simplification, we assume that all suppliers have the same quality distribution for their production. Without loss of generality we normalize the number of producers to be one, and we denote by $q(b)$ the number of units of quality b. Let $Q(b)$ be the number of units of quality b or higher, in other words:

$$Q(b) = \int_b^1 q(\beta)d\beta$$

The choice of units implies that one unit of quality b is equal to b units of quality 1. The effective supply of goods of quality b or higher is:

$$Q^e(b) = \int_b^1 \beta q(\beta) d\beta$$

We define the mean quality of goods of quality b or higher as:

$$m(b) = \frac{Q^e(b)}{Q(b)}$$

Both the nominal supply $Q(b)$ and the effective supply $Q^e(b)$ fall with increases in the minimum quality standard b. On the other hand, an increase in b raises average quality. Let $c(b)$ be the short-term cost of producing one unit of quality b. The following condition ensures that when quality b is produced, it is profitable to produce all qualities higher than b.

Condition 2

$$c'(b) \geq 0, \; \frac{d}{db}\left(\frac{c(b)}{b}\right) \leq 0, \forall b$$

This condition means that the quality-normalized cost per unit is lower for higher-quality goods. A unit cost of production that is constant and independent of the quality of the good satisfies the above conditions. An example in which these conditions might hold is fruit growing, where the short-run production cost corresponds to the cost of harvesting, packaging and storing, and is independent of the quality of the fruit.

The total production cost of quality b or higher is:

$$C(b) = \int_b^1 c(\beta)q(\beta)d\beta$$

In order to reduce the number of potential cases, we assume that all installed capacity is used, independently of the standard. A sufficient condition for this to hold is that $m(0)c(1) < p(Q^e(0))$.

4.1 The closed economy

When the minimum quality standard is b, producer profits are:

$$\pi(b) = p(Q^e(b))Q^e(b) - C(b)$$

where p denotes the inverse demand function, which is assumed normal. Using partial equilibrium analysis and assuming the existence of a representative individual, social welfare is:

$$u(b) = v(y_0 + \pi(b), p(Q^e(b)))$$

where v represents the indirect utility function of the representative individual and y_0 his income before adding the profits derived from the firms producing the heterogenous quality good. This modelling of utility assumes that the representative individual consumes a large number of units of the good, so that his utility is a function of average quality. Taking the derivative of the utility function with respect to the quality standard b and using Hotelling's lemma we have:

$$\frac{u'(b)}{v_y} = (bp(Q^e(b)) - c(b))\frac{dQ(b)}{db} \tag{3.12}$$

where v_y denotes the marginal utility of income. Hence the quality standard b^* that maximizes social welfare, is defined by:[19]

$$b^* p(Q^e(b^*)) = c(b^*) \tag{3.13}$$

The optimal MS is that which only excludes goods whose production cost is lower than their value. Why should producers send to the market goods whose cost is higher than their value to consumers? The explanation is simple: because the price commanded by such goods reflects average quality and not the quality of each unit.

Given condition 2, an expansion in demand lowers the optimal MS b, with a limiting value of zero quality; as demand increases, lower-quality units become valuable, so the optimal standard falls. This fall in the optimal standard continues until all output is sent to the market.

The typical consumer is negatively affected by the imposition of an MS. His utility is:

$$u_c(b) = v(y_0, p(Q^e(b)))$$

Differentiating with respect to the quality standard b we have:

$$\frac{u'_c(b)}{v_y} = -Q^e(b)p'(Q^e(b))\frac{dQ^e(b)}{db} \tag{3.14}$$

This expression is negative, which implies that the increase in minimum quality harms consumers, because an increase in quality reduces the total supply of the good and raises the price. Hence consumers are always harmed by the imposition of an MS. This result is quite general, given the way we model quality. The effect of a rise in the MS on producer welfare is given by:

$$\pi'(b) = (bp(Q(b)) - c(b)) \frac{dQ(b)}{db} + Q^e(b)p'(Q^e(b)) \frac{dQ^e(b)}{db} \qquad (3.15)$$

Comparing equations (3.12) and (3.15), the quality standard that maximizes producer profits is higher than that which maximizes social welfare. An increase in the required quality benefits producers because supply decreases and the selling price rises, approaching the monopoly solution. Social welfare, on the other hand, incorporates the utility of consumers, who are hurt by a rise in standards.

Since the exclusion of lower-quality production (in certain ranges) raises social welfare and producer profits, why is it that producers cannot agree on excluding low-quality goods? The explanation is that they are unable to verify compliance with the agreement. For an individual producer, selling low-quality goods while the other producers offer only high-quality goods is a very attractive proposition, since the selling price is high. This is a form of the traditional *commons problem*.

4.2 The open economy

This section examines a two-country version of the model. The domestic economy produces and imports the heterogenous quality good, while the foreign country has no local demand for the good. An example is fruit production in Chile, where most fruit production is exported. The industries producing the good are competitive in both countries. We assume that production costs are the same in both countries, although the quality distribution differs from one country to another. We use subscripts d and f to denote local and foreign producers respectively. Variables with no subscript denote world aggregates. For example, $Q(b) = Q_d(b) + Q_f(b)$ corresponds to world supply of quality b or higher. Consider first the case where consumers can determine the good's country of origin. Here the price received by producers reflects the mean quality of each country's effective supply.

Next we examine how changes in the minimum quality standard affect the different parties. World welfare differs from national welfare by including foreign producer profits. Formally, the optimal MS is derived from the same welfare-maximization problem as in the closed economy, so the MS that maximizes world welfare is similar to (3.13). The country social welfare can be written as:

$$u(b) = v(y_0 + \pi_d(b), p(Q^e(b))) \tag{3.16}$$

where π_d denotes profits accruing to domestic producers, that is:

$$\pi_d(b) = p(Q^e(b))Q_d^e(b) - C_d(b) \tag{3.17}$$

Taking the derivative of (3.16) with respect to the MS b:

$$\frac{u'(b)}{v_y} = (bp(Q^e(b)) - c(b))\frac{dQ_d(b)}{db} - Q_f^e(b)p'(Q^e(b))\frac{dQ^e(b)}{db} \tag{3.18}$$

The second term in equation (3.18) is negative and represents the increase in import value caused by the rise in price. Since raising standards reduces effective supply, the price of both imports and local production goes up. Hence the quality standard that maximizes country welfare is lower than the standard that maximizes world welfare. This result follows from the fact that standards favor producers but harm consumers. When a fraction of local consumption is produced abroad, incentives to raise quality are lower.

Taking the derivative of the expression for the utility of local producers we obtain:

$$\pi_d'(b) = (bp(Q^e(b)) - c(b))\frac{dQ_d(b)}{db} + Q_d^e(b)p'(Q^e(b))\frac{dQ^e(b)}{db} \tag{3.19}$$

The second term on the RHS of (3.19) is positive as it corresponds to the increase in the income of local producers caused by the rise in price following the reduction in effective supply. Thus, the quality standard that maximizes domestic producer welfare is higher than the world welfare-maximizing standard, and *a fortiori* higher than the MS that maximizes domestic social welfare.

If the country imposes the standard desired by domestic producers, foreign producers are not necessarily adversely affected. Indeed, foreign producers' profits are:

$$\pi_f(b) = p(Q^e(b))Q_f^e(b) - C_f(b)$$

Differentiating with respect to b we have:

$$\pi_f'(b) = (bp(Q^e(b)) - c(b))\frac{dQ_f(b)}{db} + Q_f^e(b)p'(Q^e(b))\frac{dQ^e(b)}{db} \tag{3.20}$$

From expression (3.20), the MS that maximizes foreign producers' profits is higher than the standards that maximize world welfare and domestic welfare, respectively.

The minimum standards that maximize the profits of domestic and foreign producers are not generally the same. Before comparing the MS that maximize profits for domestic and foreign producers, we need to make some assumptions about the relative quality of domestic and foreign production.

Condition 3 $m_d(b) \geq m_f(b)$, $0 \leq b \leq 1$.

Condition 3 implies that the average quality of domestic production is higher than average foreign quality at any minimum quality level b. An additional condition is that the difference between mean domestic and foreign qualities declines as the minimum quality level rises; that is

Condition 4 $m'_d(b) \leq m'_f(b)$, $0 \leq b \leq 1$

Conditions 3 and 4 together imply that for any MS, average foreign quality is lower than domestic quality, and that this difference declines as the MS rises. It is important to note that condition 3 implies $m_d(b) \geq m(b)$ and that condition 4 implies $m'_d(b) \leq m'(b)$. Most of the results in the remainder of this paper depend on conditions 3 and 4, although some of our results require only weaker assumptions. An alternative to condition 4, is that output of quality b, as a proportion of output of quality b or higher, is smaller among domestic than foreign suppliers, i.e.,

Condition 5

$$\frac{q_d(b)}{Q_d(b)} \leq \frac{q_f(b)}{Q_f(b)}, 0 \leq b \leq 1$$

Lemma 1 *If condition 3 is satisfied, then condition 5 is necessary but not sufficient for condition 4.*

Proof: From the definition of $m(b)$, we have:

$$m'(b) = (m(b) - b)\frac{q(b)}{Q(b)} \tag{3.21}$$

From condition 3, $m_d(b) \geq m_f(b)$ and as $m(b) \geq b$, a necessary condition for condition 4 is condition 5.

Q.E.D.

4.3 Profit margins and protectionism

We have seen that the MS that maximizes domestic and foreign producer profits is higher than the one that maximizes home country welfare. However, if the profit margin is sufficiently large, i.e. if the price of the good is much higher than production costs, the differences between standards tend to disappear. Moreover, as the price rises towards infinity, the optimal quality standards of society and both local and foreign producers all converge to zero.

The domestic welfare effect of an increase in minimum quality standards can be expressed as the sum of two components (see equation (3.18)). The change in the profits of domestic producers can also be expressed as the sum of two terms (see equation (3.19)). The first term in both equations is identical while the second term has a different sign. The corresponding equation for the foreign producers also has similar terms.

Assume that the demand curve is concave, i.e. $p'' < 0$. As demand expands, the first component of equations (3.18), (3.19)) and (3.20) (the corresponding equation for foreign producers) which is identical in all three, becomes larger relative to the second term. Hence, for sufficiently large profit margins, further expansions in demand imply that the standards preferred by society and by producers converge to zero.

Explaining these results is straightforward. When the profit margin is low (low demand), profit-shifting to foreign producers is not significant, whereas consumption losses caused by a reduction in effective supply can be high. On the other hand, domestic and foreign producers benefit from a supply restriction that raises their profit margins. In this case, the socially optimal MS is much lower than that preferred by producers. On the contrary, when prices are high (high demand), any supply restriction that takes products out of the market lowers both social welfare and profits for domestic and foreign producers. Hence the optimal standard for society and producers approaches zero.

It follows that in markets where profit margins are high, there is little interest in imposing quality standards. On the other hand, if margins are low, domestic producers are likely to lobby for standards, and the standards they prefer are higher than those that maximize domestic social welfare.

4.4 The case where the origin is unknown

In this section we consider the case in which consumers cannot identify the source of the good, so domestic and foreign producers perceive the same price, which reflects the average quality of total supply. This situation harms domestic producers, since they receive a price that is lower than that corresponding to the average quality they put on the market. We show it leads to a higher MS, and hence to lower welfare compared to when the country of origin is known. Moreover, the standard that maximizes domestic welfare could be protectionist. In fact, we show that when the domestic market is large, the MS that maximizes domestic welfare is protectionist. However, these difficulties can be corrected by imposing the condition that goods have to be labeled to indicate the country of origin.

Proposition 5 *If conditions 3 and 4 are satisfied, then the fact that consumers cannot identify the source of the product raises optimal standard for the country and lowers maximum domestic welfare.*

Proof: First, note that domestic producer profits are:

$$\pi_d(b) = m(b)p(Q^e(b))Q_d(b) - C_d(b) \qquad (3.22)$$

Rewriting terms,

$$\pi_d(b) = p(Q^e(b))Q_d^e(b) - C_d(b) - A \qquad (3.23)$$

where

$$A = p(Q^e(b))Q_d(b)(m_d(b) - m(b))$$

The variable A represents the difference between effective sales by domestic producers when consumers are unaware of the origin of goods, with respect to the case where price reflects average quality of domestic production. This variable is positive if condition 3 holds, i.e. there is a loss to domestic producers because they receive a lower price than that corresponding to the average quality of their production.

The expression for domestic welfare is given by the same equation (3.16) as in the case where consumers know the origin of the good, except that the expression for π_d in (3.16) is given by (3.23) instead of (3.17). Hence for any MS the domestic social welfare is lower when consumers are unaware of the country of origin of the good.

Hence the effect of a marginal change in the MS on domestic social welfare is given by:

$$\frac{u'(b)}{v_y} = (bp(Q^e(b)) - c(b))\frac{dQ_d(b)}{db} - Q_f^e(b)p'(Q^e(b))\frac{dQ^e(b)}{db} - \frac{dA}{db} \qquad (3.24)$$

If conditions 3 and 4 hold, the loss A decreases with the increase in the MS, i.e., dA/db is negative. Hence, from the comparison of equations (3.24) and (3.18), it follows that the MS that maximizes domestic welfare is greater when the country of origin is unknown than when it is known.

Q.E.D.

There are several other differences between the case where consumers are unable to determine the origin of the goods and the case in which they can. First, it is no longer true that the MS that maximizes domestic social welfare is lower than the one that maximizes world welfare: this can be seen by comparing (3.24) and (3.12). Moreover, if the demand curve is concave, i.e. $p'' < 0$, then as demand rises the third component outweighs the second component in equation (3.24). When this occurs the MS that maximizes domestic social welfare could be greater than the optimal world MS. Hence if the profit margin in the industry is large, when the country sets the standard that maximizes domestic welfare it could well be protectionist.

In short, given the set of assumptions we have made about inter-country quality differentials, the informational asymmetry causes a welfare loss and raises the country's optimal MS. However, this problem can easily be solved by requiring imported goods to be labeled so that they can be identified by consumers.

5 Conclusions

This chapter inquires into the use of protectionist standards by welfare-maximizing local social planners. It presents two specific models to deal with different types of MS. In the first model the existence of a con-sumption externality justifies imposing an MS. The planner's desire to transfer rents to local producers may lead to a protectionist standard. In our model, profit shifting is achieved by excluding the foreign firm from the local market. Now, from the point of view of the local planner, an MS that excludes the foreign firm has two unfavorable effects: firstly, it eliminates competition in the local market; secondly, it raises domestic production costs. This implies that the profit-shifting motive does not always leads to a protectionist MS. In fact, it is shown that it is not always welfare enhancing to exclude the foreign firm, i.e. to set a protectionist standard.

In particular, when the foreign markets are relatively small, the for-eign firm has few alternatives for its production other than the local market. Hence a high MS is required to exclude it from the domestic market. The exclusion standard may turn out to be too costly for the local firm, and therefore the planner may wish to accept imports from the foreign firm. The existence of a negative consumption externality, however, always leads the LSP to set an MS higher than the one the planner would set if both firms were local. The reason is that foreign producers absorb part of the costs of raising the standard. When the MS does not exclude foreign producers, it clearly hurts the local producer who faces higher production costs but no protection from imports. Consumers benefit from lower levels of the negative externality (better environment). In this case, a MS that excluded the foreign firm could benefit the local firm, but this might not be the case because the MS chosen by a welfare-maximizing local planner could result in much higher costs for the foreign firm.

The second model allows us to consider a third reason for setting an MS: information asymmetry. In our model, standards always hurt consumers. Two cases are distinguished. First, consumers are aware of the country of origin of the good they consume. In this case, the LSP sets a standard that is lower than the one it would have set if all firms were domestic. Both local and foreign producers prefer the higher standard. Second, when consumers are unaware of the country of origin and the average quality of foreign goods is lower than the average quality of domestic production, the standard that maximizes domestic welfare could be higher than the one the LSP would use if all producers were domestic. Moreover, the standard chosen by the LSP raises profits of domestic producers at the expense of foreign producers, resulting in a protectionist standard. Note that the simple requirement of a label identifying country of origin eliminates the need to resort to a protectionist standard.

To summarize, since the objective function of the LSP does not include profits made by foreign producers, it is likely to lead to a beggar-thy-neighbor standard. In some cases, the chosen standard may be protectionist, i.e. a standard that favors domestic producers at the expense of foreign exporters.

Appendix

A.1 Proof of proposition 1

Proposition 1 *If condition 1 is fulfilled*

1 The foreign firm's profits from exports fall as the MS is raised in H.

2 Under monopoly, the domestic firm's profits fall as the MS is raised.

Proof: Differentiating the foreign firm's first-order conditions for sales in its own market with respect to τ, gives:

$$\frac{d(d\Pi^*/dq^*)}{d\tau} = \frac{d(p^{*\prime}q^* + p^* - c(\tau))}{d\tau} = (p^*q^* + 2p^*)\frac{dq^*}{d\tau} - c'(\tau) = 0$$

which implies (using condition 1)

$$\frac{dq^*}{d\tau} = \frac{c'(\tau)}{(p^*q^* + 2p^*)} < 0 \qquad (3.25)$$

Totally differentiating the two firms' first-order conditions in the local market $(d\Pi/dq_i = p'q_i + p - c = 0, i = 1, 2)$ with respect to standard τ, gives:

$$\begin{bmatrix} p''q_1 + 2p' & p''q_1 + p' \\ p''q_2 + p' & p''q_2 + 2p' \end{bmatrix} \begin{bmatrix} \frac{dq_1}{d\tau} \\ \frac{dq_2}{d\tau} \end{bmatrix} = \begin{bmatrix} c'(\tau) \\ c'(\tau) \end{bmatrix} \qquad (3.26)$$

Given the symmetry of the model in the local market, we have $q_1 = q_2$ in equilibrium, which means that the determinant of the matrix in (3.26) is $\Delta = p'(2p''q_1 + 3p') < 0$. Applying Cramer's Rule and condition 1 we have:

$$\frac{dq_i}{d\tau} = \frac{c'(\tau)}{(2p''q_i + 3p')} < 0 \qquad (3.27)$$

Thus the effect of an increase in minimum standards on the profits of the foreign firm (3.3) is:

$$\frac{d\Pi^*}{d\tau} = (p^*q^* + p^* - c)\frac{dq^*}{d\tau} - c'(\tau)q^* + (p'q_2 + p - c)\frac{dq_2}{d\tau} + p'q_2\frac{dq_1}{d\tau} - c'(\tau)q_2.$$

Given that the first-order conditions for profit maximization continue to be fulfilled (an application of the Envelope Theorem), this expression reduces to:

$$\frac{d\Pi^*}{d\tau} = -c'(\tau)(q^* + q_2) + p'q_2\frac{dq_1}{d\tau}.$$

The above expression can be rewritten using (3.27):

$$\frac{d\Pi^*}{d\tau} = c'(\tau)q_2\left(\frac{p'}{2p''q_1 + 3p'} - \left(1 + \frac{q^*}{q_2}\right)\right). \qquad (3.28)$$

The first term in the brackets is less than 1, since the denominator can be written as $p' + 2(p''q_1 + p')$, which, by condition 1, is larger in absolute value than p'. This means that the derivative $d\Pi^*/d\tau$ is negative. A similar argument shows that the profits of the domestic firm under monopoly also fall as τ is raised:

$$\frac{d\Pi^m}{d\tau} = -c'(\tau)q_1 < 0$$

Q.E.D.

6.2   Conditions on welfare

This part of the appendix finds conditions that ensure the welfare functions shown in Figure 3.4.

Condition 6 $W^d(0) < W^m(0)$, $d^2q_i/d\tau^2 < 0$, $d^2[(b-d-c)q_1]/d\tau^2 < 0$, $c'(0) = 0$, and $\lim_{\tau \to \infty} c(\tau) > p(0)$.

Lemma: *If condition 6 holds, then:*

1 *The welfare functions W^d, W^m are concave.*
2 *The welfare functions W^d, W^m have interior maxima τ_c and τ_a respectively.*
3 *These maxima satisfy $\tau_c > \tau_a$.*

Proof: The condition $c'(0) = 0$ implies that $dq_1/d\tau = 0$ at $\tau = 0$ (see equation (3.27)). This condition, combined with the fact that $b' > c'$ at $\tau = 0$ allows us to state that the social-welfare-optimizing MS is always strictly positive. To see this, note that from the social welfare expressions (3.6) and (3.5), we obtain:

$$\frac{dW^m}{d\tau} = [p^m - c(\tau) + b(\tau) - d]\frac{dq_1^m}{d\tau} + [b'(\tau) - c'(\tau)]q_1^m \tag{3.29}$$

and

$$\frac{dW^d}{d\tau} = [p^d - c(\tau) + b(\tau) - d]\frac{dq_1^d}{d\tau} + 2[b'(\tau) - c'(\tau)]q_1^d + [c'(\tau) - 2p'\frac{dq_1^d}{d\tau}]q_1^d + [b(\tau) - d]\frac{dq_1^d}{d\tau} \tag{3.30}$$

where q_1^m and q_1^d denote the quantities produced by the domestic firm under monopoly and duopoly respectively. Hence, W^m and W^d are increasing at $\tau = 0$. Concavity of W^m follows from the fact that we can write:

$$\frac{d^2W^m}{d\tau^2} = \frac{d(p[dq_1^m/d\tau])}{d\tau} + \frac{d^2[(b-d-c)q_1^m]}{d\tau^2} < 0$$

and that the first term can be written as $p'(dq_1^m/d\tau)^2 + pd^2q_1^m/d\tau$. This expression is negative because the first term is negative by (3.27) while the second is negative by condition 6. The second term in the expression for $d^2W^m/d\tau^2$ is negative, also by condition 6. An analogous derivation shows that W^d is concave.[20] Finally, to show that local optima τ_c and τ_a exist, we use the fact that when standards are high, costs are higher than prices so production ceases and welfare is zero.

The condition $c'(0) = 0$ implies that $dW^m/d\tau\,|_0 > 0$. The last two terms of the equation (3.30) are positive. Additionally, we have that $2q_1^d \geq q_1^m \geq q_1^d$, which, in turn, implies that $p^d \leq p^m$. Given condition 1, expressions (3.25) and (3.27) imply:

$$\frac{dq_1^m}{d\tau} \leq \frac{dq_1^d}{d\tau} \leq 0$$

which gives:

$$\frac{dW^d}{d\tau} \geq \frac{dW^m}{d\tau}$$

and this implies that $\tau_c > \tau_a$.

Q.E.D.

Notes

1 We use the general notion of a *minimum standard* rather than the more common *minimum quality standard*, because the standards we analyze do not necessarily affect consumers' utility.

2 Marketing orders specify characteristics of the goods that can be sold in a market.

3 Members can introduce more stringent standards only when scientific evidence for higher standards exists.

4 Asymmetric transport costs can explain this.

5 Copeland and Taylor (1995) analyze consumption externalities in a general equilibrium setting.

6 The US Agricultural Marketing Act establishes regulatory mechanisms for the producer promotion of *ordered markets*. The Act authorizes the imposition of MS, marketing limits and regulations on packaging.

7 Other liquor imports are subject to intermediate taxes.

8 This is the rationale for special taxes on alcoholic beverages.

9 Our first model shows that the effectiveness of standards as protective devices depends on the relative size of the export market.

10 Another case in which discriminatory taxes on alcoholic beverages led to a WTO panel is the recent case *Korea: Taxes on Alcoholic Beverages*: see WTO document WT/DS75/AB/R, 1999. In this case the appeals panel decided against Korea. A related case is *Japan: Taxes on Alcoholic Beverages*: see WTO document WT/DS8/R, 1996.

11 This section is based on Fischer and Serra (in press).

12 It is possible to include a fixed setup cost of introducing a standard level τ, hence providing micro- foundation for the inability of a firm to produce at more than one standard: Fischer and Serra (in press).

13 As costs are convex and increasing in τ, there exists a minimum standard such that the foreign firm operating in both markets obtains zero profits. As a corollary, there exists a τ_e such that profits are equal to those obtained from producing solely for F, at standard level $\tau = 0$.

14 This will become important since, given that the effect of the externality depends on consumption per individual, standards should be the same everywhere, in the absence of other reasons such as protection.

15 Certain segments may disappear for some functional forms of the externality.

16 If $\gamma_d > \gamma_c$, the standard desired by the firm is always below what the LSP chooses.

17 Alternative functional forms exist for the externality, giving rise to other convexity properties in the social welfare function.

18 It is easy to show that the local second-order conditions hold in this case, by condition 2.

References

Barret, S. (1994). "Strategic environmental policy and international trade", *Journal of Public Economics*, 54, 325–38.

Bockstael, N. E. (1984). "The welfare implications of minimum quality standards", *American Journal of Agricultural Economics*, 66, 466–71.

Boom, A. (1995). "Asymmetric international minimum quality standards and vertical differentiation", *Journal of Industrial Economics*, XLIII (1), 101–20.

Brander, J. D. and B. E. Spencer (1985). "Export subsidies and market share rivalry", *Journal of International Economics*, 18, 83–100.

Bredahl, M. F., A. Schmitz and J. S. Hillman (1987, February). "Rent seeking in international trade: The great tomato war", *Journal of Agricultural Economics*, 1–10.

Chambers, R. and D. Pick (1994, February). "Marketing orders as nontariff trade barriers", *American Journal of Agricultural Economics*, 76(1), 47–54.

Chambers, R. G. and M. Weiss (1992). "Revisiting minimum quality standards", *Economic Letters*, 40, 197–201.

Copeland, B. W. and M. S. Taylor (1995). "Trade and the environment: A partial synthesis", *American Journal of Agricultural Economics*, 77, 765–71.

Fischer, R. D. and P. Serra (in press). "Standards and protection," *Journal of International Economics*.

Hillman, J. (1991). *Technical Barriers to Agricultural Trade*. Westview Press.

Kennedy, P. W. (1994). "Equilibrium pollution taxes in open economies with imperfect competition", *Journal of Environmental Economics and Management*, 27, 49–63.

National Research Council (1995). *Standards, Conformity Assessment and Trade*. Washington, DC: National Academy Press.

Ronnen, U. (1991). "Minimum quality standards, fixed costs and competition", *Journal of Economics*, 22(4), 490–504.

Part II
Case Studies

4
Latin American Trade Regime Reforms and Perceptions

Ronald Fischer and Patricio Meller

1 Introduction

The so-called "Washington Consensus" has led most countries in the region to adopt broadly similar outward oriented policies which have replaced the previous Economic Commission for Latin America (ECLA) consensus that stressed import substitution. In this chapter we review the extent of these trade reforms and their effects on the growth of trade in the various countries. Even though they have liberalized their external sector, we will show that Latin American countries use the new instruments of protection *vis-a-vis* each other and other countries. These barriers have become one of the main causes of frictions between countries in South America. This descriptive analysis is supplemented by an examination of the new forms of protection used by developed countries and their effects on developing-country trade. We conclude with a short description of the perception of WTO issues in Latin America and the problems posed by the increasing intervention of multilateral trade organizations on what have been previously considered domestic policy issues.

2 Short review of Latin American policy reforms

Latin American (LA) countries implemented profound economic policy reforms during the 1980s which provide a greater role to the market mechanism and to the private sector; moreover, the old import-substitution strategy (i.e., "inwards development") has been replaced by an export oriented strategy (i.e., "outwards development"). There are differences among LA countries with respect to the degree and procedure on the implementation of these economic reforms, but there is great coincidence in the overall approach. Williamson (1990) has synthetized this recent economic reform scheme as the Washington Consensus. The so-called Washington Consensus stresses the following policy reforms:

1 State reforms, which include: (a) Fiscal discipline, i.e., fiscal deficit should not surpass the 1–2 per cent (GDP) range. To achieve this goal in the short run, the reduction of government expenditures (in real and relative terms) is the most efficient way. On the other hand, a tax reform should be oriented towards increasing its efficiency in providing revenues to the government; this requires a broad tax base with low marginal tax rates. (b) Privatization of state enterprises; the private sector is considered to be much more efficient as a producer than the public sector. Moreover, the existence of fewer public firms will make it easier to achieve the objective of fiscal discipline.

2 Liberalization and deregulation reforms, which should promote domestic competition; these include: (a) Domestic capital market liberalization which would imply free interest rates; real interest rates should be positive but moderate. In this context supervision of financial institutions is recommended. (b) Trade liberalization where quantitative restrictions and discretionary measures should be replaced by tariffs; furthermore, tariffs should be reduced. (c) National treatment to foreign investment which provides required capital, skills, and know-how.

3 High and stable real exchange rate to increase international competitiveness for export promotion.

In this section we will review the results of these trade reforms and exchange rate policies.

2.1 Trade reforms

Prior to 1980, the ISI (import substitution industrialization) strategy prevailed in LA; industrial policy was mainly commercial policy, i.e. high tariffs and non-tariff barriers. Many horror stories have been written about the inefficiencies created by the ISI strategy; one of the principal problems is related to the anti-export bias generated by the incentives in the domestic price structure.[1] In this respect it should be observed that at the overall level, LA exports had an annual average export growth rate of 3.2 per cent during the 1960–80 period; this LA export rate was much lower than the 6.1 world export growth rate.

There is a wide consensus in LA that by the end of the 1970s the ISI strategy was (in general) exhausted; the external debt shock accelerated this fact.

During the 1980s there was a profound change of focus in most LA countries; the ISI strategy (inwards development) started to be replaced by an export-oriented strategy (outwards development). The highly successful Asian export countries example became the pattern to follow; exports were promoted as the engine of growth. The new predominant rationale states that given their small relative size, LA economies should be open; the pursuit and increase of efficiency will be achieved by the integration of the domestic economy to the world.

The LA trade regime which prevailed during the ISI strategy had a highly complex and messy structure; there were different types of non-tariff barriers like import licensing, import prohibition, quotas, together with a high level and large dispersion of tariff schedule, surcharges, etc.; moreover, there were special regimes and special exemptions, some related to geographic areas and some related to type of firms (public firms).

Two sequential features characterize the changes observed in Latin American (LA) trade regimes during the 1990s. First, most LA countries have implemented a unilateral trade liberalization process, i.e., each LA country has decided to reduce its tariff and non-tariff barriers independently of what the rest of the world does.

During the 1990s there was a clear trend towards a rationalization of the trade regime; this included the simplification and reduction of bureaucratic procedures related to external trade operations (exports and imports), the elimination of most non-tariff restrictions, the elimination of most special regimes and special exemptions. With respect to tariffs, in many countries there has been a tendency towards the use of only a few tariff categories, in particular, Chile and Bolivia have a flat tariff structure, Argentina and Peru have three tariff categories, Mexico and Brazil have six and seven respectively.

In short, there have been deep changes in the LA trade regime. The sharp unilateral external liberalization process implemented in most LA countries shows up in a comparison of the tariffs and quantitative restrictions (QR) figures of the 1990s with those of the second half of the 1980s shown in Table 4.1.

(a)   Maximum nominal tariffs have been reduced from a three digit level to around 20 per cent. There has been a clear change of perception in LA; from the 1960s through the 1980s, tariffs lower that 20 per cent were considered to be too low, while now, tariffs higher than 20 per cent are considered to be too high. In 1997, most LA countries had weighted average tariffs in the 10 per cent to 15 per cent range.

(b) Most LA countries had surcharges prior to 1990; these surcharges were significatively reduced or eliminated during the 1990s.

(c) A large percentage of LA imports were subjected to QRs prior to 1990; at present QRs play a null or minor role in most LA countries.

In short, LA is now more open and export-oriented. Comparing the years 1980 and 1997, the exports/GDP share increased in most LA countries; moreover, in several LA countries the increase in this share is larger than 50 per cent.

The second LA feature is related to the surprising proliferation of (bilateral) free trade agreements (FTA) during the 1990s: in the 1990–94 period no fewer than twenty-six bilateral agreements had been signed (Table 4.2). In addition, the decade saw the creation of important subregional preferential trading areas like NAFTA and MERCOSUR. The 1990s could therefore be called the decade of the FTA in Latin America. An important outcome has been a significant increase of intra-Latin American export growth.

Table 4.1a   Tariffs and quantitative restrictions in Latin American countries, 1990s

Country	Tariffs & surcharges (%)		Mean tariff weighted (%) 1997	Quantitative restrictions (import % affected by QR)
	Tariffs	**Surcharges**		
Argentina	0 ÷ 20	10	11.3	4[a]
Bolivia	5 ÷ 10	1 ÷ 2	9.7	2
Brazil	0 ÷ 20	–	14.8	1[a]
Chile	11	–	10.9	0
Colombia	0 ÷ 20	0 ÷ 16	12.1	14[a]
Ecuador	5 ÷ 35	–	11.8	15[a]
Mexico	0 ÷ 20	–	13.2	2
Peru	0 ÷ 15	–	13.8	5
Uruguay	0 ÷ 20	0 ÷ 5	9.8	0
Venezuela	0 ÷ 20	–	12.4	10

[a] This percentage corresponds to all tariff categories.
Source: GATT, IMF, World Bank.

Table 4.1b Tariffs and quantitative restrictions in Latin American countries, 1980s

Country	Year	Tariffs & surcharges		Quantitative restrictions[a] (import % affected by QR)
		Tariffs	(%) Surcharges	
Argentina	1986	0 ÷ 100	0 ÷ 14	60
Bolivia	1984	0 ÷ 60	0 ÷ 2	90
Brazil	1985	81[b]	–	34[c]
Chile	1984	0 ÷ 35	5 ÷ 15	0
Colombia	1984	61	0 ÷ 18	93[d]
Ecuador	1984	0 ÷ 290	1 ÷ 30	38[c]
Mexico	1984	0 ÷ 100	3 ÷ 19	38
Peru	1989	0 ÷ 117	3 ÷ 147	100[d]
Uruguay	1982	0 ÷ 75	0 ÷ 74	0
Venezuela	1988	0 ÷ 80	2 ÷ 5	65[e]

[a] QR include import restrictions through exchange control. In general, QR correspond to non-automatic requirements to import permits.
[b] Average value of all tariff categories.
[c] This percentage corresponds to all tariff categories.
[d] In this case QR corresponds to prohibitions.
[e] QR through allocation of foreign exchange.
Source: IMF, *Issues and Development in International Trade Policy*, 1992.

Table 4.2 Free trade agreements in Latin America, 1990–94

1.	Argentina – Brazil	1990	14.	NAFTA		1993
2.	Bolivia – Uruguay	1991	15.	Brazil – Peru		1993
3.	Argentina – Colombia	1991	16.	Mexico – Caricom		1993
4.	MERCOSUR	1991	17.	Mexico – Costa Rica		1994
5.	Chile – Mexico	1991	18.	Bolivia – Brazil		1994
6.	Chile – Argentina	1991	19.	Mexico – Bolivia		1994
7.	Argentina – Bolivia	1992	20.	Chile – Bolivia		1994
8.	Bolivia – Peru	1992	21.	Chile – Ecuador		1994
9.	Argentina – Venezuela	1992	22.	Colombia – Venezuela – Mexico		1994
10.	Argentina – Ecuador	1993	23.	Venezuela – Caricom		1994
11.	Bolivia – Chile	1993	24.	Colombia – Caricom		1994
12.	Chile – Venezuela	1993	25.	Brazil – Venezuela		1994
13.	Chile – Colombia	1993	26.	Bolivia – Paraguay		1994

Source: BID, División de Integración, Comercio y Asuntos Hemisféricos y CEPAL.

Changes in the LA trade regime have had an important effect upon LA export growth rates. Prior to 1990, LA exports had annual growth rates below 5 per cent. In the 1990s, LA exports grew on average at 8 per cent per year, which is higher than the 6.9 per cent world export expansion (Table 4.3a). There are several LA countries which show export growth rate higher than 11 per cent (Mexico, El Salvador, Paraguay) (Table 4.3b).

Table 4.3a   Export growth by regions (annual average; %)

	1970–80	1980–90	1990–95
East Asia & Pacific	9.64	9.31	13.24
OECD	6.61	4.64	6.10
Latin America & Caribbean	4.63	4.84	7.95
World	6.38	4.97	6.91

Source: World Bank.

Table 4.3b.   Latin American export growth (annual average; %)

	1970–80	1980–90	1990–95
Argentina	4.45	4.04	9.00
Bolivia	−1.31	1.29	7.03
Brazil	9.58	8.40	4.58
Colombia	5.30	6.00	8.13
Chile	9.47	6.93	9.59
Costa Rica	6.73	5.46	9.27
Dominican Republic	8.73	5.55	9.15
Ecuador	13.22	4.50	7.98
El Salvador	2.90	−4.85	12.80
Guatemala	5.70	−1.44	5.96
Mexico	6.98	7.65	11.88
Nicaragua	−1.66	−4.75	8.18
Panama	n.a.	n.a.	6.01
Paraguay	6.80	5.49	11.95
Peru	2.60	−2.63	4.35
Puerto Rico	n.a.	n.a.	n.a.
Uruguay	6.77	4.61	6.70
Venezuela	n.a.	0.63	6.46

Source: World Bank.

Table 4.4   Latin American per capita exports (1987 US$)

	1970	1980	1990	1995
Argentina	210	286	402	531
Bolivia	144	121	147	175
Brazil	64	131	212	272
Chile	193	436	679	988
Colombia	115	158	236	293
Ecuador	98	272	350	451
Mexico	135	228	385	654
Paraguay	138	187	417	599
Peru	168	166	114	157
Uruguay	242	466	696	886
Venezuela	n.a.	699	685	779

Source: World Bank.

However, Latin America is still a region with a relatively low export level. Using the export per capita indicator for comparison purposes, LA (including the Caribbean countries) had US$ 516 of export per capita in 1995 compared with a world figure of US$ 951 (World Bank). OECD countries had an average higher than US$ 4,000 of exports per capita, while several East-Asian countries were in the US$ 2,000 to US$ 4,000 range. The LA countries that had the highest export/capita in 1995 were Chile (US$ 988), Uruguay (US$ 886) and Venezuela (US$ 779) (Table 4.4).

2.2 New protectionism in selected Latin American countries and their trade partners

Despite the impressive trend towards trade liberalization in Latin American countries and the massive increase in intraregion trade documented in the previous sections, new forms of protection have become important in restricting intra-Latin American trade. The larger countries in the region have begun using contingent protection mechanisms such as anti-dumping, countervailing subsidies and safeguard provisions in efforts to protect individual sectors.[2] Table 4.5 shows some protective mechanisms used in Latin America.[3]

The data shown in Table 4.5 warrants the examination of individual countries to determine the extent to which they attempt to evade the spirit, and often the letter, of their obligations under the WTO. In particular, we concentrate on measures which affect other LA countries and omit the issues relevant to developed countries, such as intellectual property issues, investment and others.

Table 4.5 Protection in Latin America

Measure	Countries
Import procedures Import and custom encumbrances Import licenses Other taxes and charges Advanced payment of VAT and other taxes	Salvador, Paraguay, Argentina, Brazil, Uruguay
Unexpected tariff increases	Mercosur, esp. Brazil
Antidumping and countervailing	Mexico, Argentina
Safeguards	Brazil
Tariff escalation	Salvador, Mercosur, Mexico
Tariff quotas	Salvador, Mexico
Labeling requirements	Mexico, Chile
Sanitary and phytosanitary restrictions	Chile, Mexico, Brazil
Special agricultural protection	All

Source: Derived from Trade Policy Reviews of WTO.

2.2.1 Brazil

Among Latin American countries the larger countries are most prone to the use of non-tariff, non-quota forms of protection. Brazil, which is the largest Latin American economy, is the country that uses the new forms of protection most effectively. Brazil uses a large variety of instruments, such as unexpected tariff increases, changes in import procedures and the more classical anti-dumping safeguards and countervailing subsidy procedures. Many of these measures are introduced with suddenness and often violating basic commitments. According to the Report of the Trade Policy Review of the OMC of 1996, "... frequent tariff adjustments give an appearance of uncertainty to Brazil's trade and investment regime."

Until as recently as 1996, the Brazilian anti-dumping (AD) and countervailing subsidy regulations did not follow the Antidumping and Countervailing Subsidy code of the WTO. During the period from 1992 to 1995 Brazil introduced 66 AD and 13 countervailing subsidy cases. Given the complex levels of protection in its economy, Brazil tries to compensate for the various distortions created by the complex system of state and federal taxes with subsidies that in some cases become net export subsidies. These subsidies include tax and tariff exemptions for equipment and material used for exports and excise and sales tax exemptions and subsidized export credits.

Within MERCOSUR itself, the behavior of Brazil has caused serious strains, as for example, when in March 1999 it started unilateral negotiations with the Andean community countries (Venezuela, Colombia, Perú and Ecuador) with the object of achieving trade and customs agreements or the imposition of the obligation of cash payment of imports from other MERCOSUR members (*El Mercurio*, April 17, 1999). The reduction in tariffs that have been negotiated appear to be illegal under MERCOSUR, according to Argentine officials. The Associated members of MERCOSUR (Bolivia and Chile) labor under worse conditions. For example, before Chilean textiles can be exported to Brazil, the importer must obtain an import license, which, though theoretically automatic, takes about three weeks to process. These licenses can only be obtained in one office in the whole of Brazil. In January 1997, Brazil introduced legislation that regulates wine imports, introducing bureaucratic measures such as certificates, Portuguese labels,[4] registration with the Agriculture ministry, etc., that, even though they are not overtly discriminatory, are aimed at imports (*Estrategia*, January 21, 1997). In general, Brazil's trade partners, even within MERCOSUR, complain of the great ingenuity in slowing administrative procedures employed by Brazil as a trade barrier.

2.2.2. Mexico

Under NAFTA, the trade policies of Mexico *vis-à-vis* its northern partners are regulated strictly according to the accords and it appears that this more formal approach seems to have spilled into the conduct of trade with other partners. Hence Mexico has substantially improved its trade relations with its LA partners, establishing free trade agreements with several Latin American countries and generally reducing the use of non-tariff barriers. There is still substantial use of contingency measures such as anti-dumping, with 90 measures in force at the end of 1997, and this has become an important impediment to trade.[5] Some areas continue to receive special protection: the automotive sector, textiles, clothing and footwear. Mexico appears to be increasing the use of technical and labelling requirements that do not conform to international standards. Moreover, there are complaints about the introduction of new procedures without sufficient advance notification to trade partners. Certain sensitive products require the presentation of original documents at the central offices of the Health ministry, imposing a large burden on exporters. Mexico sometimes employs "emergency" phytosanitary standards (as in the fishmeal case mentioned in the introductory chapter) which bypass the normal advance notice procedures.

Mexico has also started requiring certification by the national metrology center for products subject to technical regulations. The problem is that there are product areas without local capability or areas in which testing must be performed by the local competition, which adds cost and uncertainty to the certification process. Under new regulations, supposedly less-stringent foreign producers can certify products under broader rulings, but this only applies to ISO 9000 certified plants, accredited by the Mexican quality system. Overall Mexico seems to have graduated from the primitive restrictions used in the past to "modern" methods such as contingent and phytosanitary measures.[6]

2.2.3   Argentina

Argentina has changed its economy from a substantially closed system to an open-oriented economy, with important increases in the stability of the trade regime. Nevertheless, some areas which are problematic remain, such as protection in some agricultural sectors, and special protection for some manufactures such as toys, textiles, clothing and footwear. Moreover Argentina has imposed "statistical" levies on imports, which introduce uncertainty among exporters. These levies seem to be related to a desire to increase fiscal revenues rather than having a protectionist intent, since they are applied across the board, but they still affect exports from other LA countries. There are sectors where it is difficult to evaluate the overall tariff equivalent rate, due to the fact that there are several different para-tariff measures that are applied. Argentina is also a frequent user of AD measures, but mainly against imports from Brazil within LA. Argentina still retains free trade zones whose exemption from all taxes can be construed as export subsidies, but these are scheduled for future removal. There is strong protection in the automotive sector and this has been one of the critical sectors in the negotiations within MERCOSUR. Overall, Argentina is a country that has eliminated most of the important restrictions of trade and still has not begun to use more sophisticated trade measures (contingent protection or phytosanitary restrictions) in a coherent protective program, though they have been used in specific cases such as safeguard actions in the shoe industry and quarantines and fumigation procedures (which add cost and sometimes harm) on certain fruit.

2.2.4   Chile

Chile is generally regarded as an extreme case of a classical trade stance, though this is not altogether true. The country sets a uniform tariff of 10 per cent on all goods and there are no quantitative restrictions. Moreover, this tariff is scheduled to decrease unilaterally to 6 per cent in the 2000–03 period. There are no quotas and import licenses are granted automatically. There is an exemption for three agricultural sectors: sugar, wheat (and wheat flour) and edible oil. In these sectors price bands operate, supposedly to buffer changes in international prices but which in practice have a bias towards higher than international prices, sometimes going above WTO tariff bindings.

Despite appearences, the effective tariff is far from uniform, since Chile has signed FTAs with most LA countries. The effect is that the tariff schedule has become complex, as there are sometimes hundreds of exceptions and time schedules for the free trade agreements. Furthermore, Chile uses stringent phytosanitary restrictions that have, until recently, kept out US fruit and still bans imports of chickens from the US. As mentioned in the introductory chapter, Chile uses an idiosyncratic labelling system and classification for meat cuts that effectively exclude imports of meat from the US and are difficult to comply with for Argentina.

For several years, import competing sectors have asked for a change in the composition of the Distortions Committee which decides on dumping and subsidy allegations. Their lobbying has led to the introduction of legislation on Safeguards which, while complying with article XIX of the Uruguay Round, represents an increase in perceived protection.

2.2.5 European Union

Even though the European Union boasts fairly low tariff rates, these are much higher in the agricultural sector with extreme peaks for some products such as poultry, dairy products, meat, cereals, sugar and tobacco. The structure of tariffs shows some degree of escalation. There exist tariff quotas for fruit and other agricultural products.The EU is a regular user of AD regulations, especially in the textile sector.

The zero risk approach in safety and environmental directives may also be considered a trade barrier. Moreover, the new ISO 9000 and 14000 standards increase the difficulties of exporting to the EU market for small companies in LA, and share many of the characteristics of technical barriers to trade.

Europe has also become involved in various trade disputes regarding products exported by Latin American countries. For example, the discrimination against bananas produced in Ecuador and Central America has led to a serious trade dispute between the US and the EU. Wine exports can also be vulnerable to trade disputes, since Europe requires that wine must be produced under wine-making practices acceptable to the EU, violating basic principles of the WTO.

2.2.6   The United States

While in many respects the US is an open market, there are several indications that there remains a substantial level of protection. The indiscriminate use of AD and countervailing subsidy allegations against steel, soyabeans and oranges from Brazil, salmon and flowers from Chile, and other uses of contingent protection measures impose a degree of uncertainty on LA exporters. This is compounded by the application of marketing orders for fruit that are biased against foreign exporters and the introduction of phytosanitary restrictions with what appears to be randomness.[7]

There is concern with respect to the administrative features of the US contingent protection regulations, some of which do not seem to agree with the WTO codes. Some LA (apart from Mexico) countries were possible candidates for an FTA agreement with the US, but the lack of "fast track" authority made the prospects unattractive. There is also some concern about the way in which the US certifies countries for anti-drug efforts and its influence on trade. Similarly, the US efforts to impose its own standards of intellectual property protection are viewed with concern in LA, specially because lack of compliance can lead to sanctions.

2.2.7   Japan

Japan used to be a country which imposed myriad administrative measures that impeded agricultural imports. These barriers have decreased, even though phytosanitary procedures remain complex. There remain some high tariff peaks in specific products. Japan imposes stringent conditions on fresh fruits, vegetables and other horticultural products, many of them without scientific evidence. Imported fruit and flowers are often subjected to fumigation which destroys their commercial potential. This increases the risks for exporters and acts as an efficient trade barrier. Certain derived food products such as snack foods, ice cream, fruit juices, confectionary and others are subject to tariff escalation. Sectors such as shoes enjoy the protection of tariff-quotas, while value-added wood products are protected by tariff escalation.

Administrative procedures are cumbersome and slow, while charging high fees. Japan also uses standards that are unique and outdated but successful in reducing foreign competition. In conclusion, though the changes in Japan's economic policies have reduced the extent of the new forms of protection, substantial barriers remain for Latin American exporters.

2.3 Exchange rate policies

Multiple exchange rates were used in many LA countries during the ISI period as a complement to the trade regime; a dual exchange rate regime, with a controlled official rate for the trade balance components and a free rate for the capital account, was used by a few countries. Moreover, access to official foreign exchange market was in some countries a stricter barrier than that related to the trade regime. In short, both trade and exchange rate regimes were heavy and burdensome obstacles to LA import and export activities.

However, at the beginning of the 1990s, a unified exchange rate system prevailed in most countries of the region. Strict exchange controls, which were a normal feature in most LA countries prior to 1980, were relaxed considerably in many economies during the 1990s; foreign exchange transactions and dollar deposits are now legal operations to which most agents have an easy access. The foreign exchange market has almost become a normal market.

Distinct exchange rate regimes have been used in LA countries; even individual countries have changed the exchange rate regime often. Prior to 1980, some countries such as Mexico and Venezuela had a fixed nominal exchange rate (pegged to the dollar) in order to keep a stable real exchange rate in an inflationary environment. Brazil and Colombia used a passive crawling peg for more than two decades. Argentina and Chile used an active crawling peg to guide inflationary expectations at the end of the 1970s. A fixed nominal exchange rate was used as the nominal anchor in the stabilization programs of Chile (1979–82), Bolivia (1985–86), and Argentina during the 1990s. Free (or dirty) floating has been used by Venezuela (1989) and Peru (1990–91). A combination of a passive crawling peg with a (dirty) float within a band was used by Chile during the 1990s.

The changes in the exchange rate regime should be related to the policy role assigned to the exchange rate. There are several roles that are connected to the use of the exchange rate as the mechanism to modify relative prices (price of tradables/price of non-tradables) or as the nominal anchor of the general price level.

The use of the exchange rate for resource reallocation plays an important role in trade liberalization and export expansion processes. High and stable real exchange rates are a necessary condition for export growth. After the external debt shock, many LA countries implemented substantial real devaluations during the 1980s. During the 1990s, the increased financial flows to LA induced pressures for exchange rate appreciation; which has had a negative effect on LA competitiveness. In some LA countries, the exchange rate has been used as a mechanism to stop inflation. For example, in Argentina, the use of the exchange rate as a nominal anchor is considered as the most fundamental part of the stabilization program. The exchange rate has clear advantages over monetary targets as a nominal anchor since it is clearly easier for agents to monitor (and to understand) a fixed nominal exchange rate than to monitor changes in monetary aggregates such as M_1, M_2 or any M_i. The end result, however, is that the overall credibility of the stabilization program becomes inseparable from the permanence of the nominal value of the exchange rate.

In short, there is a trade-off between both roles assigned to the exchange rate. Export growth requires a depreciated domestic currency, while appreciation helps fight inflation. Moreover, in relatively small economies such as most Latin American countries, with their shallow capital markets, the exchange rate becomes a key variable for economic stability. Hence, exchange rate volatility generates a highly unstable environment for business and investment.

Finally, in spite of this trade-off, it must be stressed that nowadays in Latin America, any economic agent, consumer or producer, has easy access to the foreign exchange market.

3   Latin American perspectives on foreign investment and GATT issues during the 1990s

3.1   Latin American foreign investment perceptions

Latin American trade and foreign investment regimes and the associated perceptions experienced profound changes during the 1990s. The region now believes it is highly desirable to become fully integrated to the world economy. In LA, isolationism is a phenomenon of the past.

But while the region has become a supporter of multilateralism and free trade, world events such as the formation of economic blocs (European Union) and the increasing protectionist forces in DC (developed countries) appear to be moving in the opposite direction. Moreover, a highly integrated global trading system creates a new set of issues; since almost every internal policy has implications for trade, avoiding distortions and non-economic advantages seems to imply a high level of harmonization in other policy areas.

Furthermore, there has been a profound change in the perception of LA policy makers with respect to foreign investment. During the 1960s foreign investors were considered almost as "exploiters"; in brief, it was widely believed the costs of foreign investment were higher than the benefits. For this reason, expropriation and nationalization were considered desirable. During the past decade, most LA countries have held the opposite view; with foreign investors being now considered "saviors". Foreign investment is held to be a key link to the world economy by bringing large amounts of capital, modern technology, and know-how. For these reasons, LA countries are engaged in a competition to attract as much foreign investment as possible.

Meanwhile a new phenomenon has happened: LA firms are investing in other LA countries; i.e., LA firms have become foreign investors. In addition, joint ventures between Latin American neighbors are beginning to appear. It used to be a common perception that each LA country had excellent relations with all LA countries with which it did not share a common border. Hence the new joint ventures between LA neighbors will have important political and economic implications. Furthermore, the fact that LA firms are now foreign investors makes it very difficult to revive the old LA antagonism against foreign investment.

FTA also have foreign investment clauses. NAFTA is a trade agreement which LA has found extremely attractive and one in which most LA countries would like to be admitted. Empirical studies generally suggest only small static trade gains (or losses) from entry to NAFTA, a result which is due to the low tariffs that LA exports already face in the US, given the combination of the Generalized System of Preferences (GSP) and the low tariffs in the US for natural resource imports. Easily identifiable dynamic benefits are also of modest proportions, except for Mexico, where estimated benefits from NAFTA entry range between 1 per cent GDP and 7 per cent GDP, considering static and dynamic (including static) gains respectively (Brown 1992); dynamic gains include the effect of entry into NAFTA on foreign investment expansion. However, LA countries, and even Canada, see NAFTA membership as an insurance against potential future US trade restrictions and as a possible seal of approval that would help attract foreign investment. The seal of approval argument reflects the fact that dynamic effects are widely viewed as more important than static effects in the computation of trade gains. As in the case of trade diversion, Mexico's present membership in NAFTA leads to investment diversion away from the other LA countries.

Latin American foreign investment codes have been modified in order to apply "national treatment" to foreign investors. This implies that there is no discrimination between domestic and foreign investors in any issue relevant for business, such as taxation and access to the foreign exchange market. Moreover, in general there are no sectors from which foreign ownership or participation is excluded.

3.2 Latin American perception of WTO issues

The range of trade issues dealt with by GATT-WTO has expanded over time.[8] Prior to the Uruguay Round, it included only policies directly affecting trade in goods, and focused on tariff and non-tariff barriers at the border. The main guiding principle was that foreign goods should be treated equally with domestic goods. Furthermore, DCs accepted the existence of positive discrimination with respect to LDCs (less developed countries, which includes LA); i.e., they allowed LDCs to benefit from the MFN (most favored nation) clause from reciprocal liberalization agreements among themselves, without any reciprocity requirements by LDCs.

In the more trade-integrated world that provided the backdrop for the Uruguay Round, all domestic policies are considered to have trade effects, i.e., are thought of as "trade policies", and have begun to come under international scrutiny; the focus of attention has shifted from goods to policies. Furthermore, in order to avoid free riders, DC tolerance for positive LDC discrimination has disappeared. In fact, during the Uruguay Round debate the LDCs "weren't trying to trade off their liberalization against concessions elsewhere. The blockades came from the DCs. The real problems of protectionism are increasingly to be found in the DC" (Sutherland 1994, p. 29). However, it could be argued that LDC achievements included the delayed elimination of the MFA (Multifiber Arrangement, a system of protection for textiles which discriminated against LDC textile exports) and the eventual incorporation of the agriculture sector under the overall goods trade rules. On the other hand, DC obtained the agreement on intellectual property protection (TRIP, trade related intellectual property rights) which implies a constraint on domestic policies in LDCs.

In recent decades many LA countries have been highly successful in expanding exports and diversifying their exports to DC markets. They are thus extremely interested in the functional world trade system; therefore, many LA countries now support multilateralism and free trade. But the growing "new protectionism" in DC, in some cases accompanied by discretionary regionalism (EU), threatens to thwart the goals of the LA countries.

The new protectionism in some cases has been a response to the successful export performance of LDC which are displacing domestic DC production. LA perceives that DC criticism of low environmental and labor standards (in LA) is related to DC producers' difficulties in facing up to external competition. More generally, DC pressure is transforming trade negotiations into policy and institutional negotiations. Laws, institutions, and LA government regulations are being targeted as "distortions" to trade. To obtain increased access to DC markets, LA laws and regulations are required to be harmonized, i.e. closer to those of the DC (Tussie 1993; Agosin and Tussie 1993).

In this new world economy, the pressure for policy harmonization has become strong. LA will find it difficult to prevent pressure for "harmonization of standards" in areas such as the environment, health and technical quality from becoming non-tariff barriers. DC institutions will become the "harmonization reference model" and LA countries not meeting the DC model will risk exclusion from DC markets. Trading blocs will become policy (and/or police?) blocs (Tussie 1993). A good example of such policing is the US government's questioning of the Chilean intellectual property (IP) law because it uses 15 instead of 20 years as the duration of the property rights and hence "does not meet world standards". But where in the Holy Texts is it written that an IP law must have a 20-year period? Which is the empirical evidence that supports the need for 20 years of intellectual protection through a monopoly? It would seem that the Washington pharmaceutical lobby has more powerful arguments than those related to economic rationality or empirical evidence.

Ironically, the logic of any specific DC harmonization model is weakened by the many differences among the DC. In Europe and Japan, the public sector provides much direct support to the private sector in its production, export, and technology activities, while in the US there is a different and highly regulated relationship between the two sectors. On trade issues, the EEC and Japan are more protectionist, considering it socially beneficial to provide heavy subsidies to farmers; the US has up to now taken a more free-trade stance.

Notes

1   In some Latin American countries, the political economy rationale for an anti-export bias was related to the fact that traditional commodity (natural resources) exports were controlled by foreign firms or by landed oligarchs.
2   From the WTO Trade Policy Reviews for Argentina, Brazil and Mexico.

3 Sources for this section are the latest Trade Policy Reviews of the WTO for the various countries and the 1999 annual report of the US Trade Representative.

4 Apparently at times even rejecting products bearing labels in other languages in addition to Portuguese (*El Mercurio*, October 7, 1999).

5 In 1993, just a short time after signing a free trade agreement with Chile, Mexico imposed phytosanitary restrictions on the entry of Chilean fishmeal into Mexico. After some negotiations this restriction was lifted, but immediately afterwards Mexico initiated AD actions against Chilean fishmeal. The investigations led to a rejection of the dumping accusation and at the end of 1994 Mexico introduced safeguards against imported fishmeal (*Estrategia*, November 21, 1994).

6 A recent example is illuminating in this respect. A Chilean exporter of matches was informed by its distributors in Mexico that they would have to stop shipments because a new ruling requires that distribution from the central storage deposit be done in special trucks certified by the Departments of Transportation and Defense, under unknown regulations. Moreover, this delay implies that renewal of the quality certification would require certification to be performed by its domestic competitor (*El Diario*, May 17, 1999).

7 Consider, for example, the (subsequently lifted) restrictions on imports of Chilean lumber due to the possibility of pests, even though the wood had been previously treated against them.

8 For good reviews on this subject see Low (1990), Tussie (1993), Paiva Abreu (1994).

References

Agosin, M. and D. Tussie (eds) (1993). *Trade and Growth: New Dilemmas in Trade Policy*. New York: St. Martin's Press.

Brown, D. (1992). "The impact of a North American free trade area: Applied general equilibrium models", in N. Lusting, B. Bosworth and R. Lawrence (eds), *North American Free Trade. Assessing the Impact*. Washington, DC: Brookings Institution, pp. 26–68.

Low, P. (1990). "The GATT system in transition: The relevance of 'traditional' issues", *Ensaios*, no. 1, Río de Janeiro: Departamento de Economía, PUC, September.

Paiva Abreu, M. (1994). "O Brasil na rodada Uruguai do GATT: 1982–1993", *Texto para Discussao*, no. 311, Río de Janeiro: Departamento de Economía, PUC, January.

Saborio, S. et al. (1992). *The Premise and the Promise: Free Trade in the Americas*. Washington, D.C.: ODC.

Steil, B. (1994). "Social correctness is the new protectionism", *Foreign Affairs*, 3 (1), January, pp. 14–20.

Sutherland, P. (1994). "Trading places", *World Link*, London, March, pp. 28–31.

Tussie, D. (1993). "The Uruguay Round and the trading system in the balance: Dilemmas for developing countries", in Agosin and Tussie (eds) pp. 69–90.

US Trade Representative (1999). "National Trade Estimate Report on Foreign Trade Barriers", various countries.

Williamson, J. (1990). "What Washington means by policy reform", in J. Williamson (ed.), *Latin American Adjustment. How Much Has Happened?* Washington DC: Institute for International Economics.

World Trade Organization: "Trade Policy Reviews", various countries, latest issue for each country.

5
Poisoned Grapes, Mad Cows and Protectionism

Eduardo Engel[*]

1 Introduction

A good definition of "protectionist measure" would be useful from both a conceptual and a practical point of view. In fact, in order to better define the elements of the new faces of protectionism we need a clear sense of what constitutes a protectionist measure. From a practical point of view, the effective resolution of disputes, whether these occur within multilateral organizations like the World Trade Organization or stem from free trade agreements such as NAFTA, depends heavily on being able to decide when a measure is protectionist.

This chapter proposes a new definition, in which a measure becomes "protectionist" when it differs from the measures that would otherwise have been taken, if the welfare of all countries affected by the measure had been considered. I discuss the implications of this new definition in the context of two case studies. The first deals with the poisoned grapes crisis between Chile and the US in 1989. The second is the "mad cows" dispute, which broke out in 1996, between the UK and the European Union. Comparing the two cases serves not only to illustrate how difficult it can be to determine whether a measure is protectionist, but also provides lessons on what a small, developing country like Chile can

* This chapter was originally published in the *Journal of Policy Reform*, Vol. 4, No. 2, 2000, and is reproduced with the permission of Gordon & Breach Publishers © Overseas Publishers Association N.V. 2000. It was partly written while the author visited the Center for Research on Economic Development and Policy Reform at Stanford University; the Center's hospitality is gratefully acknowledged. The author thanks Claudio Rammsy for outstanding research assistance, and Alexander Galetovic, James Hines, Anne Krueger and Pablo Serra for helpful comments and suggestions.

do to mitigate the effects of unilateral measures that dramatically affect its commercial interests.

On March 13th, 1989, the US Food and Drug Administration (FDA) announced it had found two grapes from Chile contaminated with cyanide. Without consulting the Chilean Government, the FDA promptly banned Chilean fruit, triggering the "poisoned grapes crisis" as it became known, which hit one of Chile's main exports hard. Four days later, following tough bargaining between government representatives from Chile and the US, and the signing of agreements on strict sanitary controls, the US formally ended the embargo. In the meantime, Chile had lost over US$400 million. Section 2 describes this case in detail.

In the second case, on March 27th, 1996 the European Union imposed a worldwide ban on beef exports from the United Kingdom, thereby setting off the "mad cow crisis." Scientific evidence published at the time suggested that there was a real possibility that mad cow disease, which causes fatal encephalopathy, could affect people. Section 3 describes the "mad cows" case.

In both cases, the main purpose of the resulting embargo was to safeguard people's health, so one could reasonably argue that these measures were not protectionist. However, Section 4 argues that using the new definition of "protectionist measure" proposed in this chapter, one of the bans would not qualify as protectionist, whereas the other would. Finally, Section 5 presents the chapter's main conclusions. Any reader who recalls the main events associated with both cases is welcome to skip directly to Section 4 for the main thesis of this chapter.

2 The poisoned grapes crisis[1]

2.1 The March crisis: the embargo

On Monday March 13th, 1989, the FDA announced it had detected two Chilean grapes containing cyanide in the port of Philadelphia. Although the dose was not lethal, the FDA issued a national news release announcing its decision to quarantine all fruit from Chile headed for the US market, calling on stores to take it off their shelves and consumers to avoid consuming the fruit. This measure not only affected half of Chile's production for the season, already being loaded for shipment or on its way to the US, it particularly affected Chilean fruit that had already entered the country and was then being stored in commercial distributors' refrigerators or warehouses, and whose destruction was now recommended. The FDA decision to ban the fruit and to publicize this throughout the country created real panic. Just hours after Dr Frank Young, FDA Commissioner, made the announcement, the main supermarket chains had removed the fruit from their shelves. The ban on Chilean fruit due to cyanide-contaminated grapes became the lead story on national television news and in newspapers throughout the country.

Media accounts after the event revealed that, during the week leading up to the announcement, the US embassy in Santiago had received several telephone calls threatening to poison fruit destined for the North American and Japanese markets. This initially led to some restrictions on Chilean fruit entering the US, but these were lifted a few days later when exhaustive checks found nothing, and in light of what the US government called "notable safety measures adopted in Chile." Knowledge of these precautionary measures was restricted to the authorities of each country and exporters, with no information provided to the public at large.

FDA checks were stepped up, however, after a second threatening call, with more than 100 officials being deployed at exporters' expense to inspect and check approximately 10 per cent of the 600,000 boxes of Chilean fruit arriving daily at US ports. On the morning of March 12th, FDA inspectors going through cargo from the "Almería Star", containing produce exported by Julia Saavedra of Curacaví, Chile, found two grapes showing signs of tampering in a box of Flame Seedless "Crispy". Specifically, the grapes were discolored, with a ring of crystalline material surrounding an apparent pinprick. Laboratory analysis confirmed the presence of cyanide, although the dose would not have been lethal to human beings. Due to cyanide's high volatility in an acid medium such as a grape, technicians could not determine the original dose injected.

Other importing countries, among them Canada, Japan and certain European countries, took immediate measures when they heard of the FDA *communiquée*. The Canadian government simply copied US measures, suspending the entry of Chilean fruit for two days following the first threat. Later, with the discovery of the contaminated grapes in the US, Canada applied a total embargo on fruit and vegetables imported from Chile.

Japan, which had also received telephone threats in its Santiago Embassy, also suspended Chilean fruit imports, while the European Commission alerted its twelve member countries, leaving them to take the corresponding measures, without recommending a ban.

In Chile, the measure caused huge public outcry, because of the enormous losses it would cause. Share prices fell immediately, with shipping company stocks, whose prices dropped 10.7 per cent, the most affected. The US ban on Chilean fruit was felt immediately not only by producers, but all the way along the production chain of what had become a flourishing fruit export industry. More serious still was the damage to foreign consumers' confidence in Chilean fruit. Such a public measure threatened to produce not only major financial losses but also the loss of entire markets, as consumers were becoming particularly sensitive to food additives generally.

That same Monday 13th, in a nationally broadcast address, Carlos Cáceres, Chile's Minister of the Interior, told the people of Chile that while he did not support the decision by US Authorities, he did understand their concern for consumers' health. He called the incident a terrorist attack supported by the Communist Party and announced an investigation to identify those responsible. Similarly, he announced that security measures would be strengthened throughout the fruit processing chain, from the moment of harvest until its arrival at the port of destination.

General Pinochet's government set up a crisis committee, made up of the Ministers of Interior, Government, Foreign Relations, Agriculture, Finance and the Presidency. This committee operated round-the-clock throughout the critical days that followed, designing strategies to deal with the emergency.

The military government's immediate response included three courses of action. Firstly, the Foreign and Agriculture Ministries moved quickly to initiate top-level negotiations with the US, to obtain a speedy reversal of the ban. With this in mind, by the next day, an official delegation was on its way to Washington, where it began an intensive lobbying effort directed at members of congress, business leaders and US government officials, who were informed of the measures' impacts, as well as safeguards adopted by Chile to protect its exports.

Secondly, sanitary controls were tightened, and the government launched an investigation to identify those responsible. Charges were filed in the courts under the Internal Security Act.

Lastly, the government commissioned studies to assess the impact of the measure on the export sector and the national economy as a whole, and to define possible supportive measures.

Once in the US, the Government delegation headed by Foreign Minister Errázuriz contacted US counterparts, industry representatives and members of Congress. In a news conference, Senator Heinz[2] underlined the urgent need for a rapid solution, in view of the damage to both US and Chilean interests. Before the FDA, he argued in favor of a plan to restore confidence in Chilean produce.

Three days after the ban, James Baker, the US Secretary of State, met with Chile's Ministers of Foreign Affairs and Agriculture and they agreed to work together to find solutions to the critical situation affecting Chilean fruit exports. They announced that a team of FDA experts would travel to Santiago to confirm security controls on shipments. In response to stories in the Chilean media suggesting political motives behind the FDA's measure, Baker said that the decision was made "strictly on the grounds of health and safety and not, in any way, for political motives", adding that both Chilean producers' and US citizens' interests were being hurt.

The Chilean Agriculture Minister and the FDA Commissioner agreed in principle on a solution to the crisis, and technical experts from both countries began to draw up the details. On Friday March 17th, four days after the embargo was imposed, and following tough negotiations and agreements on strict sanitary controls, authorities announced that Chilean fruit exports to the US market would resume, as of March 21st.

2.2   The reaction in Chile

Chile's military authorities were convinced that the poisoning of the grapes was a terrorist act, of Marxist origin. On March 16th, Miguel Angel Poduje, Minister of the General Secretariat of the Government, announced that the Communist Party had put together a "Fruit Plan" to sabotage Chilean fruit exports.

Likewise, the Agriculture Minister blamed the Communist Party and the opposition in general, linking the incident to a boycott then being promoted by the CUT (Chile's National Association of Unions) and US labor organizations, among them the AFL-CIO,[3] while naval commander-in-chief, Admiral Merino, called it "one of the many low blows the US has hit us with." He added that the decision to suspend exports of Chilean fruit to the US market was a "malicious act intended to attack Chile, planned by the Communists in Chile."[4] Only Foreign Affairs Minister Errázuriz was more cautious, emphasizing the importance of resolving the crisis and avoiding new areas of conflict with the US. He criticized the US government for having made the decision to impose the ban without prior consultation, an attitude considered inconsistent in a trading partner relationship.

The coalition of political parties opposing Pinochet in the "Concertación de Partidos por la Democracia" called the ban a hurried measure, out of proportion to the alleged risk.

Luis Maira, at the time leader of a coalition of parties to the left of the Concertación, speculated that the embargo could have been the result of dissatisfaction with progress in the Letelier case.[5] Communist Party leaders, on the other hand, formally requested that a special judge be appointed to investigate and clarify the military government's charges. The harshest criticism of the FDA decision came from lawyer and shipping magnate Ricardo Claro in a series of public statements. After hearing that the US Secretary of State had telexed other countries advising them of the poisoned grapes, he argued that the Chilean government should take the US to the International Court of The Hague, for what he considered an unspeakable outrage.[6]

In response, the US ambassador to Chile told the media that his government had given no instructions to other countries on the issue, and insisted that tampering had occurred in Chile or on the way to the US. He ruled out any protectionist motives on the part of his government, because "there is no possibility of substituting a North American product for the Chilean product."[7] In effect, virtually all fresh grapes on sale in the US at the time were from Chile.

The embargo's economic impact

When the embargo was announced, the export fruit sector was one of Chile's most booming sectors, with annual growth averaging almost 20 per cent throughout the previous decade. Exporters had even broken into demanding markets like Japan's. A year earlier, in 1989, fruit exports to the US reached US$582 million, accounting for 8.3 per cent of total Chilean exports, making it the second largest export industry. The fruit industry had 120,000 hectares under production, employing almost 500,000 workers.

The FDA embargo hit as the export season peaked, when 45 per cent of the fruit had already left the country. This was also the moment when agricultural sector debts were at their highest. The Superintendency of Banks reported that when the ban was announced export sector debts with private local banks amounted to almost US$400 million.

Although it was short (just four days), the ban's impact on the economy was widespread. An Official Report on the Grapes Case, prepared by the Chilean Congress, confirmed exporters' estimates that private-sector losses reached some US$330 million.

The sheer magnitude of losses forced the military government to support producers and exporters. To provide some relief, and prevent the fruit export sector's collapse, on March 19th General Pinochet announced measures to bail out the export sector, including compensation and special lines of credit to producers and exporters. Measures also included a debt swap mechanism, which allowed exporters to buy

Chilean foreign debt papers abroad, then trading at 60 per cent of face value, with the Central Bank of Chile then buying them back at par. At the same time, the Association of Banks agreed to let exporters roll over financial liabilities falling due between March 13th and June 30th.

These measures, according to a report by the Chilean Chamber of Deputies, cost the Treasury some US$198.2 million,[8] while a Central Bank report stated that US$263 million from the Copper Stabilization Fund were used to alleviate the crisis.[9]

2.3 New investigations and revelations: accusations and new information

Once the US government lifted the embargo, the media in both countries revealed new information, publishing allegations and raising suspicions about the motives of those taking the measures in the US.

Some US newspapers suggested that one possible explanation for the excessive zeal of the FDA (supported by the White House) was the bitter experience of the Bush administration in December 1988, when it took no measures in response to a bomb threat affecting a PanAm flight over Scotland and the plane blew up, killing 207 people. Dr Young acknowledged that this event had influenced his decision.[10]

In July 1989, four months after the embargo, Herb Denenberg, a journalist with CBS, did a three-part series for Philadelphia's Channel 10 news network on the poisoned grapes case. After two months' research with a team of experts, he questioned the alleged poisoning of the grapes, arguing that FDA analyses had been inconclusive and suffered from numerous defects which violated their own procedural rules.

On November 16th, 1989, the *Wall Street Journal* published an extensive report by journalist Bruce Ingersoll, presenting evidence that strongly suggested the fruit had been poisoned in the US and not in Chile.

Chilean and US experts argued that the grapes couldn't have been poisoned in Chile, nor could cyanide have been injected. Some specialists cast doubt on the "miraculous" way in which the two contaminated grapes were found amidst a shipment of millions of bunches of grapes. Among them, Herman Chernoff, professor of statistics at Harvard University, noted that just 26 of the 4,045 pallets in the "Almería Star" came from Julia Saavedra's vineyard and yet a large number of boxes from her vineyards were among those inspected, and suggested that this indicated that the FDA had prior information on where to look for the poisoned grapes. He added that the probability of Mrs Saavedra's vineyards being so over-represented in a random sample was less than one in ten thousand.[11]

Finally, critics also attacked the unusually harsh measure taken by US authorities in banning all exports, compared with the insignificant quantity of poison actually discovered. Measures were taken without considering the disastrous impact they would have on the Chilean economy. They also pointed out that the FDA had never taken such a drastic step before, even faced with more serious cases.

2.4 Investigations into the grape case

On February 27th, 1990, the judge who was investigating the possibility that the grapes were poisoned in Chile temporarily closed the case, amidst reports that the US authorities had failed to cooperate with judicial requests, and having found no evidence to indicate who was responsible.

In June 1990, the Association of Chilean Exporters published their own detailed report of laboratory studies that concluded that the grapes had been poisoned in the FDA laboratory in Philadelphia.

On January 24th, 1991, the Chilean Chamber of Deputies approved the report of a Special Commission looking into the case. To date, this is the only document on the case published by a regular Chilean governmental agency. It is also the one official document that brings together all public and private reports and testimony to date. After a detailed history of events leading up to the ban, the Commission analyzed the legal responsibilities of the US government, and concluded that there was manifest bad faith in its dealing with the situation. The report, which examines the many laboratory reports and expert testimony, argues that the poisoning did not occur in Chile. It also draws attention to a series of events that demonstrate total non-compliance with the legally accepted procedures for responding to the poisoning: "We can, with some certainty, state that the FDA had prior knowledge of the whereabouts of the contaminated grapes," so that when the ship arrived, it was inspected in such a way as to ensure that the poisoned grapes were found.

In the light of this and other information, the Commission concluded that the poisoning could not have occurred in Chile or on the way to the US. Given the characteristics of the poison, the difficulties of injecting cyanide into individual grapes, as well as a series of anomalies in FDA procedures, contamination a few hours before inspection, possibly in the FDA laboratories, was the most likely explanation.

2.4.1   *The quest for compensation*

From 1990 on, the newly-elected coalition government of the Concertación, together with fruit exporters and producers, focused their energies on obtaining compensation from the US government for Chile's economic losses. Legal action was backed up by numerous examples of irregularities and negligence committed by FDA officials when making their decision, in the eyes of the Chilean government and exporters, as well as arguments supporting their belief that the fruit had been contaminated outside Chile.

After studying several courses of action, on February 28th, 1991, President Aylwin's government and exporters themselves launched separate administrative and legal actions (for US$246 and US$212 million respectively) against the FDA for material damages resulting from the US measure.

In August, the FDA rejected the Chilean claims. In February 1992, the Chilean private sector filed a lawsuit in the Federal Court of the District of Philadelphia. However, the US government invoked "jurisdictional immunity" to reject legal proceedings against it, and on December 30th 1992 the court's preliminary ruling came down against the Chilean claim. In view of this, and after studying other alternatives, on March 30th 1993 the Aylwin government invited its US counterpart to use the 1914 Bryan-Suárez Mujica Treaty, to resolve their differences.[12] Three months later the US government rejected the Chilean request, suggesting the alternative of using diplomatic channels, specifically the creation of a binational working group. The Chilean government accepted this proposal, with negotiations culminating, in February 1994, in the proposal of a series of tariff compensations to favor Chilean exports. These measures were rejected outright by producers and exporters, while President Frei's government described them as insufficient. Thus, the work of the binational commission ground to a halt.

At the same time, lawyers representing Chilean producers appealed the initial ruling in Philadelphia's Appeals Court, achieving their first (and so far only) judicial victory (February 25th, 1994). The US government in turn appealed and, in late 1995, the US Supreme Court issued a final ruling on the case, rejecting Chile's petition to have the US administration brought to trial for the ban. In response, Chile's Foreign Minister appointed Ambassador Fabio Vio to coordinate an *ad hoc* commission to report on possible courses of action open to Chile. This commission also recommended using the diplomatic route. To this day, the case remains unresolved, and continues to be a major problem in Chile/US relations.

2.5   What caused the embargo?

To understand the origin of this crisis, we need to answer two questions. Firstly, who contaminated the two grapes found by the FDA, on Monday March the 13th? Secondly, assuming that the FDA acted in good faith, why, once the grapes had been found, did the Bush administration apply so drastic a measure with such grave economic consequences for Chile?

In terms of who contaminated the grapes and why, there are three main hypotheses. First, there is the conspiracy and sabotage theory that several public figures and organizations have insisted upon. The facts that have come to light suggest that there could have been a political motivation behind the FDA decision. What might this have been? Some people suggest a strategy to intimidate General Pinochet, to prevent him from making any changes to plans for a return to democracy, following his defeat at the polls in the 1988 plebiscite. This theory suggests that the US government, concerned that Pinochet might try to stay in power beyond the deadline set out in the 1980 constitution, put together a plan to apply pressure to a highly sensitive area of the economy. Luis Maira, mentioned above, put forward a less conspiratorial version of this hypothesis, suggesting that this action was taken in reprisal for the military government's lack of interest in resolving the Letelier case.

Secondly, there is the *protectionist hypothesis*, according to which the embargo responded to strong pressures being exerted on the US Congress by Californian fruit growers, anxious to protect themselves from growing competition from Chilean fruit. This hypothesis has been rejected by official circles in Chile. However, some elements suggest a degree of collusion between the State Department, US health agencies and the US Congress to restrict the entry of Chilean fruit. A controversial telex sent by the Secretary of State to countries importing Chilean fruit shortly after the crisis erupted, as well as the curious behavior of the US agricultural attaché in Saudi Arabia, who contacted importers in that country to persuade them to cancel contracts with Chilean exporters,[13] lends some support to this hypothesis. However, the protectionist hypothesis is ultimately unconvincing, because Chile's grape export season does not overlap with grape production in California. Furthermore, neither Chilean nor North American producers can significantly lengthen their export seasons, making potential competition between producers in the two countries unlikely. To sustain this hypothesis, therefore, requires demonstrating irrational behavior on the part of agricultural producers in California.

A third hypothesis suggests negligence by the FDA. Numerous anomalies and unanswered questions point to the possibility that FDA researchers, concerned about telephone threats in Santiago, may have been testing the effects of cyanide in fruit. According to this hypothesis, one cannot rule out the possibility that the tainted grapes formed part of experiments being carried out by the FDA, and that they got mixed up with other grapes that were being examined for preventive reasons.

This leads us to ask whether the FDA, while not involved in the actual tampering, can be blamed for applying a disproportionate measure that caused significant damage to the Chilean economy. What could explain an attitude of this nature? Elements singled out by the media at the time include the weakness of Commissioner Young's position, the lesson of the attack on the PanAm aircraft, and pressure from consumer organizations alarmed at the FDA's failure to ban apples with "Alar".[14] Nor can we discard the possibility that the FDA may have agreed to take part in a political operation mounted inside the federal government.

Finally, it is worth questioning whether Commissioner Young's decision to apply an embargo was a rational response. To do this, we must examine the facts he had at his command at the time, rather than information that became available months, days or even hours later. This analysis clearly assumes that Young did not participate in any plot. When news of the discovery of two poisoned grapes reached him on Monday March 13th, how would Commissioner Young have reasoned? Section 4 argues that this last explanation is the most convincing, and that any official in the position of FDA Commissioner would have acted the same way. However, this does not change the fact, as also argued in that section, that Commissioner Young's measure can be classified as protectionist.

2.6   The embargo in the context of free trade

In the media, some analysts suggested that Chile resort to the General Agreement of Tariffs and Trade (GATT) to file a trade dispute with the US on the grounds of a unilateral and arbitrary measure that restricted free trade. According to this point of view, Chile should use the GATT to appeal to the good sense of the international community, and to publicize the US over-reaction. According to GATT provisions, countries can unilaterally apply measures to protect the life and health of their citizens, provided these measures are not "arbitrary" or "unjustified".

However, Luis Escobar Cerda, Chile's former Ambassador to International Organizations, said GATT wouldn't work in this case. There was no way the Chileans could prove that the US government had acted in bad faith (either due to protectionism or a political boycott), since two grapes had actually contained remains of cyanide, and the telephone threats had some credibility. The US argument that it was acting to protect the health of its citizens was unimpeachable and there was no hard evidence of other motives. What could be argued was the haste with which a unilateral measure had been applied, accompanied by publicity that affected Chile's access not only to the North American market but also to markets elsewhere. According to Escobar, "immediately following the ban, Geneva was rife with rumors about what had happened. One rumor had it that the Communist Party was responsible. Another version was that North American producers had warned or threatened that Chile should reduce exports to the US, but the Chilean Government and producers had not heeded these warnings."[15] However there was no way of confirming these rumors, so there was no basis for filing a trade action against the US: "The only option left to Chile was to complain about the unilateral reaction, or overreaction, of a country affected by an act of this type which decided to ban all imports from the country of origin."

No one disputed the public health argument used by the United States. However, what the Chileans could not accept was "that the way to protect consumers' health is to make a media announcement banning imports of grapes and other fruit and vegetables on the grounds that they had arrived poisoned, without really knowing what had happened or where."

In view of the serious damage done to a key sector of Chile's economy, Ambassador Escobar nonetheless decided to approach the GATT council, as this was the organization responsible for dealing with anti-trade actions. In his presentation, made on April 12th, 1989 at GATT headquarters in Geneva, the Chilean ambassador proposed setting up mechanisms to reconcile public health and safety measures with stable market access for exports. He argued that in response to this kind of action, governments should act quickly and confidentially and thus avoid harming mutual interests: "There is an urgent need to reconcile the right of every contracting party to defend the consumers' health with the legitimate right of an exporter to stable, barrier-free international trade, and to avoid measures which, for lack of consultation run the risk of being disproportionate."[16]

Section 4.3's proposed definition of protectionism rests on the intuitions underlying Ambassador Escobar's argument. The definition makes it possible to decide when measures to protect public health are protectionist, and, in particular, it confirms the ambassador's intuition concerning the protectionist nature of the embargo imposed by the US.

3   The mad cow case

3.1   The embargo

On March 27th, 1996 the European Union (EU) imposed a worldwide ban on beef exports from the UK, thereby giving rise to the so-called "mad cow crisis".[17] In 1995, exports of British beef and related products had reached US$1 billion.

Just one week earlier, the UK Agriculture and Health ministers had assured the House of Commons that eating British beef did not involve any risk: Health Minister Stephen Dorrell stated that the risk of contracting Creutzfeldt-Jakob Disease by eating beef was "very low" and he himself would continue eating it. However, as this followed years of the British government assuring its citizens that there was no connection whatsoever between eating beef and contracting brain disease, the ministers' declarations did little good.

The British ministers made their statement to preempt a news conference about to be held by a government commission set up to study the relation between mad cow disease and brain illnesses in humans. In this news conference new scientific evidence would be announced indicating that "bovine spongiform encephalopathy" – commonly known as mad cow disease – could be transmitted to human beings. The Commission stated that there was no evidence that this had indeed occurred, but the mere fact that it was possible was extremely worrying.

Beef sales plummeted throughout the European Union. In the UK, beef cattle sales fell by nearly 90 per cent the week after the ban was declared. Two weeks later, beef prices had fallen by 20 to 50 per cent throughout the countries of the European Union. Sales volumes had dropped even further, with consumption falling 50 per cent in Belgium, 30 per cent in France, 50 per cent in Portugal and 60 per cent in Italy. In Germany, where there had long been concern among consumers about mad cow disease, beef sales ground to a virtual halt. European export markets also were threatened, with Ghana and Libya among others responding by banning all European beef, regardless of whether it was British or not.

3.2 Background

Bovine Spongiform Encephalopathy (BSE) belongs to a group of degenerative illnesses that attack animals' brains. The human equivalent is Creutzfeldt-Jakob Disease (CJD), an extremely rare disease, affecting on average one person in a million, particularly the elderly. One famous victim of CJD was George Balanchine, the well-known Russian choreographer, who died of it at 79.

During the previous decade, 160,000 cases of BSE were detected in British cattle, many more than elsewhere in the world, the next country being Switzerland with 206 cases. In fact, just 0.3 per cent of BSE cases have been in non-British cows. British cattle probably contracted the disease by eating fodder made from brain, spinal cord and other sheep derivatives (BSE hides in the central nervous system). Sheep typically suffer from "scrapie", a BSE-related disease that has killed sheep and goats for centuries.

The first case of BSE occurred in England in 1986. In 1988, with Britain's fields full of mad cows, the government banned the use of fodder based on dead animals (goats and sheep as well as cattle). It also warned of the potential hazards involved in people eating these animals' viscera, at the same time as it went on insisting that there was no relation whatsoever between BSE and CJD.

However, the way the British government adopted these measures was inept. Among the mistakes it made in its handling of the BSE epidemic at the end of the 1980s, at least four are worth mentioning. First, it only paid half the market value for infected cattle, which probably led many farmers to rush infected cattle to the slaughterhouse, rather than sell them to the government.

A second error was the slow enforcement of measures designed to prevent cows belonging to herds affected by BSE outbreaks from reaching the food chain. The same was true of measures to avoid slaughterhouse contamination. The third mistake was to keep insisting for a long time that there was no risk at all. An extreme example was Agriculture Minister, John Gummer, who fed a hamburger to his four-year-old daughter in front of the television cameras.

A fourth mistake made by the British government was to allow British slaughterhouses during the 1980s to eliminate carcasses at very low temperatures, often less than 100 degrees centigrade, whereby potential sources of infection were not completely destroyed. This, despite the fact that in the early 1980s a British commission of experts had suggested raising temperatures. Other countries require much higher temperatures.

•

Possible explanations for the BSE epidemic in the UK therefore include: (a) this is one of the few countries that simultaneously have a large number of cattle and sheep; (b) historically the UK has had more scrapie among its sheep than any other country; and (c) temperatures for rendering down cattle carcasses in the UK were considerably lower than in other countries during the 1980s.

3.3   New scientific evidence

The evidence that led British scientists to argue for a possible link between BSE and CJD was the appearance of a new variant of CJD in the UK. Robert Will, director of a panel studying Creutzfeldt-Jakob Disease at the University of Edinburgh, and a member of the government panel, identified "an unknown and consistent pattern" of the disease in ten victims with CJD-type symptoms. None of the victims seemed to suffer from the genetic deficiencies commonly associated with the illness. Even more worrying was the fact that their average age was 27 years; all were under 42. Until this group was identified, the average age of those sick with CJD was 63. The kind of brain damage, initial symptoms and disease duration were all different from earlier cases.

This led scientists to conclude that, in the absence of a better explanation, these cases could be the result of contagion via infected beef. There was no proof that this had in fact occurred, and it was possible that the new form of the disease had been identified in the UK simply because British scientists were studying the disease much more assiduously than their peers elsewhere.

There was great uncertainty about how many British people could be incubating this new variant of CJD if the cattle population infected with BSE really was responsible. Even if cow to human contagion was difficult, millions of people could have been exposed to BSE-infected cows before 1988, the year in which the British government introduced measures to eradicate contaminated cattle and banned the use of brains and spinal cords in products for human consumption. Even though the number of CJD cases was small, the disease's long incubation period – estimated at between five and ten years – made it difficult to predict what would happen. John Pattison, director of the government advisory committee, ventured the opinion that "it would indeed be a question of a large-scale epidemic".

Another scientist estimated that the number of British deaths from the disease in the future at "between 500 and 500,000 per year", a reflection of scientists' almost total ignorance on the issue.

3.4 John Major vs. the European Union

The real problem facing the British government was in weighing the costs of alternative measures against their potential benefits, faced with a situation characterized by great uncertainty that was hard to quantify. When the British ministers informed the House of Commons of a possible link between BSE and CJD, they made the serious political error of "entering a room with no idea of whether there was a way out". A few days later, they were desperately trying to find one.

A basic solution required answers to two key questions. Firstly, how many people were infected by the human version of BSE during the 1980s, before the British took measures to prevent suspicious material from entering the food chain? Secondly, is there any risk in eating beef today?

As for the first question, the British government said virtually nothing during the initial months following the ban, but then there was little it could say to calm people's fears.

As to whether the authorities took sufficient measures to ensure people were sufficiently protected from then on, the biggest risks were posed by non-compliance with the rules adopted at the end of the 1980s, and the possibility of infected animals without visible symptoms reaching slaughterhouses. The solution to the first problem was to improve enforcement, but the only way to prevent the second problem would be to slaughter the entire beef cattle population, since certainly there were cows carrying the disease in a state of incubation. Nonetheless, it was clear that the number of individuals incubating CJD from these causes was a tiny fraction of those who were infected before 1988.

The British government's initial strategy to convince the European Union to lift the embargo was to deny that there was a problem. There was talk of a hysterical reaction on the part of their European partners and a plot to strike a blow against the efficient English beef export industry. This strategy, if it can be called such, produced few results. The British government's frustration became clear nearly a month after the embargo was declared, when British Prime Minister John Major referred to the European ministers as "a bloody bunch of shits".[18]

From the outset, the European Union made it clear it would share the cost of any solution to the mad cows crisis. There was a precedent for this when, during an outbreak of swine fever in Germany, the EU agreed to bear 70 per cent of the cost. Although the UK initially sought compensation of 80 per cent of the cost of any animal culled (somewhat ironic given that in the German case, the British government thought that 70 per cent of the costs had been excessive), it quickly agreed to a split whereby Britain paid 30 per cent and the EU the remaining 70 per cent.

Agreement on actions to achieve the lifting of the ban was considerably more difficult than sharing the costs of such measures. On April 16th, British Agriculture Minister, Douglas Hogg, announced a packet of minimal measures. Cows over 30-months-old would be kept out of the food chain after being slaughtered, and measures from the 1980s were to be more firmly enforced. This policy was designed more at the behest of meat producers than consumers. Producers went on selling beef from BSE-infected herds and the UK's proposed measures did little to satisfy their European partners.

Eventually the British government began to consider taking reprisals. This idea split Prime Minister Major's party between the pro- and anti-Europeans ("Eurosceptics"), because of the effects such a policy would have on relations between the UK and the rest of the EU. The conservative newspaper *The Daily Telegraph* suggested the government use a legal loophole to ban French cheese and apple imports, while others suggested that the UK ban imports from Europe, where there had also been some cases of BSE. There was also talk of the UK using its veto to paralyze the EU, or else to refuse to pay its contributions to the Community budget.

To Eurosceptics, who saw the ban as a plot to damage the efficient British beef industry, those on the continent replied that their markets were suffering as much or more than the British market. At the end of April, German consumption remained less than half of its level prior to the ban. Throughout the EU consumption was down by 30 per cent, and in the UK it fell by one-third.

On April 23rd, 66 British members of parliament belonging to the Eurosceptic wing of the ruling Tory party, voted in favor of a motion to exempt Great Britain from the decisions of the European Court of Justice, a motion that, if approved, would have forced the UK to abandon the EU.

In the end, the idea of taking retaliatory actions bordering on the illegal against the EU prevailed among the British Government. On May 22nd, the British embassy in the EU announced it would start to block Community activities in meetings of the permanent representatives who briefed the EU's Council of Ministers. In practice, this meant blocking all decisions requiring unanimous approval.

A terse announcement from London stated that "the Prime Minister hopes that there will be an agreement at the Florence summit for a partial lifting of the ban on beef products and a definitive timetable for lifting the general embargo. In the meantime, the UK's capacity to cooperate in European Union matters is impaired." Declarations in response to the British policy of non-cooperation suggested that a solution would be negotiated before the EU summit in Florence on June 20th and 21st. If the impasse remained unresolved, the European partners would begin to "retaliate against the British," announced Jacques Santer, European Commission President.

On Monday June 3rd, six of the 15 EU member states meeting in Luxembourg opposed lifting the ban on exports of gelatin, tallow and semen from British cattle. Germany, Austria, Portugal, Holland, Belgium and Luxembourg all opposed relaxing the embargo, thereby preventing the qualified majority needed for approval of this type of decision. The European Commission now had only a fortnight to adopt a decision that would satisfy the British. In the meantime, EU members' exasperation with the UK became clear: on June 9th Jacques Santer told the British newspaper *The Observer* that "the EU is reaching a moment of truth. We are reaching the limit of our tolerance."

By mid-June, signs of compromise began to emerge. The UK presented a new plan for lifting the export ban and relaxing its veto on EU decisions. Meanwhile, 70 members of the British Parliament, nearly half the government backbenchers, voted for holding a referendum on British membership in the EU, using an obviously biased question.

On June 18th, the Community executive approved a document prepared by European Agriculture Commissioner, Franz Fischler of Austria, establishing the conditions the UK must meet, in order to start relaxing the export ban. These included requiring the branding of all beef cattle herds and a ban on the use of cattle, sheep or goat offal in animal feed. It also required that all cows be incinerated on completing their productive life at 30 months of age and a selective cull of over 100,000 head of cattle.

The Commission declared that it did not accept the British demand to lift the embargo on its exports to third countries, saying that authorization of British beef exports to third countries could only be granted once the EU had lifted its own ban.

On June 19th, the European Commission finally approved the British plan to control mad cow disease. EU President, Jacques Santer, declared himself satisfied with the European Veterinary Committee's approval of Britain's proposed sanitary measures, and the London plan received unanimous approval after twelve hours of debate. The motion immediately ended the embargo on exports of gelatin, tallow and semen from British cattle and included a gradual lifting of the embargo on the export of other derivatives as well as British beef itself.

Apart from incineration of several million head of cattle on completion of their active life, the plan included the culling of about 100 thousand animals born between 1989 and 1990, still active in the reproductive cycle. It also involved an effective program of cattle identification, as well as controls to keep meal of animal origin out of beef cattle feed. At the same time, the UK ended its non-cooperation policy, whereby more than 90 issues being dealt with in the EU had been blocked.

3.5 After Florence

Despite the easing of tensions that followed the agreement reached in Florence, not everything was a bed of roses. In late July the EU Agricultural Commissioner, Franz Fischler, announced that new scientific work showed that BSE could be transmitted from cows to sheep and goats, leading him to recommend that brains and spinal cords from sheep and goats be kept out of the food chain. French and British scientists had managed to inoculate goats and sheep with BSE.

Some days later, another study suggested that cows could infect their calves with BSE, leading the EU to call for the sacrifice of two million calves. Part of the US$2.5 billion cost of this measure was to be covered by cuts in the subsidies to grain producers.

Finally, at the end of August, there was better news for the British government. In an article published in *Nature*, Roy Anderson, of Oxford University, estimated that 446,000 BSE-infected cattle had been eaten before the epidemic was identified and before measures had been taken to avoid consumption of risky meat. Another 283,000 animals would have got through the safety net because they had the disease without visible symptoms. The epidemiological model used by Anderson was similar to that used to successfully predict the evolution of the AIDS epidemic. Although the Anderson model concluded that a large number of cows were initially infected, it also showed that few infected cows remained at that time: the model estimated that, in 1995, the number of infected cows would be slightly more than the number of visible cases. This suggested that the ban on using animal fodder, combined with the sacrifice of cattle showing BSE symptoms, were effective measures to prevent risk to people currently eating British beef. It also suggested that culling additional animals, unless this involved sacrificing the entire beef cattle population, would do little to accelerate eradication of the disease. The disease's only known form of propagation was from mother to calf. The model estimated that this form of propagation would only produce 340 new cases of BSE by the end of the century. The study also calculated the effects of a variety of beef cattle sacrifice strategies. Even the most effective strategies required 30 animals to be killed for every one with BSE. On the other hand, limiting the cull to cattle showing BSE symptoms would eradicate the disease by the year 2001.

Based on the evidence of the "Oxford study", as it became known, and specially its conclusion that the disease would disappear on its own by 2001, on September 19th the British government took the unilateral decision to halt the sacrifice of about 150,000 cattle that should have begun in early August. The government made the announcement without waiting for the EU veterinary committee's opinion on the Oxford study: "The new scientific data means that supplementary work is needed to decide on the appropriate sacrifice strategy," was the statement from Downing Street, after a cabinet meeting presided over by John Major. "For the time being the government will not carry out the selective cull, but will reexamine options based on new scientific data."

In acting this way, Downing Street argued that London had not broken with the Florence Accords, pointing out that the agreement required that the British eradication plan be "adopted as necessary in line with new scientific and epidemiological developments".

In response to the British announcement, EU Agriculture Commissioner, Franz Fischler, announced on September 20th that "if the conditions are not met, then the ban on British beef exports will not be lifted." A spokesman for the European Commission, Klaus van der Pass, stated that the EU Veterinary Science Committee needed to study the new scientific evidence to see whether or not a relaxation of the culling plan was justified.

Other European countries strongly opposed the decision taken by London, in the absence of a verdict from the EU veterinary experts. Klaus Kinkel, the highest German authority at the time given that Helmut Kohl was then visiting Latin America, reminded everyone that the British proposals had been rejected by the agricultural summit in Brussels just one week before the unilateral British decision, and that the summit had repeated its insistence on the elimination of 147,000 British cows.

4   Lessons and a new definition of protectionism

4.1   Comparison of the two case studies

Following the declaration of the two embargoes discussed above, both Chile and the UK took immediate steps to eliminate risks to consumers.

In both cases, these were situations of great uncertainty, difficult to quantify. Were there more contaminated grapes out there, and if so how many? How many British citizens were incubating CJD? Could beef currently being consumed by the British people be BSE-contaminated? Chile increased phytosanitary controls, whereas the UK tightened supervision of sanitary measures adopted at the end of the 1980s.

It is worth examining the similarities and differences in the role played by scientists in both of the cases described above. In the grapes case, the possibility that contamination had occurred outside the US was ruled out on the basis of scientific studies. These studies, undertaken by the University of California at Davis, played a central role in Chile's arguments before US courts. Statements from eminent US experts also contributed to the conclusion that the FDA had prior information on where to find the poisoned grapes.

In the British case, it was only after publication of the "Oxford Study" that scientists came to support the government position. When it concluded that BSE disease would be gone by 2001 even if the selective sacrifice plan was not carried out, Anderson's study served to justify the Major government's unilateral decision to depart from the Florence Accords.

It is worth drawing attention to British scientists' independent spirit. A news conference touched off the crisis, when two members of a government-appointed commission decided to inform their fellow citizens of the conclusions they had reached on the new variant of the Creutzfeldt-Jakob Disease, namely that a link between BSE and CJD could no longer be ruled out. Knowing that the scientists would publish their conclusion, the British government could do nothing but try to preempt them by a couple of hours, announcing that in their opinion, despite the new evidence, "eating British beef remains safe in the normal sense of the word." The declaration by John Major's ministers convinced no one.

Aside from the British scientists' praiseworthy display of independence, in the US investigative journalism played a significant role in questioning the FDA's actions. Reports by the *Wall Street Journal* and Television Channel 10 in Philadelphia provided valuable information in support of Chile's case.[19]

What stands out when comparing the two case studies is the striking difference between Chile and the UK when it came time to negotiate. The relative weakness of Chile's bargaining position is evident: whereas the UK adopted an uncooperative attitude within the European Union, boycotting much of the Union's work for several weeks, it took the

Chilean delegation three days after the FDA ban to be received by a high-level government authority in the US (Secretary of State, James Baker). Moreover, the US authorities have systematically refused to cooperate with requests from the Chilean judicial system, and the Chilean government has met with little success in pressing its legal claims against the US government, which successfully appealed on the grounds of "jurisdictional immunity" and then refused to invoke the 1914 Bryan-Suárez Mujica Treaty to resolve the dispute.

The European Union's offer to pay for 70 per cent of a selective cattle cull contrasts with the fact that, today, over a decade later, Chile has still received no compensation from the US. Furthermore, one year after the grape crisis, when evidence pointing to at least some degree of negligence on the part of the FDA became public, the US Senate rejected legislation that would have established equal conditions for the inspection of Chilean fruit, and approved an extension of the marketing orders required for kiwis, plums, nectarines and apples imported into the United States.

4.2 Commissioner Young's decision

It has been widely argued in Chile that the FDA's measure was disproportionate, and that in more serious cases it had not adopted such draconian steps. To quote the report of the Chilean Chamber of Deputies, this was a "hasty and exaggerated measure" which caused serious economic damage. "From all of this one can conclude, with considerable certainty, that there was manifest bad faith on the part of the US authorities in facing up to the situation" (p. 24 of the report).

I argue below that Commissioner Young's behavior might have been justified given the conditions he faced. In doing so, I put myself in the commissioner's shoes, with the information available to him on March 13th, 1989 when the poisoned grapes were discovered. I assume that Young did not participate in any plot directed against Chile and reflect on what his decision-making process might have been.

A first possibility is that he conducted a cost–benefit analysis. What were the costs of ordering an embargo and what were the benefits? Benefits included the possibility of saving the lives of US citizens. The probability of a child dying from eating fruit injected with cyanide was small, but certainly not zero; if two grapes were found to be contaminated and there had been telephone threats in Santiago, he could not rule out the possibility of more poisoned grapes headed for the tables of US consumers. As well, eating the poisoned fruit could damage health, without necessarily killing someone.

What were the costs of an embargo? US consumers would have to assume the costs of not being able to consume Chilean fruit for a given period, and having to pay a higher price for fruit imported from elsewhere, or else having to replace fresh for other produce (e.g. canned fruit). There was also the second area of costs arising from the ban: the enormous losses to Chilean producers. From Commissioner Young's point of view, however, this cost was practically irrelevant, for his mission was to protect the health of US citizens and did not encompass the measures' impact on foreign producers. The ban also imposed costs on US firms (e.g. distributors of Chilean fruit), but these costs were much smaller than those faced by Chilean producers. This kind of analysis leads us to conclude that the ban was warranted on cost–benefit grounds alone, with no plot or conspiracy theory necessary to justify it.

A second analytical process open to Commissioner Young would also have led to a ban. This one is based on his opting for the measure posing the least risk to his position. If we assume that the Commissioner's goal in deciding whether or not to impose the embargo was to avoid putting his job on the line, how would he have acted? This analysis requires comparing costs associated with different options if these proved mistaken. The first option, for example, would be to avoid a ban and then face the consequences of consumers getting poisoned. Public outrage would have been huge; public opinion would have concluded that Commissioner Young, knowing of the possible existence of poisoned fruit, had nonetheless learned nothing from the recent PanAm disaster. He would probably have lost his job.

A second misjudgment would involve declaring the embargo, without sufficient justification. In this case, the big losers would be Chilean producers, who posed no threat to the FDA director's position. Insofar as the available evidence admitted "reasonable doubt" about the safety of Chilean fruit, the most advisable course of action was to impose the ban.

It is worth contrasting the incentives faced by Commissioner Young with those facing European Union Commissioner Fischler when he called for the ban on British beef exports. Fischler did not work for any government in particular but was an official of the European Commission, for which reason he had to put Community interests above those of individual member countries. It was therefore not surprising that well before agreeing on the measures that the UK should apply so the EU would approve the gradual lifting of the ban, the countries had agreed on how to share the costs of these measures. The EU also had a precedent set by a similar situation in which the EU had paid 70 per cent of the costs; it was therefore natural to apply similar criteria in this case.

It is true that the mad cow case generated considerable tension between John Major's government and the EU regarding the measures to be taken, with Major embarking on a course of obstructionist actions bordering on the illegal. However, Major's behavior seems to have been driven primarily by political considerations within his party, rather than being a reaction to exaggerated demands from Britain's trading partners.

The main difference between the situations faced by the two commissioners was that Young had almost no incentive to consider the impact of the ban on the exporting country, while Fischler did.

4.3 The measures taken and protectionism

Were the measures adopted by the US against Chilean fruit, or by the EU against British beef, protectionist? This section offers answers to these questions, and in doing so offers a new definition of what constitutes a protectionist measure.

There is no agreement on the best definition of a "protectionist measure", specifically, a non-tariff barrier to trade. The most general definition is credited to Walter (1972) (quoted by Chambers and Pick 1994), who defines it as any measure that distorts the volume of trade, the composition of the basket of goods traded between countries, or the direction in which goods are traded. Using this definition, both the embargo imposed by the FDA and that applied by the EU were protectionist measures. However, this definition is clearly too general, since any measure legitimately seeking to protect consumer health by banning imports of a risky product would thus be protectionist.

A second definition is provided by Baldwin (1970), also quoted by Chambers and Pick (1994). Baldwin focuses on a measure's effect on a country's real income and defines a non-tariff trade barrier as "any measure (public or private) which leads to internationally traded goods or services being reallocated in such a way that global potential real income is reduced." Under this definition, it seems natural to venture the opinion that the FDA ban constituted a protectionist measure, at least given the information available *ex-post* (there were no more poisoned grapes). In the case of the ban on British beef the situation is less obvious. Once the new evidence of a possible link between BSE and CJD became known, would global real income have been reduced to a lesser extent without the embargo?

The third definition comes from Hillman (1991) (again quoted by Chambers and Pick 1994), who defines a non-tariff barrier as "any decision or government practice, apart from the imposition of a tariff, which directly impedes the entry of imports into a country and/or discriminates against imports, i.e. a measure that is not applied equally to domestic producers or distributors."

The first half of the Hillman definition is similar to Walter's, for which reason we only consider the second half. Using this definition, neither embargo would constitute a protectionist measure, given that it can be argued that both commissioners had information justifying the ban in question, so the measure was not discriminatory. To prove otherwise, one would have to show evidence of similar situations involving US agricultural products, or those from European Union countries, where an embargo was not imposed. And even if such situations were found, there would always be differences between those cases and the ban in question, making it difficult to develop arguments along these lines.

Subsection 4.2 encourages us to seek a new definition of "protectionist measure," one in which a measure becomes "protectionist" when it differs (markedly) from the measures that would have been taken, if the welfare of all countries affected by the measure had been considered.[20] That is to say, a government measure is protectionist when, allowing for transfers between countries, there exists a Pareto superior alternative. For example, and working in partial equilibrium, a minimum quality standard is protectionist when it differs from the standard that maximizes the sum of producer and consumer surpluses both in the country setting the standard and in the country exporting the targeted good.

Using the above definition, the ban on British meat could not be classified as a protectionist measure. From the outset, the European Union knew that it would assume a significant part of the cost of any measures, so there were incentives to impose a ban only if this would increase aggregate welfare in the EU. Moreover, the case study of Section 3 provides no evidence that the EU failed to act with the welfare of the Union in mind.

The status of the ban on Chilean fruit is far from clear. Under this definition, we need to know what Commissioner Young would have decided if he'd had some incentive to internalize the effects of a possible ban on the Chilean economy. There's no clear-cut answer to this question, but it is likely that he would have chosen to seek more information – e.g. by calling a meeting of scientists to assess the potential health risk of the contaminated grapes – before declaring an embargo. If this is true, then the ban on Chilean fruit would qualify as a protectionist measure.

5 Conclusion

Among the new faces of protectionism are the trade measures that governments take, supposedly to protect the health of their citizens, without considering the disastrous effects these may have on the welfare of their trading partners. The US ban on Chilean fruit imports, discussed at length in Section 2, is an example of this type. In contrast, the degree of integration within the European Union provided a solution to this new form of protectionism among its member countries, as the case study of Section 3 illustrates. The EU's decisions in the case of the mad cows did take into account the welfare of the affected exporting country (the UK).

In the absence of such wide-ranging integration as the EU, dispute resolution mechanisms can play an important role. On September 24th, 1995, Carlos Mladinic, who at the time was Director General of Economic Relations in the Chilean Foreign Ministry, stated that "we are a very small country and cannot credibly threaten economic reprisal. Our only option is to resort to multilateral dispute resolution mechanisms." Such mechanisms may be administered either by the World Trade Organization (WTO) or else should form part of any trade agreements signed by Chile.

The two case studies considered in this chapter motivated the new definition of protectionism discussed in Section 4, whereby one country's action (affecting other countries) may be considered protectionist when it differs from other possible measures that would maximize the collective welfare of all countries involved. This definition can be extended in many directions. For example, Fischer and Serra (this volume) applied it to the case of minimum quality standards, proposing that when standards are imposed on goods with externalities in consumption, the welfare of foreign consumers should not be considered when deciding whether a measure is protectionist.

The analysis of the previous sections also brings out the importance of creating mechanisms that provide officials with the incentives to internalize the cost of protectionist measures to exporting countries. Ideally, if countries were required to bear the costs of the measures they impose, the resulting policies should improve the aggregate welfare of all countries involved. Using the definition of protectionism proposed in this chapter, the result would be that with appropriate incentives, measures adopted would never be protectionist.

Notes

1 This section is based on media reports. The main sources are cited in the footnotes.
2 Representative of the State of Pennsylvania, where the port of Philadelphia is located.
3 *El Mercurio*, March 15th, 1989.
4 *La Segunda*, March 14th, 1989.
5 Orlando Letelier, Minister of Foreign Relations under President Allende, was killed by a car bomb in Washington, DC, in 1976.
6 *La Segunda*, March 16th, 1989.
7 *La Segunda*, March 16th, 1989.
8 Report of the Investigating Committee, pp. 56–63.
9 See Basch and Engel (1993) for a description of the Copper Stabilization Fund. Although the report is not explicit about the destination of these sums, most likely it helped finance the purchase of external debt promissory notes by the Central Bank.
10 *El Mercurio*, March 26, 1989.
11 *The Wall Street Journal*, November 16th, 1989.
12 This treaty provides a mechanism for resolving disputes between both countries. It can be applied only when both countries agree to invoke it.
13 *La Segunda*, July 16th, 1989.
14 "Alar" is a chemical product harmful to health.
15 Interview with Luis Escobar Cerda, Chilean Ambassador to International Organizations between 1986 and 1990, conducted by Claudio Rammsy, Santiago, May 30th, 1996. Unless otherwise indicated, the quotes which follow are from the translated transcript of this interview.
16 *El Mercurio*, April 13th, 1989.
17 Sources for this section are contemporary press agency dispatches and articles from *The Economist*.
18 *The Economist*, April 27, 1996.
19 This contrasts with the manifest weaknesses of Chilean journalism.
20 Of course, there is the implicit assumption that the measure makes foreign countries worse off than they would be under the "world welfare maximizing" alternative.

References

Baldwin, R. (1970). *Nontariff Distortions of International Trade*. Washington, DC: The Brookings Institution.

Basch, M. and E. Engel (1993). "Temporary shocks and stabilization mechanisms: The Chilean case", in E. Engel and P. Meller (eds), *External Shocks and Stabilization Mechanisms*, chapter 2. Washington, DC: Johns Hopkins.

Chambers, R. and D. Pick (1994, February). "Marketing orders as nontariff trade barriers", *American Journal of Agricultural Economics*, 76 (1), 47–54.

Hillman, J. (1991). *Technical Barriers to Agricultural Trade*. Westview Press.

Walter, I. (1972). "Nontariff protection among industrial countries: Some preliminary empirical evidence", *Economia Internazionale*, 25, 335–54.

6
Trade and the Environment: Mining

*Raúl O'Ryan and Andrés Ulloa**

1 Introduction

Exports have become the engine of growth in the Chilean economy, having expanded at annual rates of around 6 per cent over the last decade, to represent more than 20 per cent of GDP today. Most exports have been concentrated in natural-resource-based sectors such as mining, fishing, forestry and agriculture, and this situation is likely to persist in the medium-term future.

The dominant development paradigm as the world moves into the twenty-first century is "sustainable development", which despite being somewhat vague has proved to be a powerful concept in promoting environmental awareness and stewardship. This has certainly affected international trade, above all in products that are intensive in their use of environmental inputs such as natural resources and energy, or those with polluting productive processes.

This greater concern for the environment, while legitimate *per se*, has been used as an excuse to obstruct the import of products that compete with local production, on the grounds that they supposedly involve risks to human or environmental health. Although the World Trade Organization (WTO) has rules governing such practices, new instruments of a voluntary nature have appeared which, based on the product "life-cycle" approach, in practice can be used as protectionist restrictions. The life-cycle approach attempts to identify and then reduce

* The authors are grateful for suggestions from Sergio García and Carlos Gajardo, and for comments by Alex Galetovic and participants in the New Faces of Protectionism Seminar. We also are grateful for valuable help from Cristóbal Huneeus and María T. Viertel.

121

environmental impacts throughout a product's entire existence, i.e. production, transportation, distribution, recycling and final disposal. Chile's mining sector has not been immune to such practices. In 1984 it was accused of ecological dumping, on the grounds that the country's environmental standards were very deficient, so its productive processes were more polluting and of lower cost. Unfortunately for the mining sector, this greater concern for the environment is also being expressed in several initiatives that attempt to portray metals in general, and copper in particular, as hazardous for both human health and ecosystems. If such initiatives prosper, Chile runs the risk of losing important markets.

The aims of this chapter are to analyze the environmental threats to Chile's mining sector, discuss possible causes, analyze their main impacts and make recommendations. Section 2 provides a general overview of trade restrictions based on environmental arguments, including the instruments and measures being used, the role of the WTO and a brief discussion of the protectionist nature of these measures. The aim is to describe the context in which these trade practices are being developed, with the analysis focused on measures that affect the mining sector.

The third section briefly analyzes the environmental performance of Chilean mining, and the protectionist threats that may arise from this. The fourth section discusses new protectionist trends that are based on product life-cycle considerations. Section 5 presents conclusions and makes recommendations.

2   Conceptual framework: the new faces of protectionism based on environmental considerations

Looking after the environment has become an issue of the utmost importance in many countries, especially in the developed world. Progressive environmental degradation has made society increasingly worried about local environmental effects caused by economic activities, and there is also a growing awareness of the regional and global impacts of pollution. As a result, consumers are demanding products that are environment-friendly, and firms have responded by building environmental considerations into their new productive processes. Governments, sometimes following and other times taking the lead, are requiring or at least encouraging private-sector decision-makers to take environmental costs into account.

This greater environmental concern has affected international trade, and tighter environmental regulations, basically in developed countries, have been blamed for a loss of competitiveness in more pollution-intensive industries. Some industries have lobbied to slow down environmental regulation in their own countries and to get similar standards complied with by their competitors, either through trade and environment agreements or else directly through trade restrictions. This attempt to harmonize environmental standards and procedures is being reinforced by a series of voluntary environmental certification incentives that have emerged over the past decade.

Some developed countries, mainly in the European Union (EU), have begun to incorporate the "precautionary" principle in their legislation, which legitimizes restrictions on the use of products that might be harmful to people's health or ecosystems, even when the suspected danger is not well supported scientifically. This can be seen in a series of international agreements on the environment, which have significant trade implications.

The above has been strengthened by the increasingly aggressive stance adopted by ecological movements, who see international trade as one of the causes of environmental degradation, due not only to the faster economic growth trade can generate, but also because ever fiercer competition to capture and consolidate domestic and foreign markets may lead to a relaxing of international environmental standards.

2.1 Loss of competitiveness and eco-dumping

The costs of environmental regulation have risen significantly over the last 25 years in developed countries. The United States Environmental Protection Agency in the (EPA) estimates that during the 1980s the annual cost to that country of complying with environmental regulations was more than 2.1 per cent of GDP, and in the 1990s the figure was even higher. In other countries of the Organization for Economic Cooperation and Development (OECD),[1] the costs of environmental regulation are put at between 1 and 2 per cent of GDP (OECD 1993).

This rising cost of environmental regulation has been used as an argument to justify a loss of competitiveness in certain industries in the United States, manifested in terms of slower productivity growth, lower exports, job loss and the relocation of more pollution-intensive industries in environmentally less-demanding countries.[2] It has even been claimed that the whole United States economy has become less competitive.[3]

A number of studies have attempted to quantify the impact of regulatory policies on the competitiveness of the industrial sector (Ugelow

1982; Robinson 1988; Tobey 1990; Jaffe *et al.* 1995). The results suggest the impacts are relatively small, ranging from 1 to 3 per cent of total costs.[4]

At the global level, the hypothesis of a loss of competitiveness among industries located in environmentally more-demanding countries has provoked different reactions from ecological groups, businessmen and politicians. Ecological groups draw attention to the danger that competition to win or maintain market share may lead countries to relax environmental standards; industrialists and politicians argue that industries in developing countries are competing unfairly as they do not have to comply with demanding environmental standards. This is seen as a sort of "environmental dumping" or "eco-dumping".

In addition, and as a consequence of the above, it is claimed that significant differences in environmental requirements between countries would lead pollution-intensive industries[5] to set up in countries with looser environmental controls.[6] However, this hypothesis has not proved sustainable empirically. Studies by Lucas *et al.* (1992) and Low and Yeats (1992) show that although there is an increase in the concentration of polluting industries in developing countries, there is no significant evidence that this type of industry has moved towards environmentally less-demanding countries as a result of differences in environmental legislation. More likely such movements would be explained by different labor costs or natural resource endowments. Actually, there are factors that discourage industries from locating in environmentally less-demanding countries, including the prestige of the firm *vis-à-vis* environmental damage or as regards their consumers, the anticipation of stricter measures in those countries in the near future, and the high costs of rapidly changing from a more polluting technology to a cleaner one compared with starting out with the cleaner one immediately (Birdsall and Wheeler 1992).

Multinational corporations are the most sensitive to international differences in environmental regulations (Walter 1982), as they use production facilities in different countries to supply multiple markets, so these corporations frequently use the environmental standards of their home country throughout their operations.

Despite a lack of empirical evidence for this type of competitive disadvantage, a series of proposals have recently been announced that aim to diminish or eliminate it; these include proposals to harmonize environmental standards and policies, at both government and industry level, to certify compliance with environmental management standards and procedures.

The harmonization of environmental standards is increasingly being put forward as a way of reducing differences in environmental costs: if countries have uniform environmental standards in goods and services production, the costs of environmental control would be equalized across countries. Such initiatives have been repeatedly criticized, especially by economists, since free trade and efficiency can perfectly well coexist with different standards.

Clearly a different valuation of the environment between countries, as well as different capacities to assimilate pollutants and differences in the costs and benefits from achieving better environmental quality, make standards differ between countries. For that reason, attempts to impose harmonization would mean a loss of world welfare.[7]

In order to impose such standards, some countries have used international trade restrictions that prohibit the entry of products that fail to comply with the environmental standards of the importing country; others have tried to impose tariff surcharges to reduce or eliminate the cost differential. There are several cases here, for example the tuna fish trade dispute between Mexico and the United States, and the attempt to impose a tariff surcharge on exports of Chilean copper. These cases are discussed below.

2.2 Standards to prevent risks to health and environment

A second issue relates to the growing concern in developed countries for people's health and care for ecological systems at the local, regional and global level. This has led to the introduction of increasingly strict legal standards for potentially harmful products. At the same time, a series of international agreements have been reached to protect global ecosystems. Three of the most important of these are the Montreal Protocol, the Basle Convention and the Convention on International Trade in Endangered Species (CITES).[8]

Although this concern is legitimate, and each country has sovereignty to impose the regulations it deems most appropriate for its inhabitants and environment, it has led to trade restrictions such as import bans on potentially harmful products.

There are several documented cases of trade measures that have been applied to provide greater protection to people's health or to the environment. In 1984 a system of returnable deposits came into operation in Denmark and the use of metal containers was banned because they are not reusable. Other members of the EU complained that this measure put their firms at a disadvantage compared to Danish firms. The Danish government justified the measure by claiming that it was based on a desire to reduce the quantity of waste products and to protect its environment. The case was taken to the European Court of Justice which upheld the measure on the grounds that it was in proportion to the aim being pursued. Shortly afterwards, for similar reasons, the German government imposed a deposit system for plastic bottles, which hurt industries in France and Belgium (Laplant and Garbutt 1992; Geradin and Stewardson 1995).

In December 1985, the European Economic Community (EEC), as it was called at that time, banned the use of hormones in the feeding of farm poultry for human consumption, and in 1989 it prohibited the import of hormone-treated meat. As a result, the United States lost a market worth approximately US$ 145 million per year.[9] The USA protested that there was no scientific evidence to demonstrate that hormones were a threat to human health, so the restrictions imposed constituted a trade barrier. The EEC, for its part, argued there was no evidence that the use of these hormones was risk-free, so they were adopting a necessary precautionary measure to protect their consumers in relation. In retaliation, United States began to apply higher tariffs on certain products from European countries.[10]

This episode illustrates one of the main weaknesses of this type of measure: namely, the fragility of their scientific underpinnings. The procedure for identifying and quantifying the risks of a substance is known as risk assessment. It aims to determine the safe dose for individuals, or the maximum permissible concentration levels of a given substance in a product or in the environment. This process is highly uncertain as regards both the identification and the quantification of risks.[11] Furthermore, as risk assessment is a relatively new discipline, there is no consensus on the tests, techniques, nor on many of the hypothesis formulated by the experts. Faced with this type of situation, it is normal that there should be different scientific viewpoints on the consequences of a given exposure level.

In response to this uncertainty, many countries have decided to invoke the "precautionary principle" in their own legislation, as well as in international agreements. This principle establishes that even when certain cause–effect relations are not well understood scientifically, measures can still be taken to prevent possible damage to health or environment.[12] The principle has been adopted by the European Union in its Article 139r (2), 1992, which has been used in many treaties, agreements and international conventions, including the North Sea Conference on marine protection; the Montreal Protocol on substances affecting the ozone layer; the Convention on Biological

Diversity and in at least ten other international agreements (Van der Zwaag 1996).

Since there are many toxic substances[13] which, in an isolated way or in combination, may cause harm to human health or ecosystems, and given that only some of the effects of a few of these substances are understood, choosing one rather than another either to research or restrict becomes a potentially discriminatory process. A variety of interest groups participate in the decision, including governmental authorities in the importing country, industry, international organizations concerned for health and the environment, as well as ecologists, the potentially affected community and scientists. This, of course, opens the door to contingent protection measures deriving from protectionist interests, albeit grounded in "scientific" research.

All of this causes problems that developing countries are not ready to cope with. Carrying out risk assessment for a substance requires a lot of information and years of basic research, and developing countries have neither the economic means nor the trained staff to undertake research aimed at rebutting the tests or risk assessment procedures on which international trade restrictions are based.

For this reason it has been suggested that rather than setting standards based on a risk concept that is often debatable, what is needed is to define and harmonize procedures for risk assessment at the international level, leaving countries themselves to decide their acceptable risk level in a sovereign way. However this is not how decisions are being taken in practice.

2.3   Processes of environmental certification

Over the past decade, mainly in OECD member countries, there has been a proliferation of measures for certifying compliance with environmental criteria, as regards both final products and productive processes. These requirements are based on the life-cycle approach, which seeks to identify environmental impacts over the entire product lifespan, from conversion of raw material to finished product, passing through the stages of transportation and distribution to consumers, and including maintenance, recycling and final disposal. The message behind these demands is that all stages of the product life-cycle should be clean, and particularly the production process.

The first certification systems used in Europe were programs of eco-labeling, eco-packaging and recycling.[14] Other programs have also been discussed such as extending producer responsibility (Oldenburg 1994). There has been a recent process towards harmonizing procedures and criteria in Europe to enable certification systems to become more adaptable, homogeneous and transparent. One of these processes is the work done by the International Standards Organization (ISO), known as ISO 14000.[15] This consists of setting up a model Environmental Management System and a series of standard guidelines that firms should comply with. Although this procedure has only recently come into use,[16] it is expected to have a big impact in the future.

In general, these certification initiatives are voluntary, although in some countries it is the governments themselves that are promoting them. Industries that wish to do so, or products destined for markets which require it, must apply to obtain this certificate. In 1994, 22 of the 24 OECD countries had one of these programs in operation (Stevens 1994). They have been used mainly in textiles, footwear and forestry products, and in the future may be extended to other sectors including mining.

2.4   The role of the WTO in environmental disputes

The GATT and its succesor, the World Trade Organization (WTO), whose main aim is to promote free trade, has played an important role in reducing the use of environmental arguments to restrict trade. Articles I, II and III of the GATT trade code establish non-discrimination and equal national treatment. This means that if a standard or some other trade measure is applied to a product coming from a given country, the same measure should also apply to the local product and to products from other countries. However, there are exceptions, for the GATT establishes that the imposition of standards may be justified when they are needed to protect human, animal and plant life and health. For this purpose, standards should be based on scientific principles, as well as on the international norms, directives and recommendations relating to the issue, and should not involve unnecessary restrictions to trade (Article XX).

In practice, as mentioned in the previous section, such exceptions have repeatedly been used as arguments for imposing trade restrictions, and the GATT-WTO has had to arbitrate in many of the resulting disputes. One of the best known is the trade dispute between Mexico and the United States concerning the impact of tuna fishing on dolphins: since tuna exporting countries were not complying with the mammal protection standards imposed by the United States on its own producers, the US banned tuna imports from Mexico and Venezuela, as well as Costa Rica, France, Italy, Japan and Panama – the latter being intermediary countries.

In February 1991, Mexico asked the WTO to convene a special dispute solution panel, arguing that with this measure the United States was in breach of WTO rules. The United States, for its part, replied that by virtue of Article III (national treatment) it could impose the same protective standards for dolphins at the border as were in force inside their country. Moreover, by virtue of Article XX, the measures were justified in terms of promoting animal health. The panel concluded that the United States could not extend compliance with its legislation to other countries, for which reason it could not ban these imports. In response, the USA decided to adopt tuna product labeling that provided information on the methods used in production. This practice is not incompatible with WTO provisions, as it merely amounted to providing information to the consumer.

Due to the repeated imposition of restrictions invoking exceptions permitted by the WTO, this institution has incorporated certain additional precepts, so as to make clear that the use of trade measures under Article XX is only valid when it can be shown that there is no other way of obtaining the same benefit. For example, in response to a Canadian demand that the US fishing fleet operating in its waters should unload in Canadian ports,[17] the WTO, while recognizing that the measure was legitimate, asked for it to be changed as in its judgment the same goals could be achieved without affecting international trade.

The use of technical standards on products, processes and production methods, has been a highly controversial issue in the WTO. Such procedures make it possible to issue directives on terminology, symbols and wrapping, as well as the branding or labeling of a product, and its process or production method; moreover, their use has been on the rise. The WTO has clearly established that the regulations should not restrict trade more than is necessary to achieve legitimate goals: namely, protection of health or national security; prevention of practices that might lead to error; protection of animal or plant health, or protection of the environment. In addition, it has recommended the use of international standards whenever these exist and can be applied.

However, the ambiguity regarding what is understood by "unnecessary trade restriction", or the term "legitimate goals" gives rise to dispute, and until a clear definition exists, there is a risk that these technical barriers will be used with protectionist aims.

2.5 Protectionism and the environment

It is very difficult to prove that a given trade measure has been imposed with protectionist aims. Measures may applied on environmental grounds, but to what extent are they really an attempt to protect local industry? Would they have been imposed in the same way if there was a local industry that had to bear a significant cost? Does this constitute protectionism?

Two definitions of protectionism seem appropriate in the environmental context. Firstly, it could be argued that a trade measure is protectionist if, as a result, local firms can obtain a competitive advantage they would not have had in the absence of the measure (Laplante and Garbutt 1992). Thus, a restriction would constitute protectionism which, even though not discriminatory, might impose higher costs on foreign firms than on local ones, thus affording the latter an additional advantage. For example, it has been argued that the requirement of recycling or the reuse of containers is protectionist, as distributors prefer to buy from national producers who take responsibility for the collection, disposal or recycling of containers. For foreign producers it might be very expensive to set up their own system of collection and recycling, because, among other things, they cannot take advantage of economies of scale.

Secondly, it could be argued that a measure has protectionist characteristics when the importing country would not have imposed it if all demand were supplied by local firms. The imposition of a much tougher restriction (i.e. a standard) than would have been imposed if local costs were considered as well as those of foreign firms, is an example of this type. As a result, the restriction might reduce world welfare. For example, between 1970 and 1980 Japan made it obligatory to include labels detailing all the additives and synthetic chemicals used in edible products; a requirement that was also imposed on local industry. However, most Japanese producers were using natural additives. If instead they had been using artificial additives, it remains an open question whether the measures would have been applied .

Apart from this, explicit or implicit threats to impose restrictions on trade in certain products, on environmental grounds, constitutes contingent protectionism, i.e. it requires exporting firms to take actions in the light of measures that might possibly be taken in the future. For example, alleging a probable case of "eco-dumping", local producers might threaten to seek imports sanctions. This would result in pressure on foreign countries to improve their environmental practices. Even if such measures were not actually put into effect because of the difficulty of proving dumping, local industry would obtain a trade advantage. This can clearly be seen in the mining sector example discussed in the next section.

Finally, the proliferation of voluntary certification mechanisms, such as eco-labeling or ISO 14000, may also constitute protectionist instruments. Many of these measures have been promoted by local industry itself, along with environmentalist groups, who impose their own criteria regarding what is understood by products that do not harm the environment.[18] This has meant foreign industries in practice have had to comply with such requirements in order to enter markets, as local distributors simply do not buy products that do not use these certification systems.[19]

Such instruments are governed by the WTO, under the category of technical trade barriers, and it is stated that they should not be used to create unnecessary barriers to international trade. However, due to their voluntary nature, it is difficult to establish the WTO's role in their regulation. The WTO has no jurisdiction over private groups, for which reason it cannot prevent their use.

3 Threats to trade in mining products on environmental grounds: the problem of "ecological dumping"

Since the end of the nineteenth century, mining has contributed significantly to Chile's economic growth, and at the present time accounts for nearly 10 per cent of GDP. In addition, it has been the main export sector and currently generates 45 per cent of all foreign currency export earnings. Copper is by far the most important mining product, accounting for over 80 per cent of total mining exports.

Between 1970 and 1990 the physical production of mining products registered a remarkable increase: copper went up by 146 per cent, molybdenum by 64 per cent, gold by 942 per cent and silver by 374 per cent. These trends persisted during the nineties, and particularly copper output doubled in the decade. As a result, Chile is the world's second producer and exporter of copper, the main producer of nitrates and sodium nitrate, the world's second producer of lithium, iodine and molydenum, and a significant gold producer.

Despite the fact that mining affects the environment from the initiation of exploration activities to the abandonment of worked-out mines and even beyond, prior to 1990 little importance had been given to the environmental problems associated with mining expansion–either at the corporate or at the regulatory authority level–and consequently these problems steadily accumulated.[20] Table 6.1 provides a qualitative summary of the significant environmental problems associated with mining for each Chilean Region in 1990.[21]

The prevailing attitude towards environmental matters in this period can be described as reactive: interventions by the authority tended only to occur in response to emergency. The government's attitude to environmental issues everywhere, not only in mining, was "produce now, clean up later"; accordingly, it minimized environmental requirements and restricted access to data on pollution levels. It should be kept in mind that over 75 per cent of copper output and more than 90 per cent of smelter capacity was state-owned at the time.

This lack of concern was in stark contrast to the increasing efforts in developed countries during the 1980s to introduce appropriate environmental management in the mining sector. Chapman (1991) for example, states that the cost of environmental protection and labor safety in the United States copper industry at that time was approximately 15 cents per pound of copper produced, corresponding to between 20 and 25 per cent of total production costs. These figures are significantly higher than those estimated in other industries where generally such costs are much less significant.[22]

Consequently, Chilean mining was extremely vulnerable to allegations of unfair competition on environmental grounds, and this became reality when the US copper industry went into crisis in 1984 as a result of a fall in copper prices. The following sections of this chapter discuss the environmental situation in mining up to 1990, and the reaction of the sector in the face of pressures to improve its environmental performance.

3.1   The environmental situation up to 1990: an invitation to allegations of "ecological dumping"

Up to 1990 mining caused significant environmental impacts, as can be seen in Table 6.1. In general the main problems of pollution occurred in large-scale mining, and particularly in the operations of Chile's seven copper smelters[23] and single gold smelter.[24] Copper smelters are located in various areas of the country and have impacts on different populations. The main smelters are Chuquicamata (the largest in the world), with a capacity of 1.5 million MT/yr, and Caletones with a capacity of 1.25 MT/yr, both belonging to the state-owned company Codelco. Codelco owns nearly 75 per cent of smelting capacity in Chile; the National Mining Company (ENAMI) owns 16 per cent and the private sector (Refimet and Chagres) owns just 10 per cent.

In 1990 all smelters[25] were violating the current quality standards for sulfur oxides (SO_2), and Chuquicamata was also exceeding the standard for breathable particulate material (PM-10) (Solari 1992). In addition there was an unquantified problem – but acknowledged to be serious – relating to significant arsenic emissions that were affecting exposed populations in the areas surrounding these smelters. In general, the problem of managing toxic substances was hardly addressed at all.

Apart from this, mining has affected water quality, as well as the quantity of water available for other uses. Environmental impact studies carried out in the Mapocho, Elqui, Aconcagua and Copiapó rivers over the last fifteen years[26] show that they are contaminated beyond minimum quality standards. However, it has not been specified how much of this pollution is the result of discharges from mining and how much is due to the high natural presence of some of the substances (copper, arsenic).[27] Furthermore, although mining is presumed to pollute underground waters, there is no reliable data on the seriousness of the problem.

The permanent scarcity of water in the north of Chile – one of the driest deserts in the world – and its inadequate management have been growing causes for concern. The doubling of copper output during the 1990s significantly increased the demand for water, and has been estimated that by the end of the decade mining will use nearly 35 per cent of all available supplies in the north of Chile, way above the 15 per cent used in 1990 (Lagos 1996, p.181). There are documented examples of small rural communities that have been left without water supply due to the installation of mining works in their immediate surroundings. Moreover, mining companies have done significant prospecting work and have identified and are exploiting underground water resources, some of which are fossil reserves. The potential impact of the shrinking of these reserves on the fragile ecosystems in the north of Chile is unknown.

Finally, the environmental conditions under which small-scale mining has been carried out are extremely deficient.[28] This sector has not been concerned about environmental management and has had very limited investment capacity to improve procedures. According to Galaz (1993), small-scale mining impacts the physical environment by removing material and changing landscapes; it also emits emits particulate material and discharges liquid effluents into streams and rivers in an uncontrolled way.

This paints a worrying environmental picture, which in the second half of the 1980s seriously threatened Chile's copper exports. On January 26th, 1984 a group of North American mining companies petitioned the International Trade Commission (ITC) to totally or partially suspend

Table 6.1 Environmental impacts caused by the mining sector in Chile[1]

Region		Air		Water		Soil
I	*	Atmospheric pollution caused by various industries.	**	Excessive water consumption by mining companies (salination)		
			*	Pollution of underground, surface and sea water (La Cascada and Pozo Al Monte).		
II	***	Contamination by gases and particulates (Calama, Chuquicamata, Antofagasta, Tocopilla, María Elena and Pedro de Valdivia).	**	Underground, surface and sea water pollution (all Region).	***	Destruction of landscape and archeological sites.
			***	Excessive consumption of undergroung and surface water (mainly Río Loa).		
III	***	Pollution by gases and particulates (Copiapó, Potrerillos, Tierra Amarilla) coming from the ENAMI smelters (Paipote) and Codelco (Potrerillos).	**	Marine pollution due to mining tailings (Chañaral).	**	Pollution of agricultural areas due to the accumulation of mining tailings
			***	Pollution of river beds and water courses due to tailings and liquid industrial discharges.		
			**	Marine pollution due to waste from pellets plant (Huasco and Chapaco).	**	Risk of tailings dams overflowing.[3]
IV	**	Pollution by dust with high manganese content (Coquimbo). Pollution from high arsenic content (El Indio Mine).[2]	***	Water pollution (surface and underground) in cordilleran sectors.	*	Tailings dams with problems of stability and leakage.[3]
				Contamination of river beds and water courses (Río Elqui).	*	Alterations to landscape due to open pit activities.
					***	Arsenic pollution in hills and snow close to the El Indio Mine.

Table 6.1 (Contd.)

V	*	Air pollution caused by various industries, particularly Ventanas, Concon, Chagres, and Melon Cement	**	River pollution (Aconcagua and Blanco) from uncontrolled mining activity and tailings.	***	Contaminated agricultural soils in Ventanas (ENAMI).
					***	Chemical pollution (Cabildo, Catemu)
			**	Physical contamination of water bodies (all watersheds and mining centers).	**	Tailings dams with stability and filtration problems.[3]
Metro-politan Region	**	Contamination by particulates (Polpaico Cement)			**	Destruction of landscape and archeological sites.
					*	Tailings dams with stability and filtration problems.[3]
VI	***	Air pollution (SO2) from Caletones smelter.	**	Pollution of river beds and water courses (mainly Cachapoal river).	**	Pollution due to tailings dams (Cachapoal Province)
					*	Tailings dams with stability and filtration problems.[3]
VIII			***	Marine pollution due to coal extraction.	*	Deterioration of mechanical resistance of ground due to small mining activities in urban zones (Coroncl).
XI			*	River pollution	*	Negative impacts on landscape due to open pit mining.
			*	Coastal and marine pollution due to mineral loading.		
XII			**	Marine pollution due to oil spills.	*	Soil pollution due to oil extraction.

Notes:
1 Regions VII, IX and X have no environmental problems related to mining.
2 Not included in reference studies.
3 National Geology and Mining Service, 1990, "Inventory of Tailings Dams".

*** Highly significant.
** Significant.
* Moderate or minor significance.

Sources: Hajek, Gross and Espinoza (1990); Huepe (1994).

imports of Chilean copper into the United States. They argued that US firms' compliance with environmental standards had significantly increased their production costs, and that copper imports from Chile had forced them to close the country's 25 main mines (Lagos and Velasco 1992). Implicit in their presentation[29] was the fact that Chile's environmental standards were less demanding. A study (EULA 1995, p.61) states that in 1984 and 1985 on three occasions the ITC was petitioned to apply a tariff surcharge on the grounds of "ecological dumping", the idea being that this extraordinary tariff would compensate for the lack of environmental controls in Chile. These petitions "did not succeed at the time. Then in 1987, Chile was excluded from the US General System of Preferences (GSP), because of a lack of safeguards for labor rights, but subsequently was accepted again in 1991. When Chile was readmitted into this system, copper products were included on a list of exceptional products that did not enjoy the benefit of the GSP, and this was based on environmental considerations" (ibid).

In its defense, Codelco made a commitment to undertake environmental protection investments amounting to US$ 386 million between 1984 and 1990 (Lagos and Velasco 1992, p.185), and these were indeed carried out during that period.[30] The available data shows that the average annual investment in cleanup operations during that period was more than double that of first four years of the decade.

3.2   Reactions to the threats: environmental costs and impacts

The situation described above made it clear to both firms in the mining sector and the government, just how vulnerable their environmental situation was. It also revealed the magnitude of the costs of improving the situation and the need to develop an explicit policy in this area. The democratic government that took office in 1990 put the environmental issue explicitly on the political agenda, and adopted a more active approach towards it. As a result, concrete measures were taken to improve environmental performance from 1990 onwards. A few months after taking office the government set up the National Environment Commission (CONAMA) with a mission to generate a regulatory framework – which finally took shape, in 1994, in the Framework Law for the Environment – as well as to develop the environmental institutional framework the country needed. The Mining Ministry set three environmental goals for the sector:

- Ensure the inclusion of environmental protection in the management of the mining industry.

- Build environmental criteria into the design of all new mining projects.
- Solve critical environmental problems, especially those relating to airborne pollution caused by megasources in the mining sector.

In 1992, Mining Ministry Decree No. 185 was issued, regulating emissions from megasources. This was based on environmental standards for SO_2 and PM-10 that were identical to those required by the Environmental Protection Agency (EPA) in the United States.[31] The direct consequence of this, along with the 1994 passing of the Framework Law, has been that all smelters currently operating have had to take the environmental impact of their decisions into account. In particular the smelters at Chuquicamata, Caletones, Ventanas and Paipote all have cleanup plans that will lead to cutting SO_2 and PM-10 emissions to levels compatible with the corresponding standard by 1999.

For new mining projects, environmental impact assessments (EIA) were introduced as a preventive tool, and this was applied generally in this sector even before the corresponding regulations came into force in 1997. Since 1990, all large-scale mining projects have been subjected to these assessments. EIAs are part of an "unwritten tacit agreement, reached between the Government and the firms . . . they have used stricter standards than those already existing in Chile, and often the standards applied did not exist in Chilean legislation" (Lagos 1996, p.177). For example, the authority has demanded higher standards for tailings dams than those established in Decree No. 86 which regulates them, and the same for the quality of liquid effluents into the sea and plans for the abandonment and refurbishnment of mining works (ibid, p.178). In some cases these assessments have meant major modifications to projects.

The Framework Law provides the general ground rules and the guiding principles of Chilean environmental regulation, and defines both the corrective and preventive tools to be used. In the mining sector, since the Decree was issued, work has been going on to draw up an arsenic standard which will be one of the first standards decreed using the procedures established by this law (O'Ryan and Ulloa 1995).

This law was passed in record time for a regulation of such importance and impact, partly because of the support it received from export sectors conscious of the need to have clear rules on Chile's environmental commitment, which could be presented to the main export markets. Apart from this, the authorities needed the framework to facilitate Chile's entry into NAFTA, an important policy objective at the time.

Indeed, based on the environmental demands made on Mexico for its admission into NAFTA, it was clear that Chile would be held to similar environmental standards as those required of Mexico for its admission into NAFTA.

The main result of this effort has been a considerable reduction in smelter emissions, as shown in Figure 6.1. Unit SO_2 emissions were 0.54 tons per ton of smelted copper in 1985, whereas by the year 2000 this indicator is estimated to be 0.24. Total sulfur emissions have been reduced from 4,300 tons per day in 1990 to 3,300 tons, despite an 80 per cent increase in the output of copper from smelters over the same period. Moreover, new projects will have to build in environmental safeguard measures as well as measures for mitigating their environmental impacts.

The costs of these improvements are shown in Table 6.2. Environmental projects involved investments amounting to over US$ 1 billion during the 1990s, mostly to reduce emissions into the atmosphere. Additional investments required by recent arsenic regulation are not included in this figure, nor is data available to quantify the cost of the EIA. Nonetheless, costs are significant and represent sizeable outlays for the firms involved. Despite this, there is an increasing willingness on the part of these firms to assume responsibility for the environmental problems they cause. All large firms have set up environmental units and are undertaking or supporting research projects on environmental issues. An open question is how much would have been done in the absence of

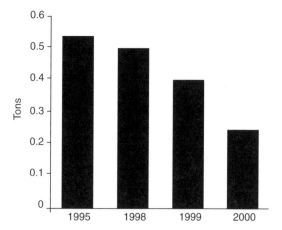

Figure 6.1 SO_2 emissions per ton of copper smelted in Chilean smelters, 1995–2000
Source: Authors' calculations based on data provided by the smelters.

Table 6.2   Investment by mining firms in decontamination, 1990–2000[1] (US$ million)

Firm	DIV	Year	Project	Total amount
CODELCO (a)	CHU	1991	Acid plant no. 3	64.0
			Others	15.0
CODELCO (b)	CHU	1993	Plant	59.0
			Replacement of acid plant module by gas cleaning	44.0
			Capture and treatment of CPS gases no. 6 and 7	33.0
CODELCO (c)	AND	1994–99	Oxygen plant no. 3	21.0
		1994–99	Reservoir IV-B contour 2134 and ancillary works	68.7
	AND	1994–99	Long-term tailings deposit (without Andina)	216.2
		1994–99	Management and cleanup of gases from the Potrerillos smelter	35.3
	SAL	1994–99	Teniente acid plant	71.2
		1994–99	Capture and treatment of CPS gases 2nd stage	62.5
			Potrerillos acid plant	61.0
	TTE	1994–99	Other minor projects	127.9
		1995–97	Ventanas acid plant	43.5
ENAMI (d)	CHU	1995–97	Paipote acid plant	68.9
REFINET (e)	SAL	1995–99	Increase in capacity and expansion of acid plant	48.3
			TOTAL	1039.5

[1] Authors' estimation.

Sources:
(a) Solari, J. (1992) "Desarrollo Sustentable y Competitividad en la Minería", in Iván Valenzuela (ed.) *Chile Exporta Minería*, pp. 136–51.
(b) CODELCO, Internal document.
(c) CODELCO, Projects Portfolio, Escenario 94–99.
(d) Ponce, R. and Reyes. J. (1996), "Enami modernizes its smelters", *Mining Magazine*, vol. 174 (5), May 1996.
(e) *Minería Chilena*, April 1996, no. 178, p. 38.

external pressure. Considering the reticence of these firms towards the issue, it can be concluded that the process of reducing emissions would at least have been slower, very likely less far-reaching and only oriented towards mitigation measures and action to avoid emergencies.

3.3   Sectoral trends: a strengthening of the clean-up process

Two current trends in the sector are helping to reinforce the process of greater environmental concern promoted by the authorities: namely, the foreign investment boom and technological change towards hydro-metallurgical production methods.

Over 80 per cent of the investment undertaken in the 60 most important projects during the 1990s was of private origin (Cochilco 1996), and currently the private sector accounts for 65 per cent of all copper produced in Chile. A central consequence of this is that expansions of productive capacity will basically come from projects that are subject to external quality standards, both in terms of the productive processes used and in environmental management.

Firms that are currently setting up in Chile are doing so "with the most modern environmental technology in equipment, processes and management" (Lagos and Velasco 1992, p. 178). An interesting case is Minera Escondida, owned by an Australian–British–Japanese consortium together with the International Finance Corporation of the World Bank. One of this firm's most important programs aims to protect the environment in both production and transport of the mineral. In producing copper it does not use highly contaminating smelters but a hydro-metallurgical process that is considerably more benign environmentally. Moreover, the plant has been designed to recover 99 per cent of the ammonia gases resulting from the process. "Consequently the plant will have no harmful effects on the air, water, deserts, beaches or sea, nor on the region's flora and fauna" (ibid, p. 191). Moreover, to avoid impact from waste water in the port of Coloso where it empties out, an investment of US$ 3.1 million was made to prevent toxic waste from reaching the part.

The Fachinal gold mine, under Canadian ownership in the extreme south of Chile, is another case where environmental impact assessment includes aspects new to Chile, such as care of the landscape, the subsequent rehabilitation of terrain and minimization of the risk of water pollution. Another example relates to Disputada de las Condes, acquired in 1978 by EXXON. According to Lagos and Velasco (1992, p.190), the strict environmental protection policy required by its main shareholders obliged the firm to implement specific strategies and environmental actions, including reforestation and water recycling, going beyond those required by Chilean legislation.

A change can also be seen in the metallurgical processes by which copper is produced. At present, the vast majority of Chilean copper is obtained via pyro-metallurgical process – smelters that process copper at high temperatures – which produces gases, particulates and liquid industrial waste that are highly contaminating and need large quantities of water. This makes clean smelter operation very expensive.

Fortunately, the technological trends are moving increasingly towards the use of hydro-metallurgy, a recently developed process. This is based on a leaching – or wet processes – to obtain copper, and does not use large amounts of energy. This form of mineral processing has significant environmental advantages over pyro-metallurgy: the absence of smelter processes, and hence the emission of polluting gases; and lower water consumption, which enables exploitable reserves to be increased by making possible the treatment of low grade copper ores.

Production increases in Chile in the future will basically occur using hydro-metallurgy, which is good news from the environmental standpoint. In 1994, only 16 per cent of all copper production used this process, currently the figure exceeds 35 per cent, thus enabling copper production to increase without a significant increase in smelter capacity.

As well as this, the increasing use of hydro-metallurgy has solved a significant environmental problem for today's smelters: namely, what to do with the huge output of sulfuric acid from the acid plants used to reduce SO_2 emissions. At the present time the consumption and production of this product is relatively in balance, thanks to the spectacular growth in demand arising from hydro-metallurgy. This demand has more than doubled since 1989, making it possible to absorb the supply increase associated with bringing on line the acid plants at Chuquicamata, Ventanas and Chagres. This equilibrium is expected to persist into the future, with acid supply increasing due to tighter emissions control, and demand growing as a result of new hydro-metallurgical processes coming on stream.

3.4 Ecological dumping: a fading threat to Chile's mining sector

Clearly, growing environmental concern internationally has forced the mining sector, in particular large copper plants, to invest huge sums in decontamination: firstly, in response to dumping accusations made in the 1980s, and secondly due to the environmental practices of foreign firms investing in Chile. Moreover, indirectly, the sector has had to invest to preempt future accusations and to facilitate Chile's entry into NAFTA. Certainly, these external pressures have joined with domestic ones – relating to health problems – to bring about a significant improvement in environmental performance as regards atmospheric emissions from mining operations. It is not possible to distinguish the relative importance of each of these factors, but – given the magnitude of the resources involved – it can be concluded that without the international concern, both the speed and the scope of this effort would have been less.

As a result of all this, the gap in environmental performance between Chile and more developed countries is bound to narrow, at least as regards the traditional pollutants relevant to mining: SO_2 and PM-10. In the near future large mining firms will produce according to international standards, hence the argument that Chile practices ecological dumping will lose force, and the chances of a threat such as in 1984 happening again will recede, at least as regards airborne emissions.

The environmental practices of the foreign firms setting up in Chile, and the application of EIA, also suggest that "pollution haven" arguments are not applicable to this sector. The entry of foreign capital responds to a combination of factors, but greater environmental permissiveness is not one of them.[32]

Nonetheless, an efficient system of environmental authorization for new projects could give Chile a potential advantage compared to countries with more long-standing environmental legislation. The increasing environmental restrictions in developed countries lead to ever more complex procedures, which are time-consuming and burdensome for firms without necessarily leading to greater environmental protection. For the Canadian-owned Fachinal gold mine in the south of Chile, it has been estimated that the project's formal acceptance process took 18 months and cost US\$ 60,000. For a similar mine in Kensington, Alaska, the same process in 1994 took 5 years and cost over US\$ 6 million, with start-up delayed because of complications and confusion over coordination between local, state and federal authority interests. The challenge for Chile is to achieve a fair balance between simplified formal requirements – keeping down both costs and the time needed to obtain permits – and adequate environmental protection. Otherwise these very facilities may give rise to claims that Chile is not adequately protecting its resources.

4   New threats to the mining sector

Although the mining sector invested over US\$ 1 billion in the 1990s to overcome its most urgent environmental problems, threats to its exports motivated by environmental considerations still persist. These stem from the increasing importance, among regulators and organizations concerned with environmental issues in developed countries (particularly European ones), of meeting environmental requirements at each stage of the life-cycle of products: (i) in the production stage, including appropriate use of inputs such as water and energy, "clean" processes and appropriate waste disposal; (ii) in product transportation, which must be safe; and (iii) in final use, which either must be risk-free, or at least of minimum risk, with safe final disposal of both the product and its container. Initiatives are being taken for mining products in each of these areas. At the transportation stage, international agreements and conventions have been discussed and established to regulate the transport of hazardous waste materials. At the stage of final use, there are several initiatives to assess the risks to health and ecosystems caused by mining products in general, and copper in particular. Finally, during the 1990s, progress was made in drawing up voluntary certification procedures for environmental processes within the firm, in particular ISO 14001.

These activities can be seen as protectionist threats, because what is understood by terms like "appropriate", "clean", "safe" and "risk-free", is debatable, and in most cases there is scant scientific evidence to underpin any definition. And it is precisely in how such concepts are interpreted – and who interprets them – that potential problems may arise for Chilean mining. Finally, international conventions and agreements have to be adopted to make these concepts operational, and these are influenced by environmentalist interests, as well as the interests of authorities, politicians, the affected industries, and their competitors. Consequently, the final outcome depends on the interests at stake. In cases where the cost of measures are basically assumed by the exporting country – as happens with Chile's mining exports – importing countries may make demands that go beyond what they would seek if their own productive sectors were affected.

The above brings us to certain initiatives affecting exports of Chilean copper and other products, which are examined in the following sections.

4.1 Initiatives to eliminate or restrict the use of metals

There is a growing trend in Europe towards reducing the use of metals, because of their potential harm to health and ecosystems. There are two groups of initiatives here. In the first place, there is a set of measures that set strict standards to limit the use of non-ferrous metals. These include:[33]

1 The standard for copper in drinking water. In 1993, the World Health Organization (WHO) adopted a new guideline for copper in drinking water, moving it from a list of comfort parameters to a list of parameters relating to health. As a result, copper ended up on the same list as cadmium, cyanide and chromium. Several countries (including Chile) sought a review of this regulation, but the European Union has

proposed following the WHO recommendation in its directive on water, thus seeking a more demanding standard for copper.

2 The OECD program to reduce risks of lead pollution, where discussion is on-going as to which applications of lead should be prohibited – gasoline, paint, batteries – to reduce exposure to this substance and so mitigate health risks. Some countries, including Canada and Australia, are seeking risk reduction through voluntary action, while others (the European Union, and United States) favor prohibition.

3 The North Sea Conference (NSC) where intergovernmental policies have been drawn up to protect the marine environment. Between 1985 and 1995 the aim was to cut copper, zinc, arsenic, chromium, and nickel effluent into the sea by more than 50 per cent among the signatory countries. This target was achieved for the biggest polluting sources.

4 The Dutch criterion document on zinc, according to which current concentrations of this substance in surface waters in Holland exceed the maximum acceptable on eco-toxicity grounds by at least six times. Consequently, voluntary reductions in zinc use is being sought, along with other mechanisms, such as international legislation on this issue.

The second group of initiatives relates to the European Union's Risk Assessment Program to identify the human health and eco-toxicity risks related to the use of different substances. This program poses a real threat to Chile, because out of 105,000 substances it has singled out copper as the first substance to be assessed for its potential risk to human health and the environment (eco-toxicity). According to the International Copper Association (ICA),[34] copper has been singled out not so much because it is a specially dangerous substance, but because of lobbying exerted by producers of substitute commodities, particularly producers of iron or PVC.[35]

What consequences would there be for Chile if this threat were materialized? The EU might stop using copper pipes for drinking water and ban the use of copper in roofing. Considering that Chile sells 40 per cent of its copper in this market, such a step could mean significant losses for the country.[36]

It should be pointed out that WTO-accepted procedures would require sufficient scientific evidence before such restrictions could be applied, and as discussed in Section 2, estimation of effects is complex and highly uncertain.[37] However even when the evidence is weak, governments can take action under the precautionary principle and recommend not using the substance, or advise using substitutes, while leaving the final decision on the issue in the hands of consumers. The latter is acceptable to the WTO, provided the requirement is the same for imported as well as local products.

Given that the choice of copper as a hazardous substance was not made with reference to any explicit criterion, and that countries deciding to restrict its use would not internalize all the costs of such a decision as they are not producers of the metal, but produce substitute materials, such measures could be considered protectionist in the sense discussed in the previous section.

4.2 Restrictions on the international transportation of copper compounds

Measures to restrict the transportation of hazardous waste between countries have affected the copper industry, because copper compounds have been put on the list of hazardous substances. There are a number of international treaties that attempt to restrict or ban this trade, namely:

1 The Basle Convention. This convention, signed by Chile in 1992, prohibits the export of hazardous waste in general, from OECD to non-OECD countries. As copper compounds are within this category, the convention represents a significant threat Chilean mining. Depending ultimately on how the term "copper compound" is interpreted, the list might include copper concentrates, which represent 30 per cent of the total value of copper exported by Chile. The hope is, however, that in the end it may only affect certain copper waste products. In 1997 negotiations took place on this very issue, with Chile putting forward a technically grounded position aimed at making sure concentrates are not included among regulated products in the original version of the Basle Convention.

2 OECD colors list. In 1992 the OECD adopted a procedure to control the trans-boundary transportation of waste products for recovery operations in member countries. Lists of substances were defined in red and amber categories, each with strong controls on their movement, and a green category for which there were no requirements apart. Some of the waste products considered hazardous by the Basle Convention are on the OECD's green list, which violates the convention according to one of its promoters – the environmental pressure group Greenpeace.

3 UNEP Protocol on responsibility and compensation. Drawn up by order of the Basle Secretariat, this protocol relates to financial

responsibility and compensation to be paid by firms involved in the international trade of any dangerous material that might be involved in an accident, or other episode resulting in environmental damage. Responsibility extends from the moment of production of the material until 30 years after its disposal.

4 International Maritime Organization (IMO) Convention on Responsibility and Compensation. The aim of this convention is to establish responsibility and compensation for the transportation of dangerous substances by sea. As of the end of 1996, the final versions included copper concentrates and other non-ferrous metals, as well as iron and coal. Chile along with Canada, Korea, Japan and several other countries, opposed this and managed to delay implementation.

Restrictions on the transportation of dangerous substances between countries clearly pose a threat to Chile's mining exports. For one thing, OECD member countries would cease to import some products, and if Chile ever joins this organization, it might be required to stop exporting them. Moreover, the increasing trade restrictions on hazardous waste, including copper compounds, makes transport more expensive and so reduces the competitiveness of copper as against other alternatives.

Additionally, the way in which the scope of agreements and conventions, and their amendments, are decided – both political and technical components are involved in the discussion process – generates uncertainty in the sector. For example, the original version of the Basle Convention – ratified by Chile – only restricted transportation but did not ban it. However, this was changed in Amendment 212, which caused concern among the firms in the sector as it raised questions as to whether changes in the rules of the game – making agreements more restrictive – will prove to be an exception or are likely to be repeated in other fields.

Lastly, there is a more general type of threat whose impact is more difficult to quantify. By being included on the lists mentioned above, copper in several of its forms, comes to be seen as belonging to the group of hazardous substances. This seriously harms the image of copper, and fuels lobbying for tighter restrictions and even its elimination for certain uses, even though the information on potential risks is very weak.

4.3 Shortcomings in environmental management in mining: new threats through ISO 14000

In keeping with the life-cycle approach, the EU is promoting the development of standardized environmental protection procedures, to be made operational through ISO 14000. Although so far they have only managed to establish procedures for environmental management systems in the firm, environmental audit and eco-certification procedures are being considered for the future, in an attempt to harmonize the environmental performance of firms across different countries. Although such norms are voluntary, it is anticipated that increasing environmental awareness in developed countries – and the promotion thereof by governments – will put pressure on the main firms that buy Chilean products to adopt them. This leads to a potential threat to the mining sector, for despite progress in the regulation of airborne emissions, there are clear shortcomings in terms of environmental performance. Firstly, the transportation, disposal and inspection of hazardous waste is deficient; the existing closure and abandonment regulations are inadequate to control the growing volumes of residues associated with both greater mining production and tighter emission limits.

At the present time, standards are being drawn up on this issue. However, the general nature of the proposed regulation[38] does not take the geographical and climatic particularities of the desertic north of Chile into account, and this will make them unnecessarily restrictive, and hence costly for mining companies. Research is needed to enable the definition of closure and abandonment procedures that are appropriate to the nation's environmental reality, for example by distinguishing low-population, low-rainfall desert areas from other regions.

Apart from this, inspection and monitoring capacity is also weak. The first of these makes it impossible to carry out follow-up procedures to ensure compliance with standards, while the lack of monitoring prevents adequate protection of potentially affected ecosystems, so although standards may be complied with on paper, it is not possible to verify their effective compliance. Improvements in regulations, as well as inspection and monitoring, are central to international certification of the quality of mining processes. Inspection and monitoring has been a recurrent issue in preliminary conversations relating to the signing of trade agreements with Canada and NAFTA.

A second area where there are shortcomings is in sustainable water management. As was mentioned above, there are conflicts between different water users in the north, as well as potential pollution and excessive use of underground waters. Specially designated uses – a key management tool – have not been established, so there is no precise definition of the water levels that have to be maintained in each stretch of river; nor are there priorities for use, nor environmental standards governing them. It should be mentioned that the European Union is developing a water directive for community countries that covers avoidance of shortages, management of subterranean waters and protection of the aquatic environment. If this directive were to extend to Chile the mining sector would have difficulty responding, particularly in the short run. It is worth mentioning here, that in March 1996 the EU was already consulting the Ministry of Foreign Relations about water management in Chile.[39]

In this climate of uncertainty, mining companies have had to prepare for compliance with ISO 14000. Both Codelco and ENAMI have established policies aimed at better environmental management. Codelco, in particular, has embarked on a wide-ranging cleanup process in its smelters which will enable it to "attain the environmental certification to be demanded by copper markets in the future" (Muñoz 1995). The process has involved an investment of over US$ 1 billion between 1990 and 2000. Likewise, ENAMI has recently initiated a study to prepare the firm for compliance with ISO 14000 standards. It is an open question whether this investment is sufficient, or excessive, in relation to the demands the ISO will impose. In particular, Chile will have to significantly improve its water administration, as well as the management and disposal of mining residues – a task that exceeds what any individual firm can do and requires concerted action between the companies and the state.

However, these standards are still in the discussion and review process, and there are two unresolved issues that make the magnitude of ISO 14000's impact on firms uncertain. Firstly, there is ambiguity about the procedures to be used to accredit compliance. How to evaluate the product life-cycle imports, and who is to do this? What standards should be complied with? What auditing procedures should be used? What should be included in eco-labeling and who accredits the information? The way these questions are answered may have non-trivial impacts on Chilean firms exporting into markets whose consumers demand compliance with such standards. If a more demanding process standard than those established in national legislation is finally imposed, some exporting firms in the sector may be forced to make additional investments.

This would specially affect small- and medium-scale mining. Although not significant as regards production volumes, these firms are important in terms of their regional importance – particularly as sources of employment. As was pointed out in the previous section, small-scale mining does not have the resources to improve its environmental performance. Nor is it possible to supervise compliance with specific regulations in small-scale mining operations, so it is highly costly to certify this sector's environmental performance, and tighter regulations could drive it out of business.

Secondly, requiring compliance with ISO 14000 is a decision for each buyer, so it might be applied to certain mining products or firms only, and not others, even though they may be similar. In fact, different markets have different requirements: the Asian market, which takes 50 per cent of Chilean copper exports, is considerably less demanding environmentally than the European one. Accordingly, a firm might decide to send its exports to those markets and reduce its environmental costs. However this policy is risky: copper is an intermediate input in the production of many products which are then exported to European countries. If these countries require compliance with environmental standards over the whole production chain, through ISO 14000 for example, then even inputs would have to be produced in a clean manner. Hence Asian markets would also be at risk.

4.4 The threat from trade agreements

Trade agreements are also used to impose environmental restrictions over and above what can be required under the WTO. Firstly, there is discussion of minimum guidelines for compliance in terms of emissions, procedures and resource management; secondly, trade treaties include the need to comply with certain agreements and conventions protecting the global environment (Basle, CITES and the Montreal Protocol).

Of the trade agreements that Chile has signed or is seeking to join, the three most important from the trade standpoint are NAFTA, the European Union and Canada.[40] Until 1997, NAFTA was the agreement that had gone furthest on environmental issues, influencing Chilean environmental legislation along the way. However this agreement would have marginal benefits for the mining sector, as less than 10 per cent of mining exports go to the United States, the main partner in this agreement. Cochilco estimates the benefits at US$ 575,000.[41]

NAFTA requires (i) compliance with the international conventions mentioned above, (ii) the need to have environmental standards that are scientifically established, and (iii) enforcement of environmental regulations. Clearly the costs of these requirements exceed the benefits of the treaty for the mining sector several times over; but they will have to be accepted if the benefits of NAFTA for other sectors of the economy justify it.

Under NAFTA, once environmental regulations are established in a member country, they cannot subsequently be relaxed and they must be enforced adequately. Although this seems quite reasonable, it may prove to be a trap for certain activities, for usually the studies used to propose standards are weak and do not take all economic factors into consideration. For example, if environmental quality standards for a given substance are based on standards applied in other countries, important economic activities might be forced either to close down or make significant investments. The same might happen if standards were set only on the basis of health considerations. In fact, in April 1994 an arsenic standard that had been decreed only months earlier was abolished, because it made it mandatory to comply with unachievable targets in certain smelters. Five years later, strict but achievable emission standards were set. If Chile had been in NAFTA it would have had a hard time turning back, with the corresponding significant social and economic impacts.

An agreement with the European Union poses different challenges. Increasing environmental awareness among European consumers, as well as concern by producers and governments, is exerting pressure for stricter regulations – both mandatory and voluntary ones. If Chile joins the EU, it will have to take care to improve the environmental performance of its processes, in keeping with the life-cycle approach and ISO 14000.

Finally, the trade agreement between Chile and Canada, the most advanced to date, contains "environmental cooperation side agreements" similar to those of NAFTA. Chile has serious difficulties here, for the agreement obliges each country to enforce its own environmental legislation. This legislation is clear and coherent in Canada, but Chile has more than 1,000 environmental standards dating back to 1916 which are not mutually coherent or consistent. In view of this situation, the Chilean regulatory team managed to postpone full application of this obligation until 1999. It committed to complying with 90 provisions at the time of the agreement coming into force (including the framework law and the SO_2 cleanup plan at Caletones); another 14 were to be clarified as regards their competence six months later; and Chile had to present a plan for the gradual implementation of the rest. However, the deadline has recently been reached and Chile is late in reaching compliance. This process will be slow and will oblige CONAMA to take serious and costly steps during the coming years.[42]

5   Conclusions

The growing environmental concern in developed countries has had a significant effect on Chile's mining sector. Since the beginning of the 1980s exporting firms have come under pressure to improve their environmental performance, and allegations of "eco-dumping" led Codelco to undertake costly cleanup investments during that decade. In the early 1990s, the political authorities also took action in this field, drawing up general standards for the environment (through the Environmental Framework Law), and making specific demands on smelters. In both cases legislators' decisions were influenced by external environmental requirements, and in fact the contents of the law clearly satisfy the requirements discussed for admitting Mexico into NAFTA. Some of the demands made on smelters are identical to those demanded by the EPA. In addition, environmental impact assessment was introduced as a requirement for new mining projects, as is common practice in developed countries. It is quite likely that in the absence of external pressure on this issue, the investment of over US$ 1 billion in environmental improvements in the 1990's, would not have been contemplated, or at best it would have been done more slowly, particularly considering that most of the investment was carried out by the state. Probably, there would also have been slower progress in domestic legislation on this issue.

It should be pointed out that many of these actions are carried out voluntarily, as under the GATT-WTO it is not possible to impose requirements or conditions on the domestic productive processes of producer countries. Despite this, an incipient tendency can be seen towards a harmonization of procedures and even standards in this sector, with those in the rest of the world. On the one hand, new mining projects, mostly foreign financed, are being set up with leading-edge technologies and processes. In addition there is a desire to present a "clean slate" so as to ease entry into NAFTA: efforts by state-owned firms to comply with the environmental management requirements of ISO 14000 – firstly by Codelco and more recently by ENAMI – are a clear manifestation of this.

The conclusion is that in the face of potential threats on environmental grounds, the mining sector has chosen to meet the external requirements. In most cases, firms in the sector act ahead of the legislation, and are even more demanding than the domestic regulators themselves. This clearly constitutes a response to a subtle and novel form of protectionism, as firms are forced to make decisions about their processes in the light of the possibility of their suffering from restrictions such as eco-labeling or other voluntary restrictions.

As well as this, there is a potential threat of major proportions for the mining sector in the environmental field: namely, the growing trend towards replacing metals by environmentally "benign" substitutes. In this context, measures aimed at restricting the uses and transportation of copper are worrying, as are tendencies that stigmatize it as a dangerous substance, notwithstanding the uncertainties in the scientific studies. In the absence of clear scientific data to establish whether the metal creates a significant risk or not, the decision by importing countries has been to apply the precautionary criterion which recommends avoiding its use when in doubt.

This is also a novel form of protectionism which may have very negative implications for Chile. The problem lies in the fact that the countries imposing restrictions do not have to bear all the costs of such decisions. As the EU does not produce copper, it is easier to choose to restrict its use and replace it by others, assumed to be less risky, albeit more costly alternatives. Hence Europe only absorbs the higher cost of the alternative, but does not internalize the impact of its decision on the copper industry.[43]

Undertaking research to assess risks is a lengthy and expensive process. Singling out a specific product like copper for analysis has negative consequences, because detailed information will become available on the harm this metal causes, but not about the alternatives that will replace it, which may also be hazardous. Moreover, the door is left open for domestic pressure groups to use risk assessment as a tool to favor their own products. As a result, the European Union may impose demands that are stricter than those it would apply if it had its own copper industry.

In conclusion, decisions on environmental issues in mining will increasingly be determined by requirements established in Chile's main export markets, particularly the EU. Considering the importance of the Chilean mining sector in world mining, and its importance in Chile's economy, the mining companies and the Chilean state must be ready to exert influence in each of these initiatives, so as to minimize their impact. They must also get ready to comply with them. Thus far, responses have been varied: the big mining companies, particularly the new ones, have been setting up with state-of-the-art technologies and environmental precautions. The government has recently taken the trouble to organize study groups, and has participated in a number of international forums where these issues are discussed. Global institutions such as ICA and ICME – to which some Chilean firms belong – have constantly been defending their members' interests. However, appropriate environmental management needs to be encouraged – essentially in state firms – and above all in small- and medium-scale mining. Progress also needs to be made in establishing coherent environmental regulations, and in reviewing and updating the more than 1,000 provisions of an environmental nature that are currently in force in Chile. In particular, water use in the north needs to be subjected to a far-reaching review, aimed at sustainable use, and efficient regulations must be established for the transport and disposal of mining residues, and the closure and abandonment of mines. These actions require policies drawn up at government level.

At the present time, there is little research on the health impacts and eco-toxicity effects of copper in Chile. Considering the risks indicated above, Chile needs to take a lead in scientific and technical studies to analyze these risks, with contributions from public and private firms in the sector. In particular the country should become a leader in analyzing the uncertainty inherent in assessing the harmful effects of copper and its possible substitutes. Finally, coordination and consultation mechanisms in the productive and public sectors should be strengthened and stabilized, with a long-term outlook. A joint approach to these issues should be developed between the state and the firms in the mining sector, so as to defend Chile's point of view wherever these issues are discussed.

Notes

1 This institution comprises 24 countries, including the member countries of the European Union as well as United States, Canada, Japan, Australia, New Zealand, Turkey and Mexico.
2 See Jaffe *et al.* (1995) for a review of this issue.
3 According to Krugman (1994), this would be a misuse of the term "competitiveness".
4 However, a study by Chapman (1991) suggests that less-stringent regulation of processes in the copper industry in developing countries could mean production cost differences of between 20 and 25 per cent.
5 The chemical and mining industries for example.
6 In the literature these are known as pollution havens.
7 See Bhagwati and Srinivasan (1996) for an analysis of the desirability of different standards in free trade in the presence of domestic pollution.
8 The Montreal Protocol aims to control the use of substances that harm the ozone layer. The Basle Agreement imposes restrictions on the trade and transportation of hazardous waste. CITES aims to control international trade in wild species.
9 See Hammonds (1990), Meng (1990).
10 The World Trade Organization recently (WT/DS26, 1999) resolved against the EU, allowing the US and Canada to impose retaliatory tariffs on their imports (euphemistically known as withdrawal of concessions).
11 These issues are dealt with very well in National Research Council (1994) and Stonehouse and Mumford (1996).
12 In the Rio Declaration (1992), Principal 15 states that "In order to protect the environment, the precautionary approach shall be widely applied by States

according to their capabilities. Where there are threats of serious or irreversible damage, lack of full scientific certainty shall not be used as a reason for postponing cost-effective measures to prevent environmental degradation."

13   It is estimated that there are 60,000 dangerous substances, but toxicological information is only available for 20 per cent of this number (CEPIS 1988).

14   Eco-labeling consists of including environmental information on a product's label, for example negative characteristics such as ecological toxicity or flammability, or positive ones such as biodegradability, energy efficiency, ozone-layer friendliness, or information relating to recycling. It is also used to include relevant environmental information over the entire product life-cycle. Eco-packaging and recycling relate to standards on material content, percentage recycled, returnable deposit systems, etc. The aim of these measures is to reduce the volume of waste (Stevens 1994).

15   There are other environmental standardization procedures such as the Forest Stewardship Council (FSC), for the sustainable management of the forestry sector, or British Standard No. 7750, which governs the implementation of a system of environmental management in the firm, or the Environmental Management Audit System, regulating the environmental auditing of environmental management systems.

16   Recently in Brazil agreement was reached to start applying ISO 14000 to the forestry sector.

17   This was done to obtain statistical and biological information.

18   For example in Canada and Germany, 70 per cent of eco-labeling initiatives come from the local industry itself (Jha and Zarrilli 1994).

19   Stevens (1994).

20   The fragmentary and scant information available is a reflection of the lack of concern that existed on this issue. See, for example, Hajek *et al.* (1990), Huepe (1994), Solari (1992), Lagos (1993), Lagos and Velasco (1992).

21   Chile is divided into 13 administrative regions.

22   They are also significantly above what other studies estimate for this same sector (Walter, 1986; Pasurka 1985).

23   The Chuquicamata, Potrerillos and Caletones smelters belong to the state-owned Codelco; Those at Las Ventanas and Hernán Videla Lira (Paipote) belong to ENAMI – also state-owned; the Chagres smelter belongs to Compañia Minera Disputada Las Condes; and the La Negra smelter is owned by Refimet.

24   Owned by the El Indio mining company.

25   La Negra (Refimet) only came into operation in 1993.

26   Intendencia de la Región Metropolitana (1988).

27   Lagos (1993).

28   Based on Huepe (1994).

29   For practical reasons this argument was not deployed explicitly, since this would have required the plaintiffs to show for each individual productive center that it was not complying with regulations similar to those required in the United States.

30   According to internal reports in Codelco this investment amounted to US$ 374 million during the period.

31   Primary standards to protect health, as well as secondary ones to protect species and ecosystems.

32 Lagos (1994 p.7) suggests the following factors: maturation of explorations carried out since the 1950s; new exploration techniques which have made it possible to discover outcrops of difficult access; the DL 600 (1974) law and the mining code (1981) which provide security to investors regarding the right of ownership of mining reserves and the profits earned therefrom; the economic political and social stability, achieved particularly with the return of democratic government in 1990; an economy that is increasingly open to foreign investment, trade and new technology; deposits which due to their high concentration and mineralogy, as well as their geographical location, afford a competitive advantage; the development in Chile of new extraction technologies; the availability of professionals and highly qualified workers, and a serious business and work culture; attractive tax conditions; and an increasingly efficient system of permits for authorizing new projects.

33 See Lagos (1996) for a full discussion of this issue.

34 An organization that brings together the world's main copper producers.

35 Personal communication from ICA staff.

36 The magnitude of these losses has not been estimated here as one would have to be specific about which copper products would be affected, the implications of this in the price of the metal, and finally how much would cease to be exported.

37 For that reason an important part of the ICA strategy for confronting this issue has been to call into question the scientific basis for estimates of lethal concentrations of copper.

38 Which would make it applicable to sectors as dissimilar as mining, the chemical industry and the forestry sector.

39 Personal communication from Sergio García of Cochilco.

40 In Mercosur, environmental questions have not been a priority issue, as reflected in the scant and extremely superficial treatment given to it in this treaty. For that reason no short-run effects are foreseen for the sector, particularly as that Chile does not have a worse record on environmental matters than the other Mercosur countries, which might otherwise have made it prone to sanctions.

41 Personal communication from a top executive at Chile's Copper Commission (Cochilco).

42 Based on an interview with Jaime Undurraga (Chief Chilean Negotiator) and W. Gyling (Collahuasi), "Dos Años Para Ordenar La Casa Ambiental", *El Mercurio*, Sunday January 27th, 1997.

43 See "Minimum Standards: A New Source of Protection", Chapter 3 in this book.

References

Bhagwati J. and R. Hudec (eds) (1996). *Fair Trade and Harmonization: Prerequisites for Free Trade?* Cambridge, Mass.: MIT Press.

Bhagwati, J. and T. Srinivasan (1996). "Trade and the Environment. Does environmental diversity detract from the case for the free trade?", in J. Bhagwati and R. Hudec (eds.), *Fair Trade and Harmonization: prerequisite for free trade?*, Vol. 1, pp. 158–223. Cambridge, Mass: MIT Press.

Birdsall, N. and N. Wheeler (1992). "Trade policy and industrial pollution in Latin America: where are the pollution havens?", in Patrick Low (ed.), *International Trade and the Environment*. Working Paper, World Bank.

CEPIS (1988). *Manual de Evaluación y Manejo de Sustancias Tóxicas en Aguas Superficiales*. Panamerican Health Organization.

Chapman, D. (1991). "Environmental standards and international trade in automobiles and copper: The case for a social tariff", *Natural Resources Journal*, 31 (Winter), 449–61.

Cochilco (1996). "Mercado internacional del cobre mundo occidental", mimeo.

EULA (1995). *Diagnóstico del Impacto de Posibles Restricciones Ambientales sobre el Sector Exportador Chileno*. University of Concepción, Center EULA-Chile. Final Report.

Galaz, J. (1993). "El sernageomin y la gestión ambiental", *Revista Minerales*, 48 (201).

Geradin, S. and P. Stewardson (1995). "Trade and environment: Some lessons from Castlemaine Tooheys (Australia) and Danish Bottles (European Community)", *International and Comparative Law Quarterly*, Vol. 44, (January).

Hajek, J. E., P. Gross and G. Espinoza (1990). *Problemas Ambientales de Chile*. Santiago, Chile.

Hammonds, Holly (1990). "A US perspective on the EC Hormones Directive", *Michigan Journal of International Law*, 11, 840–4.

Huepe, C. (1994). "Growth, the enviroment and fiscal policy in the Chilean mining sector", Mining Ministry, Mimeo, Santiago, Chile.

Intendencia Región Metropolitana (1988). *Estudio del Rio Mapocho. Final Report*.

Jaffe, M. Peterson, P. Portney and J. Stavins (1995). "Environmental regulation and the competitiveness of U.S. manufacturing", *Journal of Economic Literature*, 33(1), (March), 132–63.

Jha, Z. and V. Zarrilli (1994). OECD Documents, *Life-Cycle Management and Trade*. Paris.

Krugman P. (1994). "Competitiveness: A dangerous obsession", *Foreign Affairs*, 73(2) (March/April).

Lagos, G. (1993). "Instrumentos regulatorios y económicos para la gestión ambiental de los recursos mineros: el caso de la Pequeña y Mediana Minería", Catholic University of Chile, mimeo, Santiago, Chile. December.

Lagos, G. (1994). "Developing national policies in Chile", in Rod Eggert (ed.), *Mining and the Environment: International Perspective on Public Policy*. Resources for the Future, Washington D.C.

Lagos, G. (1996). "Requerimientos y desafios ambientales para la Minería Chilena", in CIPMA (ed.), *Inserción Global y Medio Ambiente*, pp. 173–203.

Lagos, G. and P. Velasco (1992). *Mining and the Environment: The Chilean Case*. Report for CESCO, March.

Laplante, G. and M. Garbutt (1992). "Environmental protectionism", *Land Economics*, 68 (1) (February), 116–19.

Low, P. and M. Yeats (1992). Do 'dirty' industries migrate?", in Patrick Low (ed.), *International Trade and the Environment*, World Bank, Discussion Paper.

Lucas, M., P. Wheeler and W. Hettige (1992). "Economic development, environmental regulation and the international migration of toxic industrial pollution: 1960–1988", in Patrick Low (ed.), *International Trade and the Environment*, World Bank, Discussion Paper, 67–86.

Meng, Werner (1990). "The hormone conflict between the EEC and the United States within the context of GATT", *Michigan Journal of International Law,* 11, 818–43.

Muñoz, G. (1995). "Codelco-Chile's corporate decontamination plan for its smelters", Codelco, mimeo.

National Research Council (NRC) (1994). *Science and Judgment in Risk Assessment.* Washington DC: National Academy Press.

OECD (1993). "Pollution abatement and control expenditure in OECD countries", *OECD Environment Monograph No. 75.* Paris, France: Organization for Economic Cooperation and Development.

Oldenburg, K. (1994). "Life-cycle assessment: The state of the art", in OECD Documents, *Life-Cycle Management and Trade.* Paris.

O'Ryan, R. and A. Ulloa (1995). "Marco conceptual para regular sustancias toxicas", Presented at the Vth Conference on the Environment, Temuco, Chile, 15pp.

Pasurka, C. (1985). "Environmental control costs and U.S. effective rates of protection", *Public Finance Quarterly,* 13, pp. 167,168.

Robinson, S. (1988). "Industrial pollution abatement: the impact on the balance of trade", *Canadian Journal of Economics,* 11(1), 187–99.

Solari, J. (1992). "Desarrollo Sustentable y Competitividad en la Minería", in Ivan Valenzuela (ed.) *Chile Exporta Minería.*

Stevens, C. (1994). "Synthesis report: life-cycle management and trade", in OECD Documents, *Life-Cycle Management and Trade.* Paris.

Stonehouse, R. and M. Mumford (1996). *Science, Risk Analysis and Environmental Policy Decisions.* Environmental and Trade Series, UNEP.

Tobey, J. (1990). "The effects of domestic environmental policies on patterns of world trade: an empirical test", *Kyklos,* 43 (2), 191–209.

Ugelow, G. and J. (1982). "Appendix: A survey of recent studies on costs of pollution control and the effects on trade", in Rubin and Graham (eds), *Environment and Trade.* New Jersey: Allanheld, Osmun & Co.

Van der Zwaag, D. (1996). "CEPA and the precautionary principle approach", Marine and Environmental Law Program, mimeo.

Walter, I. (1982). "International Economic Repercussions of Environmental Policy: An Economist's Perspective", in Rubin and Graham (eds.), *Environment and Trade,* New Jersey: Allanheld, Osmun & Co.

7
Trade and the Environment: Forestry

Gabriel Fierro and Raúl O'Ryan[*]

1 Introduction

Concern for environmental issues has increased significantly in recent decades. As a result new environmental agreements are signed periodically, and both national and international governmental regulations are being developed to ensure that the production, transport, use and disposal of goods and services are not harmful to eco-systemic balances or the preservation of human life. Developed countries have pioneered environmental protection measures. In less developed countries, particularly Chile, aspects relating to the protection and recovery of the environment are increasingly being incorporated into economic activities.

The trend towards globalization and economic integration processes seen in the world today affects the interests of various social groups in each country, giving rise to reactions against international trade liberalization. One of the arguments used by the power groups that are affected, supported by environmentalists, alleges ecological dumping or unfair competition owing to the lower environmental standards that foreign producers have to adhere to. These allegations are especially made against suppliers from developing countries. As a result, groups who do not want external competition, or even fear it, petition for bilateral or multilateral trade treaties to contain equivalent environmental regulations (this is known as harmonization of standards) (Bhagwati 1996). Alternatively, they lobby for trade barriers to be applied against producers from countries that have different or less stringent

* The authors are grateful for the comments and suggestions from Aldo Cerda, and the help of Georgina Paniagua and Lorena Cuenca.

environmental rules. This has given rise to the concept of "green protectionism" (*The Economist* 1993; Sheenan 1994).[1]

Protection against foreign competitors may be open and formal, as in the case of marketing orders, or else may be practiced in a concealed and informal way. The latter arises when producers or other market agents directly or indirectly threaten their foreign competitors with a variety of types of trade restrictions, forcing them to take "voluntary" preventive actions which in the end raise their costs and reduce their competitive position. In this type of protectionism, which is known as a contingent protectionism (see the discussion in Fischer, Chapter 2, this book), the effects are achieved without any explicit punishment being applied to the exporter. As a result, it is not identified by the official national or international agencies that regulate or protect trade. An example of this type of protectionism is the threats faced in European markets by suppliers of wood pulp bleached with elemental chlorine, which has forced producers to invest in new bleaching technologies in order to maintain access to that market. More generally, the life-cycle approach is now the basis for new pressures on developing country producers, based on consumer preferences. These pressures include increasing requirements for sustainable forestry management, and the reduced use of resources and generation of pollution.

In Chile, where exports have been the engine of economic growth in recent decades, possible protectionist measures arising in countries that purchase its products are a permanent source of concern, especially since the activities that have developed most in recent years (mining, forestry, fruit growing and fishing) are based on the exploitation of natural resources and therefore highly prone to allegations of environmental damage.[2] In forestry, for example, environmental pressure groups accuse the lumber chip industry of razing native forests to the ground, and they denounce forestry firms for eliminating native forests to replace them with plantations of exotic species. The campaigns these groups organize usually attract strong public support, negatively affecting the image of the forestry sector both nationally and internationally, leaving it exposed to sanctions on environmental grounds in the markets in which it competes.

Against this backdrop, this chapter seeks to answer the following questions. What trends in environmental concerns in the world affect the forestry sector? To what extent is the Chilean forestry sector vulnerable to future international trade restrictions based on environmental grounds? What consequences can be foreseen from such threats, and what are the costs for the country?

The thesis of this chapter is that, while the Chilean forestry sector does have some weak points, there are not enough objective conditions to justify any type of export restriction on environmental grounds. The main arguments are as follows: (i) the country has a well-diversified international forestry trade; (ii) national producers exploit their forests in a sustainable way; (iii) national producers of wood pulp (the forestry sector's main product) have made the necessary investments in modern low-pollution industrial plants; and (iv) although not perfect, there are well-established state institutions for regulating and controlling forestry management in Chile, modern legislation is being introduced to protect the environment, and new forestry projects have been made subject to this. Even so, the sector faces threats based on environmental considerations.

The problems of the forestry sector are fundamentally in the sphere of small-scale forest owners, where the entrepreneurs concerned have neither the technical capacity nor the savings to invest in long-term projects. The overall sectoral result is that, at least in the last two decades, both natural and planted forests in Chile have continued to grow in terms of both stumpage volume and surface area. Moreover, the conditions exist for this to continue.

The chapter is organized as follows. Section 2 reviews the sources of threats to forestry trade arising from environmental issues. Section 3 then provides data on the vulnerability of Chile's forestry exports, a comparison of production and selling costs of bleached kraft wood pulp in Europe in relation to other competitors, together with data on the country's forestry resources and on the legal and institutional framework of the Chilean forestry sector. Section 4 addresses the main sources of environmental dispute in the national forestry sector which are being brought to world attention by environmental groups, and discusses the actions taken by forestry firms to prevent future trade restrictions, as well as the costs of such actions for the country. Section 5 presents the main conclusions.

2   Environmental threats to forestry trade

During the 1980s, and very forcefully in the 1990s, environmental concerns turned towards global problems as well as local environmental impacts generated by consumption and production decisions in any part of the world. In particular, consumers in developed countries are increasingly concerned that their consumption decisions should cause the least possible environmental impact. This concern puts pressure on retailers who in turn pass the concern on to producers, who put pressure on raw material suppliers. Each of the stages of a product's life-cycle – extraction, processing, transport, consumption and disposal – must be as safe as possible for people and the environment. Furthermore, the concern has been expanded so that the exploitation of a resource must be done in a sustainable way, which includes not only environmental goals, but also social and economic goals. Thus, if a given producer can convince consumers that competing products are produced in a non-sustainable way – at any stage of the life-cycle – they will improve their competitive position in the market.

This section presents the new trends in environmental concerns, the increasing importance of the precautionary principle and the rise of NGOs and consumer groups as sources of pressure on forest firms. The importance of the life-cycle approach is discussed together with the impact of eco-labels and forestry certification initiatives on trade. The section ends with an identification of threats to trade in the forestry sector, related to environmental concerns.

2.1 New trends in environmental concerns

Governments in developed countries are imposing increasingly stringent regulations on their producers, and on ever more products, in order to safeguard the quality of the environment. In the 1970s and the early 1980s, the approach to the environment was corrective more than anything else, and had one major focus, the control of pollution discharges from industrial facilities. In recent years, a more preventive approach has been taken. National legislation and international treaties have increasingly adopted the "precautionary principle" which states that because of uncertainties, emission standards need to be established which protect health and environment with reasonable degrees of certainty[3] (Van der Zwaag 1996). Thus a recent trend observed is that preventive action should be emphasized over and above the curative, since potential damage is difficult to predict and evaluate *ex-ante* (Turner *et al.* 1993), and usually it is less costly to avert a problem than to act once it has occurred. Consequently, there are increasing requirements on firms to clean up their environmental act, even if the resulting damage is not well documented. NGOs and consumer groups have adopted this principle and push it forcefully, promoting different environmental initiatives even when the evidence of environmental damage or health effects is fairly uncertain.

Firms in developed countries have reacted to this demand for better environmental performance by improving their productive processes and the quality of their products. During the 1990s many firms began to build in environmental management as a significant part of the management of each firm. Although this process has allowed some firms to increase their profits by discovering new businesses associated with producing in a clean way (Moore and Miller 1994; Ditz *et al.* 1995; Gallon 1997), it has generally imposed significant costs on the affected firms.

In general, developing countries have lagged behind developed countries in their care for the environment. As may be expected, industries in the latter countries, which have seen their production costs rise to comply with increasingly stringent environmental standards, have lobbied to have these standards harmonized across the different countries, to reduce the alleged loss of competitiveness with industries in countries less concerned about environmental issues.[4] However, harmonization has been firmly opposed by those who defend free trade, on the grounds that it creates barriers to trade and would ultimately reduce world welfare (Bhagwati and Srinivasan 1996). Notwithstanding, the World Trade Organization (WTO) has had to arbitrate in a series of cases where one country tries to impose import restrictions on a product based on the fact that its production does not involve similar safeguards to those in force in the importing country.

This, however, does not mean that forestry firms in developing countries have a free hand. Quite to the contrary, a second important trend became apparent at the end of the 1980s and especially in the 1990s. Pressure started from NGOs and consumer groups related to the entire life-cycle of products (Roxo 1999). Moreover, an increasing alliance between social and environmental NGOs has expanded concerns to include new issues. These organizations have campaigned strongly for the preservation of biodiversity and tropical forests, as well as safeguarding the rights of local and indigenous communities which are threatened by the exploitation of natural resources (IIED 1996, p.39). Increasingly the environmental, social and economic dimensions associated with sustainable development are being considered together, not in isolation.

Moreover globalization of markets and increasingly better communications systems have made these pressures more effective. For example, in February 1998, Mitsubishi signed an agreement with the Rainforest Action Network (RAN) aimed at stopping the use of old growth forests, thus ending an eight-year boycott campaign against its products. In August of the same year RAN launched a new campaign against an American paper company this time, for allegedly using trees from old growth forests. An additional problem was that the pulp was grown on lands whose ownership was claimed by local Indians . "The campaign failed to mention [however] that the dispute between [the firm and local community] had reached a negotiated solution...four months earlier" (Roxo 1999, p.1). According to IIED (1996, p.39), "pressure groups have noted improvements in environmental performance in Canada, and are turning their attention to social issues. WWF contends that massive clear cutting...is a serious threat to some First Nations...and that local agreements with logging companies have proved unsatisfactory."

Three things stand out in these examples. First, that environmental concerns are now only part of the problem; social and economic issues are also critical. Second, there is increasing power wielded by environmental pressure groups that act both at the local and global level. Finally, local communities are now in the company of strong NGOs that help them defend their rights, but that also have their own environmental agenda that can be different from the community's.

The result is that multiple players, especially in developed countries, are receiving increasing pressures – from regulatory and non-regulatory agencies – to care about the sustainability of their production process. In addition to producers, the original targets of regulators, raw material suppliers and retailers have now been targeted also. B&Q for example, one of the largest British retailers, reacted positively to these pressures by launching a comprehensive Environmental Policy. B&Q now requires suppliers to provide information about their environmental policy, supply auditing information, and allow B&Q to disqualify any suppliers which do not show improvement in their environmental performance (Roxo 1999, p.2). In this way, the retailer passes the pressure they receive onto producers, who in turn place demands on their raw-material suppliers, who often belong to developing countries. If a producer does not respond, it runs the risk of losing important markets or simply disappearing from the shelves. Pressure is thus put indirectly on all parts of the chain, in developed and developing countries alike.

In conclusion, the protection of the environment has entered into a new dimension in the last ten years. It has become a matter of competition between companies and even countries. New concerns have surfaced, new actors are entering the scene. Up to the 1980s, environmental protection had a strictly operational dimension for firms: there were environmental regulatory standards specific to the country, which had to be complied with. Usually these standards considered a specific phase of the life-cycle of a product. Now, firms and countries must accept that this is not enough. Increasingly, the "environmental friendliness" of a product is being judged by standards external to the country where the product is produced. Moreover, environmental concerns extent to the whole life-cycle of the product, and include, together with the environmental dimension, social and economic concerns. In the forestry sector in particular, NGOs with capacity to undertake campaigns in the exporting and importing countries are having an increasing influence in the process of identifying products to be targeted.

2.2   Life-cycle and eco-labels

The growing environmental concern among governments and consumers has led to systems for certifying compliance with standards and environmental criteria at each stage of a product's life-cycle. These are becoming increasingly important in the forestry sector, and as a result, firms in this industry are faced with new challenges. Eco-labels developed to certify that a given product is "environmentally friendly", based on a set of selected criteria. Initially these criteria were fairly limited, usually considering environmental effects of the use and disposal of the product or its wrapping. Additionally, they were meant to be applied to the cleaner fraction of each product category (not more than 30 per cent of the total), and as more products comply, the environmental target is set higher. Canadian Environmental Choice and the Japanese Eco-Mark are examples. They encourage the use of recycled products to limit waste generation and limit consumption of non-renewable resources.

However the recent trend has been to extend these schemes to more extensive life-cycle criteria. They increasingly include more than one, and sometimes all, the life cycle stages: production, transport, use and disposal. The inclusion of the production stage is of particular concern because of its potential trade effects. For example the Nordic Swan, the Swedish Environmental Choice Programme (SECP), the EU Eco-label Award Scheme, and the NF Environnement generally include production related requirements in their eco-label criteria. The first two actually include requirements for the whole life-cycle of the product and the products considered include detergents, cleaning agents and paper products. Producers, both domestic and foreign, have modified processes and production methods to meet eco-label criteria and maintain their products on the market. SECP in 1996 had established 27 product groups and almost 700 products had been awarded eco-labels, including toilet tissue, paper towels, office paper and coffee filters. By the end of 1996, Nordic Swan considered 45 product groups and had labelled over 1,000 products.

A fundamental problem with labeling schemes is that the definition of the products to be targeted generally reflects the preferences of the importing country. In particular, different interests groups press to include the products they deem require attention. Additionally, even though when defining criteria for the award of eco-labels a participatory process is followed, including expert groups and public review, usually foreign producers are not included. This is not because they cannot participate, it is simply hard for foreign producers to set up the lobbying groups required in each country, in particular for exporters from smaller countries. As a result, self-serving environmentally based restrictions are imposed on foreign products.

For example, the EU Eco-label award scheme, which addresses the production phase of pulp and paper, is meant to encourage reduced consumption of non-renewable resources, to reduce the emissions of diverse gases to air, and the use of chlorinated organics, to reduce waste through recycling of previously used paper, and requires the application of sustainable forest management practices. It has been severely criticized by the governments of the US, Canada and Brazil, and also by Argentina, Japan the British paper industry and the Confederation of European Paper Industries. The main criticisms are its lack of transparency since foreign producers are shut out of the process for drawing up the criteria; discrimination in favour of Nordic countries by emphasizing recycled content; and eco-label criteria that reflect domestic environmental conditions and preferences, among others (OECD 1997, pp. 40–41).

It is also interesting to note that successful eco-labeled products often exceed 30 per cent of market coverage. As a result, "they are no longer effective in identifying a small selection of products which are environmentally preferable, but tend to become a *de facto* voluntary standard" (ibid, p.69). In this case, the need for a transparent process becomes essential and the choice of product categories covered by the scheme also becomes critical. If the product group chosen is a product which is largely imported from foreign countries and if the eco-label contains production and process related criteria, the eco-label may constitute a barrier to competing in the market place for foreign products which do not conform to the eco-label criteria. The same may apply when retailers wish to carry a majority of eco-labeled products.

2.3 Sustainable forestry management and forest certification

All pulp and paper companies have to meet a number of customer requirements such as bleaching processes without chlorine, and eco-labels based on various criteria. Sustainable forest practices were mentioned earlier as a requirement for certification under the EU Eco-label. Growing international concern over the state of the world's forests has now made the requirements of sustainable forest operations a key issue. This concern manifests itself in two ways: first, forest certification systems are being developed, and second, NGOs routinely undertake campaigns against products considered unfriendly to the environment in any of the life-cycle stages.

Forest certification systems are voluntary in nature and share the purpose of informing consumers about how well the forests from which the product to be bought originates, are being managed. Most of the systems include the same key elements and the difference among them is basically in the depth with which each element is addressed. The key elements are (Roxo 1999, p. 3):

- Compliance with national laws
- Tenure and land-use rights
- Respect for community rights
- Economic and social development
- Economic viability in the long term
- Sustainable yield of products
- Protection of biodiversity, water and soil resources
- Assessment, monitoring and prevention of adverse effects.

There are currently many forestry certification systems being developed or already in place in the various regions of the world. They can be grouped in three categories: global, when applied internationally; and regional or national, when applied to specific regions or countries. There are only two truly global certification systems: the Forest Stewardship Council (FSC) and ISO 14000. The first refers basically to environmental performance. ISO is concerned more with the environmental management process. The current status of these systems is presented in Table 7.1 for a group of selected countries.

FSC is the most developed global certification system, and consists of a coalition of environmental and social NGOs, and economic interests such as retailers and some forestry companies, especially in developed countries. It was created in 1993 to coordinate the scattered certification efforts and avoid "an excessive diversity that might confuse consumers, and harm the credibility of the seals and their commercial effectiveness" (Scholz et al. 1994, p.39). It has established 10 Principles, each considering many criteria, that include the need to comply with national laws and international agreements, define clear property rights, respect the rights of indigenous peoples, biodiversity conservation, care for water, soil and fragile ecosystems, conservation of primary and secondary forests, and restrictions on plantations, among others. It thus sets a similar playing field for all companies.

Up to mid-1999, a significant 16 million ha. had been certified internationally by FSC, by 167 companies/forest owners located in 30 countries. Sweden is the country with most certified forests (7.5 million ha), followed by Poland (3.0 million ha), United States (1.5 million ha) and Brazil (0.6 million ha). The FSC is supported by buyers groups in several countries. The most relevant one is the 95 Plus group in the UK, established under initiative of WWF. Fifteen per cent of wood consumption in UK is traded by this group.

FSC is resisted by the business sector, in particular by the strong American Forest & Paper Association (AF&PA). It is argued that the system is too complex and costly for small, independent forest owners, the process is dominated by NGOs, there is no governmental participation, and that significant differences among forests in different countries are not considered.[5]

Consequently, ISO 14000 is the forest industry's preferred certification system. These are a group of standards related to Environmental Management Systems. These standards do not apply specifically to forest operations but have been used increasingly by forest companies. Recently the so-called "Bridging Document"[6] published at the end of 1998, established the general guidelines for forest firms seeking certification under ISO 14000. Unlike eco-labels, which oblige compliance with the criteria of the entity awarding the seal, ISO only obliges compliance with the environmental standards of the origin country. Given that they set a clear framework and are not necessarily uniform across countries, this initiative is preferred by industrial sectors, particularly in exporting countries. On the other hand it does not prescribe performance standards, so that two companies with different standards can both be certified.

In addition to these global initiatives, there is an abundance of regional and national initiatives to certify sustainable forest practices, as can be seen in Table 7.1. They reflect national priorities, or the interest of specific groups within each country or region. Though they have different degrees of merits and problems, they share the common difficulty of their limited geographical comprehensiveness. They are generally not known to consumers and stakeholders in other countries, and they give a clear advantage to national products in their own markets, which makes them an effective trade barrier for foreign firms.

Table 7.1 Certification initiatives in selected countries

Country	FSC	ISO 14001	Regional or national certification initiatives
Brazil	Seven companies have been certified (0.6 million ha.).	Four companies have been certified.	• Brazilian FSC Under development. • CERFlOR, another important local initiative is being developed.
Canada	Only three companies certified today. But by 2003 will move from 0.2 to 8 million ha.	Four companies have been certified, covering 2.5 million ha. In 2003, 70 million ha. (60 of Canada) expected.	• Canadian standards under development since 1996. By 2003, eight million ha expected.
Chile	No certified company. Strong opposition.	Three forest companies certified.	• Fundación Chile has been unsuccessful in promoting FSC standards.
European Union			• New pan-European Forestry Certification initiative was launched in 1998. It is a forest owners' initiative, but others have joined.
Finland	No certified company.	All large companies have certification.	• Developed the Finnish Forest Certification System. Includes economic, environmental and social stakeholders. • Expected to certify 50% of total area in 1999.
Norway	No certified company	14,000 small forest owners certified collectively under the Living Forest Project (0.9 million ha.)	• Developed the Living Forest Project . Principles have been agreed upon by most stakeholders. • By the end of 2000, 90 per cent expected certified.

Table 7.1 (*Contd.*)

New Zealand	Only two forest companies certified. Strong opposition.	Six companies certified (0.3 million ha.)	• The NZ Forest Industry Council is working on an ISO-based tool.
South Africa	Eleven certified companies (0.5 million ha.)	One firm certified (0.4 million ha.). A number of producers in the process of getting certification.	• National auditing systems being used.
United Kingdom	No certification.	No certification.	• Developed the Woodland Assurance Scheme • British working group developing national FSC certification standards.
United States	Only 1.5 million ha. certified.	No information.	• Sustainable Forest Initiative developed by the AF&PA • 26 million ha. covered by this initiative.

Source: Based on Roxo (1999).

It can be concluded that the outstanding number and size of certified areas around the world and the projections for the future show that forestry certification has survived its difficult new-born period and is entering adolescent age. The issue now is not whether certification will be required, but rather what certification system(s) will be dominant.

2.4 Environmental threats to trade in the forestry sector

The increasing concern for the environment, together with the certification initiatives, both eco-labels and forestry certification, pose potential threats to trade, and more generally to forestry activity. As discussed above, the protection of the environment has become a matter of fierce competition between companies and countries. A first important problem is that there is no consensus on who should define what to care about. Voids like these are rapidly filled in by interested parties. Both firms and governments of developed countries – concerned for the impact of regulatory requirements on the competitiveness of their industry, and aware of the difficulties of imposing similar environmental standards to producers in other countries – have begun to focus their attention on voluntary instruments as a means of promoting better environmental stewardship in developing countries. Certification systems can easily be used as trade barriers, since through them, consumer decisions can be channeled to locally produced goods. A public that is increasingly "better" informed through an eco-label, would either choose to consume what is produced in the country in a clean way, or else more environmentally benign – locally produced – substitutes. In practice, these voluntary instruments are thus made obligatory for firms in developing countries wishing to sell in these more demanding markets. The development of global, regional and national level certification systems can thus be used as a new and subtle form of protectionism, forcing third-party countries to comply with environmental standards that are similar to those in force in the purchasing country. They are, however, fully compatible with current WTO regulations as they are based on consumer decisions and so do not constitute technical barriers to trade.

Additionally, environmental and social NGOs have been quick to propose certification standards based on their own criteria, and to promote effective boycott campaigns for products that in their opinion do not care for the environment. In many cases these are morally driven, rather than based on commercial interests. This does not make them any more desirable, since the tradeoff between environment, economic and social objectives is not necessarily done correctly by these institutions. However, their capacity to generate pressure on retailers and mobilize indigenous communities is of substantial concern for producers, especially in third world countries. Forestry decisions and ultimately trade are affected by these concerns.

Very strongly related to *who* is making the environmental requirements is the issue of *what* should be required. Defining what is actually understood by sustainable forestry management (SFM) is a second important potential threat to the trade of forestry products. For example, an important concern is the conversion of primary forests to secondary, or to non-forestry use. In particular many NGOs strongly oppose the conversion of (any) primary forests. It is argued that this can result in an irreversible loss of habitat and species diversity, soil erosion, destabilization of river basins and degradation of water quality, decreased access for the local population, a loss of cultural values and income, and an aesthetic degradation. Since developed countries, in general, have completed the process of converting forests to agricultural and urban uses, it turns out that this concern affects, in the main, developing countries. These latter countries mostly continue to deforest in order to satisfy demand for forestry products and incomes, and to allocate land to other uses (IIED 1996).

Plantations are also an important source of controversy. The replacement of primary forest by plantations leads to a loss of benefits specifically associated with primary forests which plantations cannot replace. In addition, normally there are negative social impacts on local and indigenous populations who often see their traditional forms of ownership impaired. Finally, deficient management practices are common in plantations and forests that are managed intensively. The trend towards monoculture, for example, requires external inputs, develops a very limited range of uses (only wood pulp, for example) and few users (normally a single large firm), and reduces both aesthetic and biodiversity. Again, doubts about plantations affect poorer countries. Although many developing countries have significant comparative advantages as regards growth rates, availability of land and cheap labor, the development of plantations with lax controls common in these countries, can lead to social and environmental losses, and have become a target for environmental groups.

Unfortunately, defining SFM is very difficult. Forests cannot be characterized simply. The term "forest" embraces such different ecosystems as the Amazonian rainforest and the northern or Chilean forests of eucalyptus or pine plantations. And there are so many variables involved – environmental, social and economic – that a comprehensive assessment methodology is required. However such a methodology does not exist, as discussed above. The dimensions and criteria to be considered are usually vague.[7] Moreover, apart from the problems of defining SFM criteria, there is also the question of the scale at which they are to be applied. SFM can be developed at a national or regional level, defining how much forest is left for preservation, how much for protection and how much for production. Once defined, the services of forests can be obtained at a meso scale, allowing each specific plot to develop according to a specific characteristic. For example, forestry firms could be allowed to develop plantations in a region, if, in other parts of the country, biodiversity concerns are addressed in forests that cannot be exploited. This concept is not accepted by many environmental organizations that evaluate each specific forestry project on its own merit. In their opinion, each intervention or project should be required to be multipurpose, i.e., to ensure all relevant services are accomplished at a microscopic level.

Different actors favor different criteria and scales of application. Establishing a consensus will be very difficult. Unfortunately this is not a scientific process, nor is it bias-free. SFM certification will ultimately depend on the criteria the certifying entities choose to favor. An additional complication is that many indicators will be required. Different forests (tropical, boreal and temperate) mean different environmental problems and variables to be considered. Similarly, different social and economic conditions should imply differential treatment. Including this level of specificity in any indicator is far from trivial, in particular if it is meant to seek a common ground for evaluation.

The diffuse nature of the concept of sustainable forestry management, and the difficulties related to defining indicators, implies uncertainties for the forestry sector. This is a long-term activity that requires fairly stable rules so that investment decisions can be taken with a minimum degree of certainty. Within the Forest Stewardship Council there are fierce debates about the contents SFM should support, and the multiplicity of initiatives and lack of defined criteria create room for pressure groups to lobby for specific criteria to be considered. Additionally, at the local level NGOs have their own priorities. The final result in each specific country is still being played out, case by case. This explains why many forestry companies prefer a system that regulates environmental management practices rather than performance.

In conclusion, informed consumers increasingly rely on environmental certification granted by developed-country entities based on criteria which, while trying to be objective, respond to the interests and preferences of the industries, consumers, governments and NGOs of those countries. As a result, plantations in particular, which are important development sources in many countries, have been called into question, and the exploitation of national forests has also been seriously affected. As it is very difficult to define SFM precisely – and to define appropriate indicators – forestry exploitation may come under attack from pressure groups that are hostile to forestry firms, both at the local and international level, thereby generating a negative image for the product in foreign markets.

In some cases, when concern for the environment or for affected local communities is not adequately built into the design of a forestry project, such pressures may be justified. However, disproportionate demands can also be made which respond more to the interests of a given NGO or some industry in particular, than to the welfare of the local community or protection of the environment.

The certification systems currently being developed do not solve these problems and may actually enhance them, depending on the final form they take, and the response from consumers. Additionally, campaigns by NGOs targeting specific products can make the forestry business more unstable, and as a result less investment in this sector can be expected. Trade may be affected, and forestry activity that would have developed in the absence of such pressures, may not do so.

3 Trade, natural resources and the legal framework of the forestry sector in Chile

In the last 20 years, Chile's forestry sector trade has grown spectacularly. There is a wide variety of products being exported to diverse markets all over the world. Additionally, plantations have allowed the recovery of previously eroded areas. Chile is becoming an important player in some products: it still has a great forestry potential and can produce at very competitive costs. The institutional arrangement, though far from perfect is fairly effective, and the legal framework required to protect forestry-related values is currently under intense discussion. This section presents the main figures related to Chile's forestry sector.

3.1 Growth, composition and destination of exports

Exports have been the engine of Chilean forestry development. The importance of trade for this sector is illustrated by the fact that, in recent years, over two-thirds of national primary forestry output has either been exported directly, or else has been used in the production of other export goods (INFOR 1995a). As can be seen in Table 7.2, sales of Chilean forestry products abroad grew by 127 per cent in 1995 dollars between 1985 and 1990 and by more than 160 per cent between 1990 and 1995. The US$ 2,369 million exported in 1995 was 51.5 per cent higher than the 1994 figure and represented 14.7 per cent of all national exports.

Forestry sector exports are highly concentrated in chemical wood pulp. As can be seen in Table 7.3, in 1994 this product represented more than 45 per cent of total exports from the sector, rising to nearly 54 per cent in 1995. This large increase in the value of chemical pulp exports occurred mainly because average prices in 1995 more than

Table 7.2 Chilean forestry exports (f.o.b. values). (US$ million 1995)

Year	1985	1990	1995
Values	396	900	2,369

Source: Based on CONAF figures.

doubled compared to the previous year. However, there was also a significant increase in physical sales. The remainder of forestry exports encompass a wide variety of products, each of which represents a minor share compared to chemical wood pulp. The product lines which follow in importance are lumber chips and sawn lumber, each of which represented about 10 per cent of total forestry exports in 1994 and 1995, and log exports which accounted for 6.2 per cent of the total in 1995. The category "Timber products and others", although important as a whole, is made up of exports of hundreds of different products, none of which individually accounts for more than 3 per cent of total forestry exports.

In terms of markets of destination, Chilean forestry exports show a marked concentration towards Asia. As shown in Table 7.4, nearly 50 per cent of all foreign sales in value terms were sent to this region of the world in 1994 and 1995. Moreover, within this continent, sales have concentrated in three countries: namely, Japan which accounts for 46.5 per cent of exports to Asia, South Korea (24 per cent) and Taiwan (11 per cent). The next most important destination market is Europe, where 20 per cent of Chile's forestry exports where sent in 1994. In Europe the main individual purchaser has been Belgium, with 35.6 per cent of total European purchases. Of the remaining 30 per cent of Chilean forestry exports, 17 per cent goes to South American countries, 12 per cent to the United States and a small proportion to Africa and Oceania.

As regards the destinations of the main forestry products, 35 per cent of chemical pulp is exported to Europe, 40 per cent to Asia, 13 per cent to South America and the remaining 12 per cent to other regions of the world. Lumber chips are sold entirely to Japan, two-thirds of sawn

Table 7.3   Composition of Chilean forestry exports, 1994 and 1995 (f.o.b. values)

Products	1994 US$ (millions)	(%)	1995 US$ (millions)	(%)
Wood in logs	113.9	7.3	144.3	6.2
Sawn lumber	158.1	10.1	222.9	9.4
Panels and planks	82.1	5.3	80.7	3.4
Lumber chips	163.5	10.4	232.8	9.8
Chemical pulp	717.7	45.9	1,270.4	53.6
Paper and cardboard	129.1	8.2	111.3	4.7
Timber products and others	169.9	12.8	306.8	12.9
TOTAL	1,534.3	100.0	2,369.2	100.0

Source: CONAF.

Table 7.4 Destination of Chilean forestry exports, 1994

Continents/Countries	US$ (millions) FOB	(%)
South America	260.2	16.6
North America	199.2	12.7
USA	176.2	
Others	23.0	
Europe	310.9	19.9
Germany	43.0	
Belgium	118.5	
France	30.8	
United Kingdom	44.6	
Italy	45.2	
Others	28.8	
Asia	770.6	49.3
South Korea	183.4	
Japan	360.5	
Taiwan	86.2	
Others	140.5	
Africa and Oceania	23.3	1.5
TOTAL	1,564.3	100.0

Source: Instituto Forestal (1995a).

lumber is sent to countries in Asia and Africa, logs are mainly sent to Asia, newsprint is sold almost entirely within South America and processed wood products are mainly sent to the USA (INFOR 1995a).

In brief, combining the variety of markets to which exports are sent with the variety of products being sold, it can be claimed that exports of Chilean forestry products are relatively well diversified. This means that Chilean forestry firms have managed to open markets and have created the capacity to offer competitive products in all corners of the earth.

3.2 Competitiveness of chemical pulp exports

The current volume and the growth potential of Chilean production represents a significant threat for certain competitors in developed countries. This is particularly true in the case of chemical pulp, where Chilean production accounted for 7.4 per cent of world output in 1995 (see Table 7.5). If the new pulp plant in Valdivia, which has faced strong opposition by ecological groups, comes on stream, Chile's share of world production could increase significantly. If one also considers that the bulk of North American output is destined for domestic consumption in that region, the volume of Chilean production in the world long-fiber pulp market is of clear significance for its competitors.

Table 7.5 World production capacity of kraft long-fiber wood pulp (actual 1995 figures and projections for 2000)

	Year 1995 kTons/yr	%	Year 2000 kTons/yr	%
Canada	6,984	36.35	7,159	34.94
USA	4,965	25.85	5,010	24.46
Sweden	2,495	12.98	2,780	13.57
Finland	865	4.50	1,330	6.49
Norway	160	0.83	160	0.78
Western Europe	665	3.46	695	3.39
Eastern Europe	251	1.31	251	1.23
Chile	*1,415*	*7.36*	*1,655*	*8.08*
Other Lat. Am.	450	2.34	395	1.93
Asia and Africa	265	1.38	280	1.37
Japan	335	1.74	335	1.64
Oceania	365	1.90	435	2.12
TOTAL	19,215	100.00	20,485	100.00

Note: The projection for the year 2000 assumes that the Valdivia plant will produce 200,000 tons. The project contemplates producing 400,000 of long-fiber and 150,000 tons of short fiber cellulose per year. As a result, Chile's share of world production could rise to 9 per cent. However, as of 1999 the project has been delayed for environmental and market reasons.
Source: Based on Hawkins Wright Ltd. (1996) and Chilean data.

Table 7.6 1996 production and CIF costs, long-fiber bleached kraft cellulose, main producer countries

	Production cost (US$/Ton)	CIF cost N.W. Europe (US$/Ton)
Chile	*305*	*391*
Southern USA	329	405
Sweden	408	451
Finland	421	465
Eastern Canada	427	492
France	452	493
West coast of Canada	477	534
Western Canada (inland)	495	579

Source: Hawkins Wright Ltd. (1996).

Apart from the magnitude of Chilean export supply, Chilean producers have cost advantages in the long-fiber chemical pulp market in Europe compared with Scandinavian producer countries. Similarly, in

Europe and Asia Chilean producers have an absolute cost advantage over the big North American producers. Table 7.6 presents the costs of production of the main long-fiber cellulose-producing countries together with the cost of their products placed somewhere in the North East of Europe. As can be seen, production costs in Chile are the lowest in the world, and significantly lower than in the United States, Sweden and Finland. This enables Chilean producers to compete solidly both in Europe and in Asia. Chile's advantages over Scandinavian producers arise mainly from the lower cost of timber storage, based on the rapid growth of the forest providing the raw material.

3.3 Natural resources

From the resource point of view, Chile has great potential for forestry development, because soils are naturally suitable for forestry in much of the country. In approximate figures, of a total continental surface area of 75.7 million hectares (Mha), it is estimated that 44.6 per cent (33.8 Mha) is suitable for forestry, 18 per cent is suitable for livestock and agriculture and the remaining 29.4 per cent is land which is unproductive from the agriculture or forestry point of view.

According to the recent forestry cadastre (Universidad Austral de Chile and others, 1997), the total surface area of Chile covered by forest is approximately 15.65 Mha, of which 86.5 per cent (slightly over 13.5 Mha) contains native forests[8] and the remaining 13.5 per cent (2.12 Mha) is planted. This means that only 46.3 per cent of land suitable for forestry is currently forested, so there is great potential for the development of new forests; moreover, inasmuch as this potential is not realized, the lack of tree cover leads to increasing soil degradation.

Of native forests, 29 per cent (3.92 Mha) is publicly owned and comes under the State-Protected Forestry Areas System (SNASPE). The remaining 71 per cent is privately owned. Although the total surface area of native forest within SNASPE is significant, representation of the different types of native forest is highly varied. Table 7.7 shows that for some forest types more than half the existing stock is within the SNASPE, whereas in other types the proportion is less than 2 per cent.

Annual extraction of native forests amounts to 9.3 million m^3, of which 6.1 million m^3 is destined for firewood and charcoal ((INFOR 1993), mainly for domestic use in the south of the country, and 3.2 million m^3 for industrial use (INFOR, 1995a). According to the same source, the industrial use of native wood splits into two-thirds for the production of lumber chips and one-third for sawn lumber and panels. Native wood currently accounts for just 15 per cent of the total

Table 7.7   Total native forest area by forest type and percentage included in SNASPE, 1996

Forest types	Total stocks (thousand ha.)	% within SNASPE
Alerce	264	17.9
Cipres de las Guaitecas	972	69.6
Araucaria	254	48.4
Cipres de la Cordillera	45	6.3
Lenga	3,400	16.8
Coigue de Magallanes	1,800	50.5
Hualo (White Oak)	184	0.5
Roble (Oak) – Raulí – Coigue	1,370	1.7
Coigue – Raulí – Tepa	457	9.5
Open forest	342	2.0
Evergreen	4,350	34.3
TOTAL	13,438	29.0

Source: Universidad Austral and others (1997).

consumption of the forestry industry, while the rest comes from Monterrey pine (*pino radiata*) and eucalyptus plantations. Thus, plantations are the fundamental source of timber for the forestry industry, and restrictions on their development for environmental or other reasons would have a significant impact on the sector.

From the global point of view, the extraction of 9.3 million m^3 of timber from native forests does not necessarily put them in danger. As that level of extraction is way below the annual rate of forest growth,[9] the country can be expected to expand its forestry stock in terms of native species. Of course, what is true for the whole is not necessarily true at the local level or for certain individual species; nor does it ensure adequate protection of the biodiversity associated with native forests.

When working with forests one should not forget that these are formed by living organisms which grow and develop in their respective ecological niche. For this not to happen, attacks by external agents have to be extreme (for example, burning, driving out animals, or planting other species). The destruction of forests by natural causes and their subsequent recovery (which happens everywhere in the world) shows the strength they have to regenerate and/or adapt to new conditions (Veblen *et al.* 1996).

From the point of view of the characteristics and height of native forests, Table 7.8 shows that the surface area of adult and secondary forest with heights above 12 meters accounts for 42.2 per cent of total native forests, or more than 5.67 million hectares. Adult and developing secondary-growth forests less than 12 meters high account for 35.2 per cent of total native forests and cover a surface area of 4.75 million ha. The surface area covered by open adult and secondary forests is 1.25 million ha, equivalent to 9.3 per cent of all native forests.

Table 7.8 also shows that stunted native forests whose height does not exceed 8 meters cover 3 million ha, equivalent to 22.5 of total native forest of Chile. Open stunted forests covers a surface area equivalent to 841,000 ha, representing 6.3 per cent of total native forests.

As regards existing plantations, reports state that the annual rate of forestation in the last 20 years, which approaches 63,000 ha/yr, has generated a forest mass of over 2.1 million ha. The resulting availability of timber over the next two decades will make it possible to double current physical production volumes. In other words, the forestry industry could grow from using 17 million m^3 per year at present to over 36 million m^3 as from the year 2017 (INFOR 1995a). To ensure continuous supply, estimates of future timber availability are based on harvesting

Table 7.8 Surface area of native forest by type of cover and height, 1996

Types	Cover	Height (meters)	Surface area (hectares)	(%)
Adult and secondary forests	Dense	< 12	1,727,193.9	12.8
		> 12	3,677,337.2	27.4
		Subtotal Dense	5,404,531.1	40.2
	Semi-dense	< 12	2,059,215.4	15.3
		> 12	1,710,208.1	12.7
		Subtotal Semi-dense	3,769,423.5	28.0
	Open	< 12	961,618.5	7.1
		> 12	290,375.8	2.1
		Subtotal Open	1,251,994.3	9.3
Subtotal Adult and secondary forests			10,425,948.9	77.5
Stunted forest	Dense	2 to 8	922,573.9	6.9
	Semi-dense	2 to 8	1,253,330.3	9.3
	Open	2 to 8	841,304.8	6.3
Subtotal Stunted forests			3,017,209.0	22.5
Total Native forest			13,443,157.9	100.0

Note: Dense forests are defined as those with a crown cover greater than 75 per cent, semi-dense forests those with a crown cover between 50 per cent and 75 per cent, and open forests those with a cover of less than 50 per cent. To be designated as a forest, the crown cover must be greater than 25 per cent.
Source: Universidad Austral and others (1997).

volumes equivalent to the annual rate of forest growth subject to the condition that timber supply never decreases.

3.4   Legal and institutional framework

The general legislation to prevent and rectify environmental problems in Chile is recent and still in a process of consolidation. In 1994, Law No. 19300, the Environmental Framework Law, was passed. This legislation aimed to create an institutional framework to solve existing environmental problems and avoid the creation of new ones, by setting up the instruments needed to manage the environment efficiently and give adequate protection to natural resources. It provides a general body of legislation to which all sectoral environmental legislation could be referred. In its introduction, the Law declares that the protection of the environment shall be based on the principles of prevention, gradualism, responsibility for environmental damage, participation by all affected parties, economic efficiency and "the polluter pays" principle.

As far as forestry is concerned, the main aspects of Law No. 19300 are as follows. It declares that the state will administer a National System of Forest Areas in order to "ensure biological diversity, supervise the preservation of nature and conserve environmental heritage". In this sense it reaffirms and enriches a historical function of the Chilean state. Indeed, at the present time the National System of Forest Areas protected by the state already covers 14 million hectares (18.5 per cent of continental land area) whereby 61 types of natural ecosystems are protected. This system is composed of 31 national parks, 43 forestry reserves and 14 national monuments. The system currently covers more than 3.9 million hectares of natural forest, and a program is under way to protect 85 natural ecosystems that have been identified in the country. The Law also declares that the Chilean state will encourage the creation of protected forest areas under private ownership, some of which are very large.

The Law requires the state to draw up and maintain up-to-date an inventory of forest flora and fauna species and to enforce the rules on harvesting, capture, hunting, trade and transport. It also declares that the "use and exploitation of renewable natural resources shall be carried out in such a way as to ensure their capacity for regeneration and conserve the associated biological diversity..."

One instrument for regulating the use and exploitation of natural resources in a given area are "Management Plans", which have to address aspects such as the maintenance of water flows and soil conservation, the maintenance of landscape value and protection of species which are in danger of extinction, vulnerable, rare or insufficiently known. In addition to management plans, which are obligatory for the most environmentally important projects, there is a system of environmental impact assessment (SEIA). All industrial projects in the forestry sector are subject to this requirement, and the system is being applied to all new projects of any size.[10]

The legislation regulating forestry management, both of native species and those introduced into the country, is old and has a complete institutional framework which has been operating for several decades. The main legislation governing the forestry sector is Decree Law 701, which was passed in 1974. This modified and complemented the old Forestry Law which had governed the sector in Chile since 1931. The consequence of this regulation is that all forestry exploitation in Chile must follow a management plan previously approved by the National Forestry Corporation, with the obligation to reforest or regenerate the exploited forests (Fierro and Morales 1994). In addition, several types of incentive exist for people who own forests or for those who wish to establish forests in suitable unforested areas. For over half a century, Chile has been developing regulations and institutions to protect soils and water and maintain or increase forest volume. However, issues relating to the replacement of native forests and the protection of biodiversity were not included among the goals of the public regulatory system for forestry exploitation.

In order to expand the surface area covered by native forests, the government sent a bill in 1991 to the Chilean Congress aiming to "encourage the increase, protection and recovery of native forests". This bill, while allowing the extraction of wood from some forests, gives special incentives to people carrying out forestation with native species and those who care for native forests in ways that enable them to be recovered or preserved. At the same time, it discourages those who wish to replace native forests by exotic species.

This legislation was intended to balance the interest of industry and environmental concerns. However this effort has been unsuccessful. The bill has been under discussion since the early 1990s, and has generated great controversy both among ecological groups – who oppose any replacement of native species by exotic species as allowed by the bill – and by business groups – who in turn oppose any additional restrictions to their property rights. This has had undesirable consequences. It has led to a situation of uncertainty for private owners of native forests, and therefore to a decrease in their commercial value. This environment is inadequate for the care, conservation, or expansion of forests, in particular in regions with many small owners.[11]

4   Environmental threats to trade in Chilean forestry products

The general threats to trade of forestry products discussed in Section 2, have been observed in Chile: restrictions on production technologies, protectionist eco-labels, requirements for sustainable forestry management, NGO pressures and boycotts, threats to plantations and exploitation of native forests. In this section, a selection of problems related to these threats is presented.

4.1   External threats to forestry exports: the case of chlorine

A good example of the problems posed by self-serving environmental concerns is the bleaching of wood pulp. The issue became fashionable in 1995, after a new control technology was developed which made it possible to measure concentrations of chemical compounds at the level of parts per quadrillion. An analysis of effluents from cellulose bleaching plants revealed that they contained traces of dioxins, chlorate compounds acknowledged to be dangerous for human and animal health. The presence of the chlorate compounds was linked to bleaching done with processes using elementary chlorine (Cl_2) or hypochlorite (ClO).

This discovery coincided with great public concern for the environment, and it became the central issue for world environmental movements in their campaign against the effects of the cellulose and paper industry on the natural world.

In response to this challenge, governments and industry in developed countries set up control systems and developed new technologies to obtain bleached cellulose by reducing or eliminating airborne pollution and the contamination of water courses by chlorate compounds. There are two possible ways to do this: by treating residual water before releasing it into natural water courses, or by changing the process for obtaining bleached cellulose. In fact, the secondary treatment of residual water can almost completely eliminate toxic elements without modifying the production process.

Meanwhile, Scandinavian industrialists developed two processes to reduce pollution by chlorate compounds during the bleaching process. The first of these is known as ECF (Elementary Chlorine-Free), which uses chlorine dioxide (ClO_2) for bleaching and cuts chlorate compounds by 90 per cent. The second process, known as TCF (Totally Chlorine-Free), achieves bleaching without the use of chlorine. These techniques have spread rapidly: in Scandinavian countries over 95 per cent of cellulose plants were bleaching with ECF or TCF processes by late 1995. In Western Europe, over 66 per cent of bleaching is done with these methods, while in Oceania and Canada the figures are on the order of 42 per cent. In Latin America the figure is 32 per cent, while in the United States and Eastern Europe the figure is 17 per cent. In Asia and Africa, these technologies have virtually made no impact at all (IIED 1996).

European industrialists and environmentalists, especially in Scandinavian countries, have lobbied strongly for a worldwide standard requiring cellulose bleaching to be carried out using ECF or TCF type processes.[12] At the same time there has been an intensive marketing campaign to persuade consumers to choose products that are bleached with these technologies. In particular, the requirement of chlorine-free products has been included in many important eco-labels. The result has been that in some periods Scandinavian producers have obtained higher prices for their products and, more importantly still, have obtained large profits by selling the technologies and equipment to bleach without elementary chlorine to the rest of the world (Porter and Van der Linde 1995). Accordingly, for foreigners to be able to compete in Europe they have to adopt technologies developed by Scandinavian industrialists.

From 1985 onwards, simultaneous detailed studies began to be carried out in the medical and biological fields to prove the risks to human health and the damage to aquatic fauna caused by dioxins in the effluents from traditional cellulose bleaching plants. However, it has been impossible to prove that the traces of dioxins found can cause harm to human health (Expert Panel 1995). Moreover, it was found that the harm caused to fish is identical to that caused by effluents from cellulose plants that do not carry out bleaching (Hodson 1996), and that the damage found is transient and reversible (Carey *et al.* 1993).

The cellulose export industry in Chile, which represents more than half the value of forestry sector sales abroad, has made substantial investments in the field of air and water pollution, so as to meet the most rigorous international environmental protection standards. In this way it reduces the risk of being excluded from the European market. In particular, the three most recent cellulose plants built since 1990, and another that will soon come on-stream, have incorporated leading-edge technologies and are comparable to plants in Scandinavian countries in terms of bleaching without chlorine gas (with ECF technology), and as regards the decontamination of liquid effluents, low water consumption and energy autarchy (Scholz *et al.* 1994). The environmental investment undertaken in these three plants amounted to US$ 100 million, equivalent to 6 per cent of total investment (Econoticias 1992).

In brief, this case shows how European producers, with the help of environmentalist groups, managed in practice to impose their processing standards on competitors from other parts of the world where environmental, economic and technological conditions are completely different. It is interesting to note that these producers, whose production costs are relatively high, have generated competitive advantages by differentiating themselves in terms of products bleached without chlorine and the marketing technologies and equipment required to achieve this.

4.2   The problem of sustainable management of native forests and plantations

The most controversial aspect of the forestry sector, which exposes it to possible trade restrictions, relates to allegedly unsustainable forest management. A report by the German Development Institute on the environmental challenges facing the export sector argues that Chile's forestry industry may be called into question because of "possible negative impacts on the ecological balance arising from the management of plantations" and by the exploitation of "plantations originating from the replacement of native forests" (Scholz *et al.* 1994, p.39). Additionally, ecological groups allege that there has been a steady deterioration and destruction of Chile's native forests, and this is seriously harming biodiversity. The basic causes of this process include native forests being replaced by plantations and being turned over to agriculture, the production of fire wood and charcoal, and the production of lumber chips (Lara *et al.* 1996).

The first allegation was formalized as follows: "Since 1974, due to the passing of Decree Law 701providing subsidies to forestry activity, extensive areas of native forests were replaced by plantations, and this became one of the main causes of the destruction of native forests. This situation persists to the present day". It then continues: "Although there are no precise figures, global estimates suggest that between 1974 and 1992 over 200,000 ha of native forests have been replaced" (Lara *et al.* 1996).

In reality, the situation seems to be quite different. The Forestry Institute at CORFO, a national entity with a long tradition of research and diffusion of forestry information, studied this issue and concluded that in the 30 years prior to 1990 no more than 135,000 ha of native forests had been replaced by plantations, that the substitutions occurred in the period 1974–83 and that since 1984 replacement has not been significant. Accordingly, the figures cited by Lara and others are most probably over-estimated. The apparent explanation of the difference between the two reports is that the values used by Lara *et al.* include land turned over for crop growing and livestock breeding which cannot be considered as replacement of native forest by plantations. Moreover, the estimates that exist for land turned over to agriculture are subject to wide margins of error.

Environmental groups usually claim that plantations are negative for the environment, using a variety of arguments, including the following: the acidification of soils, that the water regime is disturbed and biodiversity is reduced. These arguments have been refuted by a number of authors, who claim that the soil acidity argument is not supported by any scientific study, and that their own investigations made in Chile show that the behavior of soil acidity after several decades of pine plantations is fully comparable with that of native species (Grass 1992; Hartwig 1994). The negative effects on the water regime are linked to the fact that plantations consume more water than native forests. This seems curious, because plantations tend to be installed precisely in areas of abundant winter rainfall. Plantation forests thus play a fundamental role in the interception and infiltration of rainwater. As regards biodiversity, when a plantation is established a change clearly ensues. However, it has been shown that the variety of flora and fauna actually depends on the shrub and litter layer, or *sotobosque* (vegetation that grows up between the trees of a forest), and this in turn depends on soil quality, climate and the amount of light the forest lets in. Thus in low-density pine plantations, the flora and fauna that develops is very similar to what appears under other types of forest in the same geographical area.

Nonetheless, plantations can cause environmental problems. As can happen with the plantation of any species, negative results may arise from "bad planning that fails to consider social aspects, or a lack of correspondence between species, place and objectives" (FAO 1994). In other words, plantations are not good or bad in themselves. As in any human intervention in nature, plantations must ensure compatibility between the site, the species to be planted and the goals being pursued.

In this same line, a recent publication by the "Defenders of native forests", a militant pro-forest NGO, provides a synthesis of comparative research between plantations of introduced species and native forest. As regards effects on the soil, it concludes that forests of Monterrey pine *(pino radiata)* "do not have significant impacts, except for an increase in acidity at the humus level. However, forest soils in the south of the country naturally have a quite acid pH level". As for effects on water, it suggests that plantations lead to greater run-off than native forests: however, it adds that "sediment concentrations found are not very high in any of the river-basins analyzed" (Otero 1998).

In the case of Chile, the criticism against plantations (they have been called "green deserts") appears to be biased, considering that over 90 per cent have been created on unforested land suffering from various degrees of erosion (Hartwig 1994). Such plantations have halted erosive processes and help to regulate water cycles, thereby making a contribution to fixing carbon and releasing oxygen into the atmosphere. This has enabled a large forestry industry to develop and, as an important consequence from an environmental perspective, has made it possible to replace timber from native species in supplying the forestry industry. As a result, Chile's native forests have begun to recover strongly.

Plantations have also been instrumental in reducing the pressure on native forests for firewood. The Instituto Forestal of CORFO estimated that population extracts 6.1 million cubic meters per year from native forests for this purpose (INFOR 1993). Currently, this use accounts for two thirds of the total quantity of wood extracted from these forests.

With respect to lumber chip production, the use of native logs for this purpose is on the order of 2.2 million m^3 (INFOR 1995a), which in surface-area terms is equivalent to some 9,760 ha (assuming an average yield of 205 m^3/ha). Allegations against this activity are based on the fact that "lumber chip operators fell trees to ground level or leave individual trees very badly damaged or as stumps", and that "most lumber chip operators are supplied by third parties", most likely small- and medium-scale forest owners that might exploit the forest "with or without a management plan" (Donoso and Lara 1996).[13] In response to the first allegation, large forestry companies cannot exploit forests without a management plan previously approved by CONAF, specifying the type of felling to be carried out. So if CONAF authorizes the firm to cut to ground level this is not a breach of regulations; it is because there are technical grounds to expect that forest recovery or regeneration is assured. On the other hand, owing to social pressures that have caused lumber chip exports to gain notoriety, CONAF staff are especially diligent in making sure that the forestry harvest by companies in this business adheres to what is approved in the respective management plan. Accordingly, the greatest problem are small-scale owners that need to turn their timber stocks into cash. On this basis, the main grounds for taking action against lumber chip operators is the number of allegations made by CONAF of "illegal felling". For example, in 1990–92 there were

1,242 allegations relating to the cutting of native species (CONAF 1993), including 187,000 m^3 involving timber for lumber chips, or slightly over 62,000 m^3 per year. This figure is less than 3 per cent of the annual raw material input into lumber chip plants.

In conclusion, there is an image among environmental groups that forest activity in Chile – and particularly plantations – is undertaken in an unsustainable manner. However, the evidence seems to point in a different direction. Generalized mismanagement of the past (pre-1960), in particular to push the agricultural frontier, is all but over. In general, plantations are being beneficial for the environment, and are not growing at the expense of native forests, but at the expense of previously eroded land. Consequently, there is no technical support for opposition to plantations on environmental grounds: they sequester carbon, they improve water retention, reduce erosion, and increase the amenity value of degraded hills and plains. Moreover, as mentioned before, the availability of plantations reduces the demands for firewood from native forests, the greatest threat to these forests.

4.3 Obstacles to forestry development in Magallanes

Another issue that has been in public debate in recent years is the exploitation of native forests in the Magallanes region, in the Chilean Patagonia. Environmental groups have mobilized public opinion campaigns that have obstructed the work of both already-existing forestry firms and new start-ups. Furthermore a large forestry project in Tierra del Fuego which is about to obtain legal authorization to operate, has been threatened by environmentalists with an international boycott.

The Magallanes case is important because it has become a symbol for the institutions involved: the government, forestry firms and ecologists. For the government, the case has allowed the new institutional framework for environmental protection in the forestry sector to be put to the test. For forestry firms, the case shows what lies in store for anyone attempting carry out a project to exploit native forests. For ecological groups, it will allow them to test the real support that they can raise for their cause abroad.

To appreciate the economic significance of the forestry sector in the region, forestry exports from Magallanes in 1995 were in excess of US$ 20 million per year (four or five years earlier they were below US$ 2 million), and the potential of lenga forests in the extreme South of Chile is sufficient to double or triple the total value of current exports, an important impact in an economically depressed area. Before the final results of the forestry cadastre were known, the volume of native forest in this region, mostly lenga, had been estimated at more than three million hectares, according to figures compiled by experts on Magallanic forests (Schmidt 1994; Schmidt and Caldentey 1994); the cadastre subsequently found 3.4 million ha. Of this amount, 570,000 ha is in state ownership and the rest is privately owned. The same authors claim that there is about 1.7 million ha of protected and non-commercial forest belonging to private owners. Finally, the authors estimate that the productive forest area under private ownership (whose preferred function is neither the conservation nor the protection of resources) is some 500,000 ha, and with this resource initially 1.5 million m^3 of timber could be extracted per year for industrial use (one third suitable for sawn lumber and two-thirds for lumber chips). The same authors argue that on a managed forest basis, future extraction could be on the order of 3 million m^3 per year with a proportion of two-thirds of sawn timber and one-thirds lumber chips.

By 1994, about 4,000 ha per year was being exploited and from this 380,000 m^3 per year of timber was being extracted for industrial use: 295,000 destined for lumber chips and 85,000 for sawn lumber (INFOR 1995a). With the new Magallanica de Bosques sawmill coming on stream, the proportion of sawn lumber in the region approached the estimated potential of one-third. The Forestal Trillium project, recently approved both by the Magallanes Regional Environmental Commission and by the National Environmental Commission (CONAMA), aims to extract on the order of 350,000 m^3 of lumber per year. Thus, even including this latter project, extraction would still be far below the region's timber production potential.

The exploitation of forests in the Magallanes region has a history dating back more than 100 years. For more than 20 years there has been systematic research into the forest and the environmental effects of exploitation and harvesting techniques. Although scientific and technical research is not exhausted and uncertainty remains on certain issues, cumulative experience has made it possible to refine techniques for exploitation of lenga forest, providing reassurance on environmental protection. The results of exploitation adhering to these forestry prescriptions have been reported in the technical literature[14] and have been incorporated into CONAF requirements, with certain provisos for the design and approval of management plans.

The most important conclusion of the research carried out on these forests is, in the words of H. Schmidt, "the high capacity for regeneration among the lenga and coigue species in Magallanes, and the maintenance of accompanying *sotobosque* species". Moreover, he adds, "in practically all exploitation situations in the past, there has been a good rate of natural recovery, and in the case of very intensive exploitations secondary forests have formed, characterized by high tree density with much greater growth than the natural forest" (Schmidt 1994).

Accordingly, there is little justification for the fear that exploitation of lenga forests in Magallanes might be putting ecological balances at risk; still less that it will risk the existence of the resource. The reason is that the surface area suitable for commercial exploitation is no more than one-sixth of the total forest area, because no more than 60 per cent of the trees can be extracted in any hectare exploited (thereby ensuring regeneration), and the regulations permit intervention on less than 2 per cent of a given forest property each year.

However, environmental groups continue to campaign against forestry activity in Magallanes, especially against the production of lumber chips and forestry development projects in the region.

Their criticisms have targeted the Forestal Trillium project in Tierra del Fuego. Recently, as a result of final approval of the environmental impact study by the government of Chile and authorization to carry out the Forestal Trillium project, an international campaign has been announced in conjunction with environmental groups from other countries. In response to these announcements, the regional authorities have declared that the project is sustainable. Nevertheless, the project has become less attractive to the investors: for example the entrepreneurs had to make a commitment not to export lumber chips; a necessity from the forestry and economic point of view. In addition, they have suffered unnecessary delays (for example, as a result of injunctions filed against them which continue to delay the project). Another significant cost of the problems of the project arises from the negative signals for other forestry projects and for entrepreneurs from Magallanes and in the rest of the country.

Often, technical support for their claims are weak. Environmentalists' allegations are generally based on partial or biased information with scant scientific foundation, and they seek and find allies in respectable institutions to give credibility to their arguments.[15] As a result, the quality of the data becomes of secondary importance. Such is the case of a report by the Central Bank of Chile on Environmental Accounts and Native Forests (Banco Central de Chile, 1995). Although there is broad consensus that this study's gloomy projections for the future of native forests are mistaken (INFOR 1995b; Susaeta 1995) – it estimates for example that in the optimistic scenario there would be only 4 million ha of native forests by the year 2025 – the study continues to be used to justify the argument that native forest exploitation is not sustainable (see, for example, the article by Larraín and Menotti 1998).

These obstacles exist because environmental NGOs want to block the exploitation of all primary forests in Chile, even when legislation and technical considerations make it feasible. Lack of agreement on what is considered "sustainable" is at the root of this problem.

4.4   Impacts on the exploitation of native forest and on new plantations

As a result of the highly uncertain climate that has been created in Chile, and in the world generally, regarding trade in products from native forests, and in order not to put plantation forest businesses at risk, large Chilean forestry companies have desisted from commercial operations on land containing indigenous forests, regardless of their state of conservation. This means that companies are not exploiting the economical potential of their own native forests and have ceased to invest in the development of management techniques and regeneration of native species. They have also ceased to invest in techniques for using native timber.

In this climate of uncertainty regarding the possibility of exploiting their native forests in the future, it is also understandable that small-and medium-scale owners see the benefits of extracting the wealth of forest as quickly as possible, and this accelerates the rate of exploitation and reduces their interest in the husbandry and conservation of resources. The resulting attitude of this uncertainty among large forestry firms and the medium-and small-scale owners is tending to devalue Chile's native forests.

Obviously, banning all substitution of native forests by plantations of species that are non-native but appropriate to the conditions of the land, implies asset losses for private owners. Comparative profitability studies between forestry businesses on land covered by productive native forests (these are forests formed by abundant species, in which production would not have significant effects on global or regional biodiversity, nor on water courses or soil) put the cost of restriction at between US$ 550 and US$ 5,000 per ha, depending on the initial type of forest, its initial state, its location and the discount rate (Géminis 1995; The World Bank 1994). At the same time, in these cases the environmental benefits of maintaining the native forest would be very small or nil.

To get an idea of the importance of this type of prohibition, the surface area of productive native forests that could be replaced without causing environmental harm of any kind is estimated at 800,000 hectares or more (Géminis 1995). An analysis carried out independently at the Centro de Estudios Públicos concluded that the present value of preventing such substitutions,[16] would be on the order of US$ 520 million (Katz and del Fávero 1995).

Finally, plantations are also affected. Most of the deforested land located in areas that are suitable for developing plantations, is distributed among hundreds of thousands of small property owners, many of which have problems with the legal titles to their lands (Hartwig 1994). This fact, together with the inflexibility of the requirement of no replacement of native forests, independently of their state and size, implies that forestry companies cannot put together plots of efficient size for new plantations. For this reason, they have begun to plant abroad.[17] This is a potentially negative trend, since future exports will be affected.

5 Conclusions

Environmental trends in the forestry sector are generating significant uncertainties to this activity, and in particular Chile is being affected. First, the precautionary principle has resulted in an intense scrutiny of the exploitation of native forests generally. NGOs, consumer groups, and industry and governments in importing countries are increasingly concerned that exploitation of forests must be sustainable. Second, a life-cycle approach to forestry products has become dominant, requiring that products be environmentally friendly in all stages of the life-cycle of the product. Since the WTO does not allow harmonization of production standards, consumer-based instruments are increasingly favored as a way to get laggards to worry about the environmental impacts of their production activities. Eco-labels and sustainable forestry certification schemes have been developed, even when they do not have general acceptance. Moreover, they are much too blunt an instrument to take into account the inmense diversity among forests in the world. As a result, they have been and may continue to be used as trade barriers. Additionally, NGOs which put pressure on forestry firms have specific preferences on this subject, desiring little or no exploitation of primary forests, and the rejection of plantations. Developing countries – which in many cases base the development of their rural areas precisely on these resources – stand to lose most. Not only economically, but also – ironically – in the quality of their forests.

These concerns are not theoretical. In Chile, environmental pressures have resulted in a variety of significant uncertainties for the Chilean forestry sector. Despite the fact that the development of forestry exports in Chile is based on sustainably managed plantations, the greatest source of vulnerability relates to native forests. In the face of the uncertainty surrounding the use of native species, the country's main forestry entrepreneurs have abandoned or frozen their activities in native forests and native timber. This is particularly true for those firms whose main business is plantations of Monterrey pine (pino radiata) and eucalyptus, and who do not want to jeopardize this activity.

This can be considered a great success for the defenders of Chile's native forests. The economic cost for the country, however, will be large – and was not evaluated before the environmental campaigns began. It has led to hundreds of thousands of hectares of land with little economic value, which are not fulfilling any function in protecting natural resources or biodiversity, yet cannot be put into production. There may also be an environmental cost. Forests of no economic value cannot depend on the active protection of their owners against dangers such as those caused by humans and this is specially true for small- and medium-scale forest owners. The uncertainty surrounding the future exploitation of their native forests, added to the fact that forestry firms (except for lumber chip operators) are no longer buying native timber, may lead them to accelerate exploitation of their forests or operate clandestinely; or, ultimately, they may get rid of them and prepare the land for agriculture. Plantations are also limited. Environmental pressures have made it increasingly attractive to divert investments to neighboring countries, that have less restrictions.

Looking into the future, the risks facing the forestry industry depend on decisions taken in Chile, and internationally, on forest use. The definition of SFM, the establishment of indicators appropriate to the different conditions of countries, and the development of the certifying schemes that allow SFM are all key. In this area, both the state and private individuals need to assume an active role. They must participate in international forums where these issues are discussed and decided. In Chile, research is required on the reality of timber stocks, sustainable exploitation methods, systems of management control and protection. Scientific evidence supporting how Chile is managing its forests is important. Finally, the legal and institutional framework that will govern the recovery and development of Chile's native forests and plantations must be defined clearly. These actions will reduce uncertainty and allow the effective development of a sustainable forestry sector in Chile.

Notes

1 From the economic point of view, proposals for harmonization and uniformity of environmental standards have no justification, and would generate inefficiencies and welfare loss. For a recent demonstration, see Bhagwati and Srinivasan (1996).

2 In fact the Chilean copper industry has already faced formal allegations in United States and was excluded from the General System of Preferences for environmental reasons (O'Ryan and Ulloa, Chapter 6, this volume).

3 Of course what is "reasonable" depends on the available information and on who does the assessment. At one extreme the strict precautionary principle tends towards banning the discharge of substances with uncertain effects. At another extreme, abatement technologies and economic considerations may be combined to compare costs and benefits. The "critical load" concept is also used for this purpose.

4 In the literature, the term "harmonized standards" is used in a wide variety of ways. In some cases it refers to equalizing environmental quality standards, but in others it refers to harmonizing specific instruments such as the level of taxes to be applied or technologies to be required.

5 In a recent document, the AF&PA makes three objections to FSC eco-labelling: (1) the principles and criteria do not have a scientific base, and are not appropriate for american forests; (2) requirements for monitoring in the whole production chain are unfeasible given the industrial organization of the sector; (3) the principles and criteria do not reflect American consumer preferences and discriminates against the use of renewable resources.

6 Technical Report ISO/TR 14061, *Information to Assist Forestry Organizations in the Use of Environmental Management System Standards ISO 14001 and ISO 14004.*

7 Criteria usually considered include: *Forestry criteria* that pursue maximum conservation of forested areas, accept plantation regimes, favor the natural regeneration of the forest and accept forestry production within a forestry management scheme; *Environmental criteria* that seek functional environmental equilibrium, avoiding negative impacts on soils, water resources, biodiversity and landscape; they reject the replacement of native forest by plantations, minimize reforestation with exotic species and try to prevent the use of chemical substances in forestry management; *Criteria with a social focus* that seek to defend indigenous groups and peoples linked to the forest, and promote improvements in their living standards and their participation in decisions on forestry management; *Legal criteria* that relate to the design and fulfilment of rules relating to forestry management plans and labor safety in forestry activity; and *Organizational criteria* that include monitoring and enforcement requirements and the design of management plans.

8 The cadastre uses the definition recommended by FAO: "The native forest is a natural ecosystem in which the tree layer consists of native species more than 2 meters tall and with a canopy cover of over 25 per cent.

9 Assuming a conservative growth rate of native forests of 3 m^3 per ha/yr, total growth will be 40 million m^3 per year, i.e. more than four times the rate of consumption.

10 For example, environmental impact assessment has been carried out on the Río Cóndor project of Forestal Trillium, to industrialize a lenga forest of more 200,000 ha in Tierra del Fuego, and the Celulosa Arauco Valdivia Plant, which with an investment of US$ 1 billion aims to produce 570,000 tons of chemical pulp per year.

11 There are over 50,000 forest owners in Chile.

12 Greenpeace, meanwhile, has lobbied for all Chlorine compounds in cellulose bleaching to be eliminated (Greenpeace 1996).

13 These same authors minimize the environmental effects of firewood extraction (that is almost three times more) stating that: "... it is frequent for fire wood to be obtained through low intensity interventions, frequently from shoots, which leave part of the timber volume standing and do not prevent natural regeneration".

14 A selection of this literature can be found in Schmidt and Caldentey (1994).

15 For example, the newspaper headlines stated, "Lenga Magallanes will run out in 25 years", to inform the study by the Office National des Forêts in France on the native lenga forests in Patagonia. This report states, among other things, that there could be supply problems for the timber industry in 25 or 30 years' time if a series of conditions are met. In any event, the forests that will be exploited to extract industrial timber are only about 500,000 ha of a regional total of 3 million ha (Vanniere and Maurette 1995).

16 Assuming an annual rate of substitution of 20,000 ha per year for 40 years and a discount rate of 10 per cent.

17 CPMC Vice-President, Eliodoro Matte, has stated "The truth is that there is no more room for planting in Chile. Today we are planting in agricultural areas that used to be sown with wheat or grazed by cattle. As a result, we have been planting pine in Argentina which has large land areas in the north" (Estrategia 1996).

References

Banco Central de Chile (1995). *Proyecto de cuentas ambientales y bosque nativo*. Gerencia de Estudios, Departamento de Cuentas Ambientales, Santiago de Chile.

Bhagwati, J. (1996). "The demand to reduce domestic diversity among trading nations", in J. Bhagwati and R. E. Hudec (eds), *Fair Trade and Harmonization: Prerequisites for Free Trade?*, Volume 1, pp. 9–40. Cambridge, Mass.: MIT Press.

Bhagwati, J. and T. N. Srinivasan (1996). "Trade and the environment: does environmental diversity detract from the case for free trade?", in J. Bhagwati and R. E. Hudec (eds), *Fair Trade and Harmonization: Prerequisites for Free Trade?*, Volume 1, pp. 159–223. Cambridge, Mass.: MIT Press.

Carey, J. H. *et al.* (1993). *Recent Canadian Studies on the physiological effects of Pulp Mill Effluent on Fish*. National Water Research Institute, Burlington, Canada, cited in IIED (1996).

Corporación Nacional Forestal (CONAF) (1993). *Aplicación de la Legislación Forestal en Chile 1974–1992*. Informe Estadístico No. 39.

Decreto Ley No. 873 (1975). *Aprueba Convención sobre el Comercio Internacional de Especies Amenazadas de Fauna y Flora Silvestre*. Published in the Official Gazette of the Republic of Chile.

Ditz, D., J. Ranganathan and D. Banks (eds) (1995). *Green Ledgers: Case Studies in Corporate Environmental Accounting*. World Resources Institute Books.

Donoso, C. and A. Lara (1996). "Utilización de los bosques nativos en Chile: pasado, presente y futuro", in J. Armesto, C. Villagrán and Mary K. Arroyo (eds), *Ecología de los Bosques Nativos de Chile*. Vicerrectoría Académica, Universidad de Chile; Editorial Universitaria, Santiago de Chile, pp. 363–87.

Econoticias (1992). "175 millones de dólares en mejoramiento ambiental invirtió la industria chilena de celulosa y papel en la última década", *Ambiente y Desarrollo*, p. 75.

Economist The (1993). "The greening of protectionism", pp. 19–22.

Estrategia (1996). *Eliodoro Matte Larraín. Nuestra definición estratégica es clara: nos mantendremos en el área forestal*.

EULA – Chile (1995). *Diagnóstico del impacto de posibles restricciones ambientales sobre el sector exportador chileno*. Report prepared for the National Environment Commission, Universidad de Concepción.

Expert Panel (1995). *Summary comments of the Expert Panel Review to the US Environmental Protection Agency's Draft on Characterization of Potential Health Risks of 2,3,7,8 tetrachlorodibenzo-p-dioxin (TCDD) and Related Compounds*. Environ Corporation, Arlington, USA.

FAO (1994). *La CNUMAD en acción en el sector forestal*. Rome.

Fierro, G. and R. Morales (1994). "El subsidio forestal: evaluación y propuesta", *Revista Ingeniería de Sistemas*, vol. XI (2).

Fischer, R. D. (1996). *The Theory of Contingent Protection*. Center for Applied Economics, University of Chile. Santiago, Chile.

Gallon (1997). "The Gallon environmental letter", *Canadian Institute for Business and the Environment*, vol. 1 (20).

Géminis (1995). *Bosque Nativo en Chile. Análisis de desafíos y perspectivas. Discusión del proyecto de ley y formulación de una propuesta alternativa*. Santiago, Chile.

Grass, A. (1992). "Efectos ecológicos de las plantaciones de pino radiata", *CORMA Bulletin*.

Greenpeace (1996). *Body of Evidence*. Greenpeace UK, London. Cited in IIED, (1996).

Hartwig, C. Fernando (1994) *La tierra que recuperamos*. Editorial Los Andes, Santiago, Chile.

Hawkins Wright Ltd. (1996). *Outlook for Market Pulp Demand, Supply and Prices*.

Hodson, P. (1996). "Mixed function oxygenate induction by pulp mill effluents: advances since 1991", in M. R. Servos *et al.* (eds), *Environmental Fate and Effects of Pulp and Paper Mill Effluents*, St. Lucia Press, Delray Beach, Florida, USA. Cited in IIED (1996).

Instituto Forestal (INFOR) (1993). *Evaluación del Consumo de Leña en Chile – 1992*. National Energy Commission, Santiago, Chile.

Instituto Forestal (INFOR) (1995a). "Estadísticas forestales 1994", *Boletín Estadístico*, 40, Santiago, Chile.

Instituto Forestal (INFOR) (1995b). "Cuentas ambientales y bosque nativo" (Estudio del Banco Central), *El Mercurio*.

International Institute for Environment and Development (IIED) (1996). *Towards a Sustainable Paper Cycle*. London.

International Study Group on Sustainable Forest Management (1996). White Paper for the Second Meeting: 28 February to 1 March, Standards New Zealand Secretariat.

Katz, R. and G. del Fávero (eds) (1995). "Proposición conceptual para el uso de instrumentos económicos aplicables al bosque nativo", *Documento de trabajo* 238, Centro de Estudios Públicos.

Lara, A., C. Donoso and J. C. Aravena (1996). "La conservación del bosque nativo en Chile: problemas y desafíos", in J. Armesto, C. Villagrán and Mary K. Arroyo (eds), *Ecología de los Bosques Nativos de Chile*. Vicerrectoría Académica, Universidad de Chile; Editorial Universitaria, Santiago, Chile, pp. 335–62.

Larraín, S. and V. Menotti (1998). "Implicancias de la globalización económica y el libre comercio sobre la biodiversidad y los bosques de Chile", in Defensores del Bosque Chileno (ed.), *La Tragedia del Bosque Chileno*, Santiago, Chile, pp. 329–39.

Moore, C. and A. Miller (1994). *Green Gold*, Beacon Press, Boston, Estados Unidos.

OECD (1997). *EcoLabelling: Actual Effects of Selected Programmes*. Paris, OCDE/GD(97)105.

O'Ryan, R. and A. Ulloa (1996). *Amenazas al comercio internacional chileno por consideraciones ambientales*. Center for Applied Economics, University of Chile. Santiago, Chile.

Otero, L. (1998). "Efectos de la sustitución de bosques nativos por plantaciones de especies exóticas en Chile", in Defensores del Bosque Chileno, *La Tragedia del Bosque Chileno*, Santiago, Chile, pp. 295–7.

Porter, M. E. and C. Van der Linde (1995). "Green and competitive: ending the stalemate", *Harvard Business Review*.

Roxo, A. (1999). *Forestry Certification as a Market Instrument – Latest Developments and Challenges Ahead*. FAO Advisory Committee on Paper and Wood Products, Fortieth Session – Sao Paulo.

Schmidt, H. (1994). "Silvicultura y sustentabilidad en bosques de lenga de producción en Magallanes", in *Seminario sobre Medio Ambiente, Biodiversidad y Actividades Productivas*. Santiago, Chile, pp. 107–17.

Schmidt, H. and J. Caldentey (1994). *Silvicultura de los bosques de lenga. Notes for the third course*. CONAF, Corma-Austral, University of Chile. Punta Arenas.

Scholz, I., K. Block, K. Feil, M. Krause, K. Nakonz and C. Oberle (1994). *Medio Ambiente y Competitividad: El Caso del Sector Exportador Chileno*. Instituto Alemán de Desarrollo, Estudios e Informes No. 13/1994. Berlin.

Sheenan, M. J. (1994). *The Greening of Trade Policy. Sustainable Development and Global Trade*. CEI Environmental Studies Programs, USA.

Susaeta, Eladio (1995). "La responsabilidad del Banco Central", *El Mercurio*.

Turner, K., D. Pearce and I. Bateman (1993). *Environmental Economics, an Elementary Introduction*. Baltimore: John's Hopkins University Press.

Universidad Austral de Chile, Pontificia Universidad Católica de Chile and Universidad Católica de Temuco (1997). *Catastro y Evaluación de los Recursos Vegetacionales Nativos de Chile*. Proyecto CONAF – CONAMA – BIRF. Informe Nacional Con Variables Ambientales.

Vanniere, B. and A. Maurette (1995). *Auditoría Ambiental de los Bosques Nativos de Lenga de la Patagonia*. Office National des Forêts de Francia.

Van der Zwaag, D. (1996). "CEPA and the precautionary principle approach", Marine and Environmental Law Program, mimeo.

Veblen, T. T., T. Kitzberger, B. R. Burns and A. J. Revertus (1996). "Perturbaciones y dinámica de regeneración en bosques andinos del sur de Chile y Argentina", in J. Armesto, C. Villagrán and Mary K. Arroyo (eds), *Ecología de los Bosques Nativos de Chile*. Vicerrectoría Académica, Universidad de Chile; Editorial Universitaria, Santiago, Chile, pp. 169–98.

World Bank The (1994). *Chile. Managing Environmental Problems: Economic Analysis of Selected Issues. Latin America and Caribbean Regional Office.* Confidential Report No. 13061–CH.

8
Protection and Labor Standards

Alejandra Mizala and Pilar Romaguera[*]

1 Introduction

Discussion of labor standards has surfaced once more in the context of trade negotiations at the bilateral and multilateral level, as well as in regional trade agreements. Certain national governments, along with the European parliament and unions in industrialized countries, have argued in favor of drafting social clauses into the World Trade Organization (WTO), so as to comply more fully with the provisions of International Labor Organization (ILO) conventions. Moreover, negotiations relating to the North American Free Trade Agreement (NAFTA) raised the need to include requirements on labor standards as part of any agreement, so as to avoid the effects of so-called "social dumping".[1] The argument is that fair trade should be a precondition for free trade.

The fair-trade argument posits that producers in developed countries are not competing on equal terms, because they have to comply with more demanding labor standards than their counterparts in developing countries. Developing-country producers are thus being subsidized, and they can practice what is defined as social dumping. It is also feared that firms in developed countries might be forced to lower labor standards as a way of enhancing their ability to compete in international markets, or else shift investments to developing countries. In such conditions, it is argued, free trade with developing countries will tend to lower the real wages of unskilled workers in developed countries.[2]

[*] We are grateful for help from Andrea Butelmann, Guillermo Campero, María Ester Feres and Manuel Parra as well as comments from Alex Galetovic and participants in the "New Faces of Protectionism" seminar. We also acknowledge efficient collaboration from Claudia Araya. This chapter is indebted to the support from FONDECYT Project N°. 1960705.

Calls for fair trade focus on the harmonization of domestic labor policies and standards between countries. Labor standards include rules and regulations relating to the population's working conditions: minimum wages, restrictions on child labor, labor health and safety, freedom of association and collective bargaining, conditions for dismissal and non-discrimination by gender and race, among other issues.

The aim of this chapter is to analyze the interaction between labor standards and trade, in particular the extent to which labor standards could be used to justify restrictions on Chilean exports. We are interested in restrictions actually in force, as well as more subtle ones whereby the possibility of sanctions being imposed could force Chilean producers to raise their standards and so increase costs (potential protection).

Potential protection might be less important in labor issues than in environmental ones, because the changes needed in the environmental domain involve investments that take time to carry out. Raising labor standards, on the other hand, although as costly in resource terms as investing in cleaner technologies, can be done in a shorter time thus affording quicker reaction against possible export restrictions.[3] Moreover, verification of compliance with labor standards is more difficult, so these are easier to evade. One area where potential protection might be relevant is labor health and safety, since raising standards here might require investments that would take longer to carry out.

This study focuses on the USA and Canada, because, among Chile's potential trade partners, these are the most likely to threaten trade restrictions on the grounds of non-compliance with labor standards. In fact, a labor side agreement was included in the treaty Chile negotiated with Canada similar to that signed by the NAFTA countries,[4] although it does not contemplate trade sanctions.

The rest of this chapter is organized as follows. The first section critically analyzes the arguments in favor of making labor standards a condition for international trade. The second section describes negotiations on labor issues that have been carried out in the context of NAFTA, and the labor disputes that have arisen between the member countries of that agreement. In the third section we compare a series of current labor standards in Chile and the NAFTA countries, to determine whether there are significant differences that might give rise to demands to harmonize standards, or justify protectionist actions that would harm Chile. In this section also the analysis is taken further by making case studies of the main export sectors; the aim here is to analyze whether there are labor problems in these sectors that could be used against Chile in future trade negotiations. The final section presents the conclusions of this study.

2 Labor regulations as a justification for protection

A series of arguments have been put forward for making international trade conditional on compliance with labor standards. In the first place, there is concern that low labor standards might be unfair, in the sense of distorting international trade by artificially reducing production costs in the country with lower standards. It is argued that trade liberalization should be undertaken subject to the condition that countries ratify compliance with minimum labor standards (Edgren 1979; Charnovitz 1987; Walwei and Werner 1993). The second argument in favor of establishing similar labor standards between countries is that stronger international competition might lead certain countries to lower their standards, or else not enforce them, as a means of maintaining their ability to compete in foreign markets; in other words it could lead to social dumping.[5] Finally, a moral-type argument has been put forward which holds that trade should not be an end in itself, but should make possible an increase in workers' living standards by ensuring adequate working conditions; this would be achieved by establishing minimum standards at the international level (Collingsworth, Goold and Harvey 1994; Charnovitz 1994).[6] However, several authors stress that the labor standards chosen by a country are a function of its development level, so the imposition of predetermined labor standards might have harmful effects on growth and trade. According to this view, working conditions will naturally improve with economic development, so it is more important to worry about increasing trade than about imposing restrictions and regulations (Fields 1990; Park 1993).

It has also been argued (Bhagwati 1994; Lawrence 1995; Bhagwati and Srinivasan 1996) that the harmonization and enforcement of standards is not necessary for international trade to provide mutual gains to participating countries. On the contrary, a *diversity* of domestic policies, institutions and standards is perfectly compatible with mutually beneficial free trade. According to the traditional theory of international trade, the gains from trade come precisely from the differences between countries, which specialize in producing goods where they have comparative advantages, and import from other countries those goods in which domestic production is relatively more expensive; leading to increase in national consumption and welfare. Differences that generate comparative advantages for a country relate not only to its endowment of productive factors, its technology or its preferences, but also to differences in the social determinants of costs such as regulations, institutions and public policies.

Studies carried out among OECD countries (Ehrenberg 1994; OECD 1994) conclude that the different social-benefit systems and labor regulations of these countries has not been a significant barrier to economic integration. It is argued that while different labor regulations might slightly change the pattern of losers and gainers from economic integration, the number of losers would not increase significantly. For this reason some governments, employers and economists have opposed setting up social clauses, as these would reduce the competitive advantages of developing nations and facilitate disguised protection by countries with higher labor costs. However, there is significant disagreement among the governments of the G7 countries as to whether social clauses need to be included in trade agreements. France and the USA argue that labor standards should be included on the trade agenda; the United Kingdom, Germany and Japan strongly oppose discussing them.[7]

The arguments for and against setting minimum labor standards need to be assessed in terms of international trade theory. In what follows, we try to answer the following question: are there situations where, from the economic-efficiency standpoint, it is justified to make international trade conditional on compliance with minimum labor standards? Three cases need to be distinguished, depending on the effects that labor standards may have on production costs in the country imposing them (Cooper 1994; Lawrence 1995). The first is the case where labor standards and policies may have no effect at all on production costs in the country imposing them, and therefore would not have any effect on other countries. The second is the situation where labor policies and standards might have an effect on production costs in the country imposing them, and hence its capacity to compete internationally. Finally, there is the case where the existence of externalities implies that labor policies and regulations in one country might affect other countries even if they do not directly alter production costs: for example, migration flows from one country to the other, caused by sharp differences in labor standards. Each of these situations is analyzed below.

The first case occurs when labor standards are financed by payroll taxes, and the supply of labor is inelastic. In these circumstances the higher costs are borne by workers through lower salaries, and international trade is not affected. The same would happen if workers' valuation of the benefits associated with the standards were equal to the cost to their employers.[8] If, for these reasons, the standards one country imposes do not affect its labor costs and hence its capacity to compete in foreign markets, there is no efficiency justification for making trade conditional on the imposition of such standards.

The second case involves labor policies or standards that do impact the market through their effect on production costs. These are standards whose costs cannot be completely passed on to workers, either because their valuation of the benefits is not equal to the cost incurred by employers, or because they are not transferable – for example, the prohibition of child labor. In these circumstances, the setting of standards affects production costs and therefore could affect trade, provided there are other countries that can produce the goods the country trades internationally, at lower cost.

When regulations or standards affect costs, their incidence falls on the least mobile factor of production. For this reason, as labor is less mobile than capital, it is common for groups interested in raising domestic labor standards to oppose trade liberalization with countries whose standards are lower.[9] This would explain why organized workers in the United States lobbied strongly for common labor standards to be imposed on all NAFTA member countries, as this treaty would increase capital mobility (Lawrence 1995).

Nevertheless, from the economic-efficiency standpoint, it is not clear that any given country's standards should be imposed on other countries, or that their adoption should be a precondition for trade agreements. As was mentioned above, the traditional theory of international trade argues that the benefits of trade come precisely from allowing countries to be different: there is no reason why differences in labor standards should have to play a different role to differences in factor endowments (Bhagwati 1994).[10]

Furthermore, insofar as labor standards are established to compensate for failures in domestic labor markets, and as these market failures are very unlikely to be uniform across countries, the harmonization of standards will not necessarily lead to an increase in welfare. Thus, as a rule, one should expect a wide diversity of labor conditions between countries, and trade that arises on the basis of such differences should not be deemed unfair, provided standards are consistent with an efficient use of resources (Brown, Deardorff and Stern 1996).

Moreover, uncertainty about the optimum standard to be imposed on all countries suggests the need for caution and flexibility. Imposing an incorrect standard on all countries could have negative welfare consequences, and prevent learning opportunities based on experimentation with different standards (Klerovic 1996).

Finally, the third case to be considered is where the market does not allocate resources efficiently, due to the presence of externalities. For example, labor regulations and standards in one country might affect a second country through migratory flows provoked by the differences in standards.[11] In cases where the effects are not only pecuniary, the harmonization of standards might be justified. For example, the European Union, whose goals include the free movement of workers between member countries, has taken steps to establish common standards.

One final issue that cannot be ignored is the degree of compliance with standards. Many countries have made commitments to respect the labor standards imposed by the ILO; however, they do not necessarily enforce them. The question here is whether it is advisable to use international trade restrictions to punish those who do not comply with the standards they have signed up to. Some authors (Lawrence 1995; De Castro 1995; Steil 1994) argue that the long-term solution to this problem is not to restrict trade but to raise these countries' incomes, because the problem arises from income differences rather than different ethical values.[12] If this is so, trade restrictions would tend to retard growth and hence the improvement of labor standards.

In the short run, compliance with labor standards can be encouraged through explicit compensation systems, whereby the country obtains something in exchange for complying with the regulation. This is the approach followed in NAFTA with Mexico. In this treaty, no new standards were imposed on Mexico, but it was required to enforce its own legislation; in exchange, preferential access was granted to Canadian and US markets. Along the same lines, a cooperative approach, as opposed to a coercive one, has been followed by the European Union. No standards were imposed on the more backward member-countries, but they were paid from Brussels to raise their standards. It could be argued that US policy fits into the same framework with its Generalized System of Preferences (GSP), which since 1984 has been granting lower tariffs to developing countries that adhere to basic labor standards (although some would argue that the USA has managed the GSP basically to serve its own political interests (De Castro 1995)).[13]

One alternative is to use a system of labeling, where labels publicize the fact that a product was made by workers who are not protected by certain standards. Thus informed, consumers may freely decide whether or not to buy the product. This mechanism has mostly been used in cases of non-compliance with environmental standards, but it could be extended to the labor field in the future. Obviously, such a solution assumes labelers act in good faith.

From the analytical discussion above, it can be inferred that arguments for linking labor standards to trade are only justified in the case of a common market with free movement of labor.[14] In the other cases there are no solid economic reasons for making labor standards a precondition for international trade. Furthermore, in our judgment, there is sufficient evidence to support the view that economic development is one of the main determinants of the labor standards adopted by a country.

In addition, if one wants to encourage compliance with universally valid minimum labor standards for ethical reasons, one should reward or compensate those who comply with them, rather than punishing those who do not through trade restrictions, as this worsens the working conditions of the population in the sanctioned countries.

The analysis above suggests that there is no justification for the demand of harmonization of labor standards in negotiations between Chile and NAFTA, or when entering into bilateral free trade agreements with developed countries. However, Chile can be required to enforce its own legislation, since their aim should be resolving failures in the domestic labor market, as well as being consistent with the country's development level. In this way, conditions demanded of Chile would be similar to those established with Mexico in the Labor Cooperation Agreement. The next section describes this NAFTA side-agreement and analyzes certain labor disputes that have arisen between Mexico and the USA.

3   The labor agreement in NAFTA

Labor standards take on a special importance in discussions concerning economic integration agreements. In this section we describe the labor negotiations and agreements that have been reached in NAFTA; in addition, labor disputes that have arisen between member countries are analyzed, and lessons are drawn which may be of interest to Chile and other developing countries considering a FTA with developed countries.

The NAFTA case is relevant, for in the 1990s Chile chose to complement its unilateral liberalization policy by signing economic integration treaties with specific countries. Of their current or future trade partners in such agreements, the USA and Canada are those most likely to be able to threaten trade restrictions on the grounds of noncompliance with labor standards. In fact, a labor side-agreement similar to that signed by the NAFTA countries was included in the agreement Chile negotiated with Canada, However, the free trade agreement Chile signed with Mexico in 1991 does not have one.[15]

3.1 Negotiations in NAFTA

Although the initial NAFTA treaty did not address labor issues, they were introduced by the Clinton administration in the labor side-agreement known as the North American Agreement on Labor Cooperation (NAALC). This seeks to take account of the concerns of unions and worker organizations that had been ignored in the initial stages of the negotiations, when they were deemed inappropriate for discussion in the context of a free trade agreement. The NAALC recognizes that each NAFTA country has autonomous and distinct labor legislation, but it requires this to be enforced by each country. The strengthening of legislation is aimed firstly at the tradable-goods production sector, as non-compliance with standards in this sector might affect trade flows between member countries. Secondly, it relates specifically to three types of labor regulations: minimum wages, child labor and labor health and safety standards. Action can only be taken when there is evidence that some of these mutually recognized standards are persistently not being complied with.

In addition, countries commit themselves to promoting a set of labor principles such as the prohibition of bonded labor, the elimination of job discrimination by gender, race and social condition, the equalization of wages between men and women in the same establishment, protection for child and immigrant labor, and the existence of insurance for job-related illnesses. In these areas, an expert appraisal committee can be called to investigate, but only in productive sectors that trade internationally, and only if the country concerned has national laws protecting such rights.

The NAALC seeks to raise new issues for discussion in the labor field, and improve the level of information and public knowledge concerning countries' labor legislation, both through access to information and by education. The issues considered are: union organization, collective bargaining, gender equality at work, productivity and quality, and labor training, as well as other issues which the three countries may agree to include.[16]

Basically, the NAALC promotes the development of supervisory institutions in member countries, as well as adequate access to labor tribunals for employers and workers as a way of strengthening compliance with national labor legislation.

The institutional framework on which the agreement rests, consists of a trinational commission known as the Commission for Labor

Cooperation, consisting of a Council of Ministers, and a small secretariat (with a maximum team of 15 people located in the USA) assisted by groups of national experts and national government organizations. The Ministerial Council is the governing body of the Commission for Labor Cooperation, and its aim is to promote cooperation activities between the parties. In addition, a National Administrative Office (NAO) was set up in each of the countries, to act as liaison with other government agencies, as well as with other NAOs and with the Executive Secretariat of the Agreement. These offices hear complaints on labor issues arising in the other countries, and have to review them in accordance with the legislation of the country in question.

Disputes have to be resolved in accordance with a strict (and lengthy) procedure that includes discussion, investigation and, ultimately, during the first year of the agreement, fines of up to US$ 20 million. In subsequent years, the size of the fine depends on the growth of intraregional trade. Fines are imposed on governments (not firms) for non-compliance with national standards. The possibility of suspending NAFTA tariff benefits (by an amount equivalent to the fine) is only contemplated if monetary sanctions are not respected. Thus, trade restrictions are considered only as a last resort to compel a country to enforce its own labor standards. The possibility of trade restrictions would only affect Mexico and the USA, as Canada did not agree to this measure.[17]

The NAALC has been criticized for being less comprehensive and less complete than the environmental agreement, which is said to be better in terms of transparency, coverage and accessibility. Some sectors hoped the NAALC would include the imposition of minimum labor standards on all countries, and would consider the issue of human rights as part of workers rights (see Collingsworth, Goold and Harvey 1994).

3.2 Cases of labor dispute in NAFTA

It would be premature at this stage to assess the extent to which the NAALC will cover other issues in the future, or move towards more homogeneous labor standards between member countries. However, an analysis of certain labor disputes that have arisen within the NAALC framework are already suggesting interesting conclusions. In what follows, we analyze four labor disputes that have been brought before the relevant NAALC agencies. These have revolved around issues of union freedom, in terms of principles and degree of compliance, and correspond to the broadest group of labor standards, covered by the NAALC, which can give rise to consultations between the respective governments but do not lead to sanctions.

The first case was presented by a coalition of United States unions, non-governmental groups and Mexican workers, who complained against a *maquiladora* (a subsidiary of SONY Corporation located in Nuevo Laredo, Mexico) for firing workers who tried to set up an independent union.[18] The complaint was upheld by the United States National Administrative Office (NAO), which ruled that there were responsibilities and/or failings on the part of the Mexican labor authority.[19] The case went as far as the Labor Commission, which carried out a formal consultation process between the Mexican and the United States labor authorities. The outcome of these consultations led to the Mexican labor authorities assisting SONY workers with legal funds to register their independent union.

The second case involves a complaint by a Mexican telephonists' union and two North American unions against the Sprint company, which closed down one of its plants in California and dismissed workers before they voted to affiliate to the Communications Union.[20] The petitions placed before the Mexican NAO included the rehiring of the 235 fired workers and a ban on Sprint setting up in Mexico. This is an interesting case, as it alleges non-compliance with labor legislation in the United States, and the negotiations involved political authorities at the Labor Secretary level in the USA and Mexico. Moreover, it has generated widespread publicity because, as a result of an agreement between the Labor Secretaries of Mexico and United States, the US Department of Labor held a public forum to allow the interested parties to express their points of view. It was finally decided to take the case to the Labor Commission, which is currently studying the case.

Two other cases have attracted less attention, as they have been rejected by the Mexican NAO. In one of them, an electricians' union filed a complaint against General Electric of Mexico for the unfair dismissal of workers who were trying to set up a union. The same happened when a Mexican truckers' union brought an action against the Honeywell company.

Although these experiences are very recent, certain interesting conclusions can be drawn.

In the first place, despite the short time that has elapsed and the criticisms that have been made against the NAALC for being difficult to operate, the agreement has proved its effectiveness on member countries. This is because its very existence turns each country's labor legislation into a "binding constraint" – a relevant issue when one considers that many developing countries have legislation involving a mountain of rules that seek to protect workers, many of which are not enforced. A labor side-agreement with the characteristics discussed above, acts as an additional external pressure to enforce legislation that might be more important than direct supervision by Labor Ministries. The inclusion of labor side-agreements in free trade treaties can also help get socially desirable labor standards adopted. By acting under the auspices of international treaties, governments increase their bargaining power in relation to powerful interest groups that might oppose the introduction of rules that are not to their liking.

Pressure to enforce national legislation has been strengthened not only by defining rules, but also by setting up a specific institutional framework. This has the virtue of making it possible to analyze "limiting cases" which, while not directly contravening the legislation (or this is difficult to prove), do act against its spirit. The existence of these agreements raises the political cost of not enforcing a country's own labor legislation.

Secondly, side-agreements and the institutions set up under their auspices have indirectly provided the possibility of international union coordination, on issues such as the promotion of standards similar to those in developed countries for subsidiaries of multinational firms located in developing countries.

The NAFTA labor side-agreement could be used as a tool of potential protection, although it has not been so used up to now. Parties to the agreement can force a member to take measures that raise labor costs, in order to avoid possible restrictions on its exports. However, the cases analyzed suggest that the agreement is being used more as a tool to improve the domestic enforcement of labor legislation than as a tool of protection.

4 Labor legislation: is there scope for protectionist arguments against Chile?

This section analyzes Chile's labor laws compared to legislation in the countries that would be its trading partners in NAFTA: Canada, USA and Mexico, focusing on NAALC issues as well as those that have arisen in the negotiations for a treaty with Canada. The comparison with Mexican labor legislation is interesting, not so much to assess whether differences might give rise to protectionist arguments, but because Mexico is an example of a developing country that has joined an association with developed countries, and thus serves as a reference point.

The fact that agreements like NAFTA put pressure on countries to respect their own legislation, increases the importance of studying the legislation *per se*, as they turn it into a set of binding constraints. In this sense the degree to which legislation is enforced becomes a critical issue, as it is precisely non-compliance that gives rise to fines and trade restrictions. Finally, while the "quality" of the legislation (the degree of protection it affords to workers) is not an issue that arises in the letter of the Agreements, it does feature strongly in the international press and the platforms of certain pressure groups, in the context of bilateral and multilateral agreements.

As we shall see, Chilean legislation satisfies the principles discussed in NAFTA. Furthermore, Chile is one of the countries that have ratified most ILO conventions, and its legislation is quite uniform, with few exceptions favoring specific pressure groups. In this sense, from the standpoint of the letter of the law, it would seem there are no substantial issues of controversy, which might be turned into arguments for potential protection in the future.

However, USA and particularly Canada have expressed worries about certain Chilean export sectors where there might be problems of non-compliance with labor legislation, and/or working conditions that are particularly risky or harmful to workers' health. This concern has been expressed in the press, as well as in trade treaty negotiations and through demands made by international union organizations.

Against this backdrop, our research combines formal analysis of labor legislation with a discussion of controversial issues that come up in negotiations, and it provides a more in-depth study of four Chilean export sectors: forestry, salmon farming, mining and export fruit-growing. We have chosen these sectors because they account for a high percentage of Chile's exports and have been identified by opinion groups in Canada and USA as sectors where labor legislation is not fully enforced.

4.1 Comparative analysis of legislation: Chile and the NAFTA countries

The comparison of Chile's labor standards with those of the NAFTA countries is complicated by the fact that both Canada and the USA have highly decentralized legislation, with significant differences at the provincial and state level.

These countries obviously have the legislation that the NAALC establishes as a minimum requirement: minimum wages, protection for minors and standards on labor health and safety. As regards the more general regulations, Table 8.1 gives comparative figures for hours of work, termination of labor contracts, collective bargaining, the right to strike and maternity leave. Table 8.A1 in the Appendix details Chile's rules on labor health and safety.

The characteristics of Chilean regulations place the country in an intermediate position between Mexico, on the one hand, and Canada and USA, on the other. Chile has highly regulated legislation which requires formalization of the labor relation through a job contract, and establishes well-defined and homogeneous procedures across sectors of economic activity and regions of the country: for example, collective bargaining is regulated, as are strikes, dismissal, maternity leave, etc. At the same time, the legislation curtails intervention by workers (or unions) in aspects of company management and restricts state intervention in the private employer–employee relationship.

Mexico's legislation has more rigid rules in aspects such as hiring and firing, but gives more room for discretion or intervention by the public apparatus in labor relations, a characteristic that might make enforcing the legislation more difficult. For example, in Mexico there are preference clauses in hiring that do not exist in the other countries: unionized over non-unionized workers, Mexicans over non-Mexicans, and heads of households over non-heads.

Dismissal costs and conditions also vary between countries. Chile and Mexico use severance payments based on years of service as the main form of protection against unemployment, but, unlike Chile, severance pay in Mexico does not have a limit to the number of years that are considered in the severance payment. In the USA and Canada the employer is not obliged to pay redundancy on dismissal (unless this forms part of a voluntary agreement), the prevailing system of protection being unemployment insurance which does not exist in many Latin American countries. In the case of Mexico there are further difficulties in dismissing a worker: dismissal due to the economic needs of the firm is not considered a just cause, nor are technological change or the need to replace workers with others with different skills. It is compulsory to reinstate a worker who has been fired without just cause; the worker has the right to claim lost wages (due to unjustified dismissal or strike) and there are penalties on the employer for unjustified dismissal.

In the collective bargaining sphere, the differences between national legislations relate to who can represent workers, and how regulated the bargaining and strike process is. In all countries, strikes have to be declared by a majority of the workers involved, through a voting process in a workers' assembly. However, in Mexico alone, the vote does not have to be secret, replacements cannot be hired during the strike,

Table 8.1 Aspects of labor legislation: NAFTA

	Canada	Mexico	United States	Chile
Working day				
Maximum length	40 to 48 hrs per week.[1]	48 hrs per week and 8 per day.	40hrs. [2]	10hrs per day and 48 per week.
Overtime pay	50%	50–75% (more than 9hrs a week).	50%	50%
Termination of labor relation				
Unemployment insurance	Yes	No	Yes	No[3]
Maximum duration	50 weeks		26 weeks	
Initial gross replacement rate (per cent)	50 %		60 %	
Compensation	No	Yes. 3 months' wages plus 32 days per year.	No	Yes. One month per year, to a maximum of 330 days.
Collective bargaining				
Who can negotiate?	Unions certified by the Labor Relations Board (in each jurisdiction).	Unions registered in the STYPS[4] (Federal jurisdiction).	Unions registered in the NLRB.[5]	Firm unions or worker groups.
Only one union negotiates per firm?		Yes	Yes	No
Validity of a union	Certified by the Labor Relations Board.	Show affiliation, not necessary to represent the majority; minimum of 20 workers.	The NLRB organizes elections and recognizes the union representing the majority; minimum 2 workers.	Depends on the percentage they represent or whether membership exceeds 250; minimum 8 people.
Workers can vote for "no union"?		No.	Yes.	No.
Duration of collective bargaining contracts		Definite or indefinite time period, but subject to review every two years with regard to general working conditions, and every year regarding wages.	Not regulated but in practice contracts last three years.	Cannot be less than two years.

(*Cont. overleaf*)

Table 8.1 (contd.)

	Canada	Mexico	United States	Chile
Are exclusion clauses allowed?[6]	Allowed but under certain conditions.	Yes.	Yes, under certain conditions.	No.
Right to strike clause	If no agreement is reached in the collective bargaining process.	This right can be exercised where the employer refuses to sign a collective bargaining contract.	If there is no agreement in the collective bargaining process.	If there is no agreement in the collective bargaining process.
Notice of strike		6 days and 10 in public service.	60 days.	Within the bargaining process.
When is a strike legal?	Within the collective bargaining process.	For breach of contract, for imbalance between factors of production.	Decided by the NLRB: economic causes for undesirable work practices.	Within the collective bargaining process.
Strike within duration of a collective bargaining contract	Prohibited.	Yes. (Strike in solidarity or for political ends.)	Not prohibited but there are voluntary prohibition clauses.	Prohibited.
Hiring replacements	Permitted (except in Quebec).	Not allowed.	Allowed. (Depends on circumstances).	Allowed.
Maternity leave				
Maternity rest period	17–18 weeks, without pay.	12 weeks, with pay.	Does not exist.	18 weeks, with a right to 100 % of the wage.

Notes:
[1] Depends on the provinces. Contractual hours =48.
[2] Federal Law does not establish the maximum number of hours for workers in general, but stipulates that overtime should be paid when more than 40 hours are worked per week.
[3] There is an unemployment subsidy, but only for low-income workers and with reduced coverage.
[4] STYPS: Labor Secretariat.
[5] NLRB: National Labor Relations Board.
[6] In Collective Bargaining Contracts so-called "Exclusion Clauses" oblige the employer to hire exclusively union members and to terminate labor contracts with those who resign or are expelled from the union. This does not affect workers who were employed before the signing of the collective bargaining contract.
Source: Prepared by the authors on the basis of official data from the respective countries.

strikes in essential services are tolerated and, in practice, a strike can be ended by Labor Ministry intervention.

In contrast, in neither Chile nor the USA can strikes be called within the duration of a collective bargaining contract, and when strikes are legally called, replacements can be hired while it lasts.

Thus in Mexico – unlike what happens in Chile, USA and Canada – interference by state and unions takes precedence over the individual actions of employers and workers.

Chile, meanwhile, has more uniform and regulated legislation than the USA in aspects such as conditions for hiring and firing and maternity protection. In both Chile and Mexico there are rules guaranteeing maternity leave on full pay, whereas the USA has no legislation regulating this, and Canada gives only 17 weeks' leave without pay. In this sense, while the USA and Canada have more developed legislation for gender equality as regards employment and wages, Mexico and Chile have more protective rules on maternity.

In the spirit of the NAFTA agreement discussed above, Chile would seem not to have problems on labor legislation issues, as it already has the required rules and procedures in place. Nor does it have regulations that could be classified as excessive or very tough, which would be more difficult to enforce, as NAFTA would require.

The biggest difference between Chile's legislation and Mexico's is that the latter is less flexible and more discretionary. Compared to the USA and Canada, the biggest differences would seem to relate to labor health and safety regulations and aspects of gender discrimination, where the North American legislation is more comprehensive.

On aspects of labor health and safety, Chile has quite an elaborate system of regulations compared with other Latin American countries; for example, it is compulsory for firms to take out insurance against workplace accidents with private mutual-fund insurance companies, known as Mutuales de Seguridad, which also have the function (and incentive) to prevent work accidents. However, there appear to be specific compliance problems in certain export sectors.[21]

4.2   Case study: Are there potential conflicts for Chilean exporters?

The analysis of labor legislation in Chile compared to the NAFTA countries enables us to conclude that there are no labor legislation problems that might give rise to trade restrictions.

However, there does seem to be concern about legislation in certain export-oriented sectors, either because the legislation is not enforced, or because it fails to protect workers' rights adequately. Our interest in this section is to look deeper into this issue, with an analysis of the mining, fruit growing, salmon farming and forestry sectors.[22]

It is worth mentioning that although aspects of labor health and safety may be the most serious in terms of threatening Chile's exports, these are not necessarily the most serious labor problems facing the country.[23]

Our aim here is not to make an overall assessment of the degree to which Chile's labor legislation is enforced, nor discuss whether the arguments put forward are ethically correct or not. The aim is to establish whether there are situations that could be used as justification for trade restrictions on labor-related grounds. Such restrictions may arise either through the cancellation of an existing concession or the denial of new ones, by refusing to sign a preferential trade agreement.

4.2.1 Aggregate indicators

An initial indicator of a high degree of compliance with labor legislation is the fact that 82 per cent of wage-earners report that they have a formal job contract (according to data from the 1992 National household survey). The existence of a contract generally means that the worker is affiliated to a pension fund and health insurance scheme (in either the private or public system).[24]

In addition, as part of the social security system, employers have to insure workers against workplace accidents and professional illnesses.[25] The most general scheme is social security against the risk of Workplace Accidents and Professional Illnesses (Law 16.744, 1968).[26]

This mandatory insurance is financed by employers who pay a basic premium of 0.9 per cent of the taxable payroll, on top of which there is an additional differentiated premium that depends on the risks involved in the activity, not exceeding 3.4 per cent of taxable wages.

Despite the obligatory nature of this insurance, not all the labor force is protected; however, coverage has increased steadily, thereby indicating a greater degree of formalization of labor relations. According to the Department of Occupational Health, 63 per cent of the employed labor force in 1993 was covered by the insurance,[27] a figure that rises to 93 per cent if only dependent workers (i.e. not self-employed) are included; that is, there is a high affiliation rate for dependent workers.

The law has established a series of instruments for preventing workplace hazards, including Risk Prevention Departments in firms with more than 100 workers, as well as Joint Hygiene and Safety Committees (Comités Paritarios de Higiene y Seguridad) in firms with more than 25 workers, and premiums that rise according to a firm's accident rate.

Table 8.2 Fatal professional injuries (no. of injuries per 1,000 workers)

Country	1985	1986	1987	1988
Chile[1]	0.030	0.080	0.060	0.100
Peru[1]	0.060	0.050	0.057	0.060
Mexico[2]	0.160	0.180	0.150	0.140
Spain[2]	0.138	0.129	0.134	0.139
Netherlands[2]	0.050	0.040	0.040	0.040
Canada[3]	0.080	0.077	0.079	0.086
France[3]	0.079	0.074	0.075	0.081

Notes:
[1] Compensated injuries to insured workers.
[2] Injuries declared among insured workers.
[3] Compensated injuries among employed workers.
Source: Labor Statistics Yearbook, 1995.

The available data on job accident rates is quite fragmentary, and international comparisons are difficult because the information is not always compatible. However, the figures presented in Table 8.2 are a useful illustration of the fact that the rate of professional injuries in Chile is at intermediate level between developed and developing countries.[28]

The figures for Chile also show that during the initial years of the insurance – the system was set up in 1969 – the rate of workplace accidents fell sharply, but then it leveled out at around 12 per cent, according to data from the Chilean Insurance Association (ACHS); further significant reductions have not been achieved over the past ten years (see Table 8.3).

In addition to this, the work carried out by the Mutual Associations to reduce workplace hazards has reduced the seriousness of accidents. Information from the SNSS, the National Health Service System for 1993, shows that only 0.08 per cent of workplace accidents in firms affiliated to Mutual Associations resulted in the death of a worker, and in 99.6 per cent of cases disability was only temporary.[29]

Accident rates vary between different economic activities, the highest rates occurring in construction, mining, industry and agriculture.

Table 8.3 Accident rate (rate per 100 workers)

1969	1973	1978	1983	1988	1992	1993
35.3	17.0	12.7	9.1	10.8	11.9	11.8

Source: ACHS (affiliated firms).

Differences are reflected in hazard rates which, in turn, are a reflection of the effect of professional accidents and illnesses in terms of lost working days. The ratio between hazard rates in mining and in the services sector is between five and eight, among firms affiliated to Mutual Associations. Hazard rates also go down as firm-size increases. As regards professional illnesses, data problems are even greater, for illnesses tend not to be declared as it is sometimes difficult to associate an illness with undertaking a specific job. Moreover, administrative agencies do not have a legal obligation or incentive to undertake biological monitoring programs or early investigation of illnesses.

One of the main problems faced in the labor health and safety field is a lack of state supervisory capacity. This deficiency relates partly to the absence of suitable database systems and shortcomings in the capacity to process existing information. There are also problems in the demarcation of supervisory responsibilities between different state agencies.[30] Problems also stem from workers' low education levels and workplace attitudes that favor risky conduct. For example, one of the factors underlying the scant protection against pesticide use in agriculture is said to be the functional illiteracy of the rural population.[31]

Against this, it should be acknowledged that concern for labor health and safety issues has increased, both on the part of government agencies and in the business sector, especially among export-oriented firms.[32] In this context, there has been a notable increase in government supervision, which has meant increases in budget and staff assigned to these tasks, as well as a rise in the number of inspection units and an improvement in the institutional framework.[33]

Table 8.A2 in the Appendix shows how Labor Department budgets and staff have increased, as has the number of firms inspected.

Studies made by the Labor Department and NGOs, as well as conversations between government representatives and union and professional organizations responsible for inspection, show that the problems tend to be concentrated in specific areas:

- Sub-contracting firms: a lower degree of compliance with labor legislation can be seen here in terms of workers without contracts, noncompliance with work periods (hours, days and rest periods), higher accident rates and the repeated use of temporary contracts for permanent workers. In the export sector sub-contracting firms are important in mining and forestry.
- Duration of work periods in mining and export fruit-growing. Although the general rule in Chile is a 48–hour working week, with

a weekly rest period that should include Sunday, the legislation allows quite a lot of flexibility for the employer to define "special work routines".[34]

- Job safety rules in primary-sector activities. These are activities that are exposed to greater physical risk, either because the conditions of the activity itself are hazardous (use of explosives, felling of trees, work at sea), or due to the use of inputs (pesticides and chemical products) that may have adverse side-effects on workers.

These are the problems that seem to cause the greatest concern among our potential partners in developed countries – concerns that are expressed both in conversations held in the stages prior to treaty negotiations, and in articles in the international press.

4.2.2 Case studies

Below we analyze the labor health and safety situation in the four export sectors mentioned above: forestry, salmon farming, mining and fruit-growing. Table 8.4 shows the importance of these sectors in total exports in 1995.

The data we have collected on labor problems affecting these activities is based on surveys, interviews and analyses of specific cases, as well as partial inspections by the Labor Department. Accordingly, the information cannot be considered representative of the sector as a whole – still less of the Chilean economy as a whole. However, the data does show that there are certain labor problems in these sectors, which have given rise to allegations from abroad and which could become an issue in the context of a free trade agreement. It should be recalled that, in NAFTA, complaints brought before the NAO and the Labor Commission do not have to fulfill any criterion of representativeness.

Table 8.4 Chilean exports of selected products, 1995 (US$ million)

	Value	Percentage
Mining	7,785.2	48.5
Fresh fruit	1,027.4	6.4
Forestry	2,494.2	15.6
Salmon farming	388.0	2.4
Total exports	16,038.6	100.0

Source: Central Bank of Chile.

(i) The forestry sector.   Forestry activity has grown tremendously over the last few decades. Forested areas expanded by 277 per cent between 1973 and 1993, and this has meant a significant increase in the share of forestry products in total exports, rising by 245 per cent over the last two decades to 15.6 per cent in 1995. Forestry activities are mainly divided into two areas: artificial forestry plantation and exploitation of native forests. The latter activity is basically concentrated in Chilean Regions XI and XII.

Chile has adequate regulations in the field of health and safety, but these are not always complied with, owing partly to a lack of inspection capacity. An additional decisive factor is the nature of the work in certain sectors.

Such is the case in forestry, where many of the tasks are carried out by sub-contractors who do not have the skills needed to introduce satisfactory health and safety measures. Moreover, because of Chile's geographical characteristics, forests are located in zones of difficult access and far from urban areas, which, together with the seasonal nature of forestry activities, requires setting up temporary camps.

In the early 1980s, these camps were extremely precarious and did not provide workers with even minimal amenities (drinking water, toilets, showers, canteen). Over time, firms have gradually improved their infrastructure so as to ensure the provision of certain basic services (Apud and Valdés 1995).

A study carried out by Fundación Chile on a sample of 50 sub-contractors revealed that only 37 of them were providing their workers with satisfactory living conditions (drinking water, showers, toilet, canteen, light); the rest did not offer any kind of amenities. Out of the sample, 20 had regulations on labor health and safety, but only one had an organized system to ensure compliance with legal regulations, such as joint health and safety committees[35] (Apud and Ilabaca 1991). The big firms are supposed to make sub-contractors comply with the legislation, but not all of them do so.

The forestry sector has a high rate of accidents; according to Torres (1991) the accident rate in forestry management fluctuated between 22.1 per cent in 1987 and 18.6 per cent in 1990.[36] Figures are similar for the harvesting stage: 22.1 per cent in 1987 and 18.6 per cent in 1990.[37] Another source (Raga 1993) states that the accident rate in forestry harvesting was 17.2 per cent in 1992 – significantly higher than in New Zealand (3.6 per cent) or Canada (0.3 per cent). These rates are also nearly twice the average in Chile's industrial sector.

Another element that stands out is the seriousness of accidents. According to the available data, the average number of days lost in 1988 to accidents was 21.3 in forestry management and harvest (Apud and Valdés, 1995). Unfortunately we do not have figures to compare accident seriousness with other countries. However, the mortality rate in Chile per 1,000 workers exposed is three times higher than in Finland (0.51 in Chile, as an average for the periods 1984–87 and 1988, and 0.16 for Finland as an average of the period 1984–88 (ILO 1991)).

The causes of accidents can be ascribed to unsafe actions (73 per cent) and unsafe conditions (27 per cent). The former relate to the incorrect use, maintenance and transport of implements (52 per cent of cases), as well as incorrect handling of materials (35.8 per cent). In each case the problem is a lack of appropriate working methods, which in turn is a manifestation of lack of training. Training in the forestry sector is deficient because most contracts are temporary and there is high turn-over among the work force.[38] Failure to use personal protection elements accounts for 8.9 per cent of accidents. Unsafe conditions are caused by the topography of the terrain, a lack of protection and deficient maintenance of machinery, as well as vegetation and climate (Torres 1991).

Forestry workers also suffer from a variety of health problems deriving from their work: muscle and bone ailments caused by the manual handling of tree trunks, problems deriving from noise and vibration cause by chain saws, and illnesses resulting from exposure to extreme climatic conditions – scorching heat in summer and bitter cold in winter.

Below we discuss the results of the Labor Department inspection of the forestry sector carried out in 1994 and 1995, covering both artificial plantations and native forests. Problems were detected, although there are differences between regions.[39]

In Regions VII and VIII, where artificial plantations are mostly found, there has been greater formalization over recent years, as well as an increase in the mechanization of firms, which is evidence of higher investment levels.[40] Greater industrialization has led to improved working conditions and labor relations. However, in Region VII problems persist in camps that still do not meet standards. In Region VIII irregularities were detected such as out-of-date or unregistered job contracts, badly kept attendance records, excessive working hours, non-compliance with the weekly rest period, deficient operation or non-existence of joint committees, and the non-provision of personal protection elements to workers. Table 8.5 summarizes the inspections carried out in these regions in 1994 and 1995, and also indicates the existence of social security problems such as non-payment or non-declaration of social security contributions.

In Region IX few irregularities have been detected on matters relating to attendance records, weekly wage payments and rest periods. The Labor Department does not have information on compliance with standards relating to labor health and safety as it has not inspected this. However, a survey carried out in 1995 on 91 forestry workers from 13 camps in the region shows that less than 5 per cent of them had a permanent job contract, 84 per cent had a temporary contract for a specific job, and 7 per cent are in an irregular situation with no contract at all. Workers' average education level was six years of schooling, and two-thirds of workers had never received any training. In the period 1990–95 one-third of all workers suffered accidents – a lower figure than the forestry average, which is explained by the fact that it basically involved plantation maintenance activities (Unda and Stuardo 1996).

From Region X southward, there is even greater non-compliance, as this zone is basically given over to native forest management programs, an activity that is less industrialized and where living conditions are more precarious. In Region X itself there is not much forestry activity, and compliance with labor legislation is low, as revealed by a failure to make on-time wage payments in full, unwritten job contracts, excessive working hours, lack of continuity in the payment of social security contributions, poorly maintained camps, absence of prevention programs, and workplace accidents either badly cared for or not dealt with in timely fashion.

Inspections carried out in recent years in Region XI also detected non-compliance with labor standards: camps were in poor condition with egregious deficiencies as regards food and drinking water. Moreover, working days and times spent at distant work sites were excessively long, and there was an absence of accident prevention programs. Finally, various labor problems were also detected in Region XII, where there is an incipient forestry activity involving single firms operating with sub-contractors. Table 8.6 summarizes the deficiencies found in the 29 camps in this region, where 998 people are working, 50 per cent of whom are subject to some irregularity such as deficient labor health and safety (lack of drinking water, lack or insufficiency of hygiene services), illegal hours, arrears in wage payments, non-compliance with weekly rest periods, excessive hours of overtime and job contracts that fail to indicate the day or hours of work.

Table 8.5 Inspection of forestry sector in the VIIth and VIIIth Regions, 1994 and 1995

	Region VII		Region VIII	
	1994	1995	1994	1995
Firms inspected	175	85	198	283
No. of workers	3251	2549	4919	6301
Labor problems	17 fines for different reasons. Arrears in wage payments.	5 fines for different reasons. Arrears in wage payments.	Irregularities in job contracts. Excessive hours in the working day. Problems with weekly rest period. Irregularities in attendance records.	Irregularities in job contracts. Excessive hours in the working day. Problems with weekly rest period. Irregularities in attendance records.
Social security problems	17 fines.	4 fines.	Non-payment of social security contributions. Non-declaration of social security payments. Difference relating to taxable income	Difference relating to taxable income.
Safety and hygiene problems		No CPHS[1]	No CPHS	
			Non-provision of PPE[2]	Non-provision of PPE

Notes:
[1] Joint Hygiene and Safety Committee.
[2] Personal Protection Elements.
Source: Regional office, Labor Department.

Forestry activities involve a high risk of physical accident and illness in all countries.[41] However, over the last 20 years the accident rate in developed countries such as Finland and Sweden has fallen considerably. In Finland two elements have been crucial in improving the health and safety of forestry workers: mechanization, which has significantly reduced the number of forestry workers (from 35,000 in 1980 to 20,000 in 1992), and the emphasis placed on training.[42]

Chile's relative endowment of factors of production does not justify increasing the mechanization of forestry activities to the same degree but training can play an important role in improving worker safety. However, despite the problems the forestry sector has in complying with existing labor health and safety regulations, there have been improvements. In particular, firms and organizations such as CORMA (Corporación de la Madera) and Fundación Chile are promoting significant changes in the attitudes of firms and their sub-contractors in this area. Research is being carried out and seminars organized to this end, as well as talks given by specialists aimed at educating and training firms and sub-contractors. In addition, a tripartite sectoral commission has been set up, consisting of firms (participating through CORMA), the

Table 8.6 Summary of main labor problems in the forestry sector in the XIIth Region

Type of problems	Result of inspection	Number of firms	Number of workers in firm	Number of workers affected
Labor problems:				
Not keeping attendance records.	9 fines: $946,480	9	212	106
Excessive overtime.	2 Fines: $242,832	3	41	7
Arrears in wage payments.	No fines	4	119	77
Non-compliance with weekly rest periods.	1 fine: $122,688	3	220	28
Failure to stipulate working hours and timetable in the contract.	No fines.	4	141	76
Illegal working day.		2	54	36
Hygiene and safety problems:				
Absence of drinking water.	Report on hygiene and safety to the Health Service	10	451	191
Absence or insufficiency of hygiene services.		17	504	290
Social security problems:				
Non-declaration of social security contributions.	2 fines: $62,558	2	55	11
Without problems:		4	94	66

Notes: Total no. of firms =29.
  Total no. of workers =998.
  Total no. of workers affected = 495.
  1US$=Ch$404 (1993).
Source: Regional Office, Labor Department.

Confederation of Forestry Workers and the Ministry of Labor. The commission's main activities are in the field of labor health and safety: drawing up a code of forestry practices, for example. Without doubt, these activities will enhance compliance with labor health and safety standards and contribute to lowering the accident rate.

(ii) Salmon farming. Salmon farming is a recently developed industry which emerged at the end of the 1970s as a semi-experimental project to exploit the country's natural advantages for the farming of this species. Output grew from 70 tons in 1980 to 200,000 tons in 1999, making Chile the world's second largest producer of farmed salmon. In 1998, salmon exports amounted to US$ 714 million – 43 per cent of total exports from the fishing sector. It was estimated that the activity employed 8,000 people directly in 1993, and a similar number indirectly. Most are low-skilled workers and operators working in the salmon "harvest", drawn from the local population, whose alternative jobs would be in small-scale fishing or farming. According to Labor Department data, the average wage in Region X was Ch$ 90,000 (US$222) per month (ranging between $67,000 (US$165) and $120,000 (US$297)).

Salmon farming is carried out on raft-cages placed in the sea or in lakes. The working area consists of a large central space surrounded by walkways with railings from which nets are suspended to form pens for the salmon. The work of harvesting, feeding the fish and raising the nets is done almost entirely manually.[43]

The hazards of this activity are associated firstly with the ever-present risk of illness due to the harsh environmental conditions (the work is obviously done outdoors), as well as specific risks inherent in the activity itself, which, according to the ACHS, arise from both dangerous conditions and hazardous actions.[44]

Salmon farming has an accident rate way above the national average: close to 23.4 per cent as against a national average of 11.8 per cent (ACHS 1994).[45] On the other hand, the sectoral accident rate was 25.2 per cent in 1991, so it has come down slightly.

The fall in accident rates also relates to changes in installations and materials use. When salmon farming began, wooden rafts were used, but these have gradually been replaced by walkways and railings made of non-slip galvanized metal.

Accidents tend to occur mostly among permanent workers, during normal working hours, and among workers doing a regular day's work; i.e. under normal working conditions.[46]

Data from the Labor Department inspection program gives more detailed information on the difficult working conditions in the salmon sector.[47] These vary a lot between firms: the more isolated the workplace, the worse the conditions tend to be.[48] Thus, conditions of work tend to be better in Puerto Montt, on the mainland, than offshore on the Island of Chiloé.

Inspection of the sector has been stepped up in recent years. Tables 8.7 and 8.8 give the results of salmon firm inspections carried out by the Labor Department. The representativeness of the figures is limited, since the firms are not selected at random, nor can results be compared over time. However, the information is useful for visualizing the type of problems facing the sector.

In the 1993 inspection, problems centered on compliance with working hours, with the maximum legal limit being exceeded by two extra hours per day, and the ten-hour maximum normal workday also being breached. Inspection was carried out in summer, a time when a rest period of up to four hours is given during the lunch break (which is illegal), because the salmon have to be fed in dim light, early in the morning and in the evening. In fact, on the basis of the inspection a special permit was requested to spread out the working day. Apart from this, the twoday rest period corresponding to the two-week labor period was not being granted, and a system of three weeks' work for one rest day was being used without giving a weekday off in lieu of weekends worked.

In the 1995 inspection, 63 workplaces were visited in Region X, covering contractual aspects as well as safety issues. Table 8.8 gives a

Table 8.7 Inspection of salmon firms in the Xth Region, 1993[1] (no. firms inspected =63)

Infractions	Number of firms	% of firms fined
Non-existence or defects in the job contract	6	10
Excessive working hours (> 10 hours)	25	40
Absence of weekly rest period	14	22
Control of attendance (non existent or incorrect)	11	17
Social security	3	5
Others	4	6

Note:
[1] Inspection does not cover labor safety conditions.
Source: Labor Department.

Table 8.8 Inspection of salmon firms in the Xth Region, 1995 (no. firms inspected =68)

Infractions	No. of firms	% of firms fined
Inadequate floors and railings	30	44
Non-existence of toilets on rafts	45	66
Lack (or poor quality) of toilets on land	12	18
Lack of drinking water on rafts	20	29
Absence of non-slip netting	9	13
No life-jackets on rafts	5	7
Others	17	25
Absence of weekly rest period[1]	7	10
Excessive working hours[1]	4	6

Note:
[1] Figures correspond to sanctions rather than infractions.
Source: Labor Department.

breakdown of the results.[49] Problems centered on deficient safety and hygiene standards (for example, inadequate floors and railings, or lack of toilets), with fewer problems of non-compliance being detected in the other labor standards (for example, absence of contracts, illegal working hours, non-payment).[50]

The indicators suggest that, although the job is more than averagely dangerous, advances have been made in labor and safety conditions, for example with the replacement of wooden railings. This positive trend seems to reflect a greater concern among the firms themselves and in government spheres, as well as the preventive work of the Mutual Associations. However, it is difficult to obtain figures to determine whether these changes are merely a consequence of the consolidation of sectoral development, or whether pressure from foreign consumer markets has also played a role. However, the data would seem to suggest that the first of these factors is predominant.[51]

The data show that this export sector suffers from particularly difficult working conditions, with risks that are inherent in the work that is carried out. A significant part of Chile's comparative advantages in salmon production come not only from its geographical location and environmental conditions, but also from the availability of labor that is more willing to assume the risks implied in this work.[52] Nevertheless, significant progress in working conditions has been made in recent years, which reflect situations that are peculiar to this sector and are not necessarily representative of general labor conditions throughout the country.

(iii) The mining sector. In the mining sector, Canadian miners' unions have expressed concern that working conditions in Chilean mining are not good, particularly in the labor health and safety areas. This worry has been expressed particularly by those working in mines owned by Canadian investors, and it has been expressed in Canadian newspapers as well as during visits by miners' unions from that country to Chile, which are coordinated to some degree with the Chilean Mining Confederation.[53] In the light of this, it would be interesting to analyze the extent to which labor health and safety standards are not fully complied with in Chile's mining sector. However, the information is extremely precarious, as it is unsystematic; moreover, it is practically impossible to compare it with other economic sectors. Consequently, what we have done instead is to assess whether there are signs of non-compliance with labor legislation, that could be used against Chile's mining exports.

The profile of the mining workforce is one of male workers, with good levels of education, predominantly machine operators and unskilled workers, with a trend towards an increase in wage-earners *vis-à-vis* self-employed workers.

Data from the National Geology and Mining Service indicates that, apart from the nitrate segment and the smelters and concentration plants, the average hourly wage in Chilean mining was US$ 5.60 in 1994 (approximately Ch$ 2,296), which makes this one of the economy's highest paid sectors.

The average working week is 48 hours, with a wide variety of special systems for distributing the workday, as evidenced by the number of authorizations for special regimes granted by the Labor Department. Table 8.9 shows the different types of special work regimes that exist in mining, based on a sample of 220 firms.

Another feature of the mining sector is the growth of sub-contracting. In 1994, according to the National Geology and Mining Service, 32 per cent of man-hours worked were carried out by sub-contracted workers, with this proportion rising above 50 per cent in small- and medium-scale copper mining.

Labor health and safety problems faced by mine workers include the following (Parra 1996): the use of explosives and the risk of rock fall, high levels of potentially harmful dust, such as silica, accumulation of combustion gases, problems of noise and vibration caused by tools, and health problems caused by damp and the temperatures of both underground work and outdoor work in open-cast mines, as well as work at high altitudes (over 4,000 meters).

Table 8.9 Special regimes for distributing the working day in mining

Hours per day	Days of work	Rest days	No. of firms
8 or 9	<10	2 or 3	3
	10–19	3 to 8	7
	20	7 or 10	14
	21	7 or 8	11
	22	7 or 8	47
	23 or more	6 or 7	4
10 or 11	<10	1 to 7	5
	10–19	7 to 9	8
	20	10 or 11	10
	21	7	6
	22	8	4
	23 or more	≥ 7	3
12	4 or 5	2 or 3	14
	4	4	38
	7 or 8	6 to 8	35
	10 to 19	4 to 15	10
	23 or more	≥ 7	1

Source: Parra (1996).

In materials processing, there are also significant risks from exposure to dangerous chemical substances such as ammonia, cyanide, arsenic and mercury products, among others.[54] Apart from this, there is the risk of explosion, noise, vibration, heat, etc.

Ailments known to be caused by such conditions include: bronchial diseases, as well as lumbar, rheumatic and ophthalmological complaints, and arsenic poisoning.

Mine workers argue that, up to now, employers have restricted the occupational health issue to the merely curative, and have no adequate policy to prevent the problems from occurring.

They also argue that supervisory organizations are deficient, information is incomplete and out of date, and there is a lack of trained human resources to carry out the inspection work.

In general, there is no information on professional illnesses; what does exist are accident statistics published by the National Geology and Mining Service. These distinguish between the frequency rate, degree of seriousness and the fatality rate.[55] Table 8.10 shows these figures for 1987–89, 1990–91, 1993 and 1994.

The frequency of accidents is declining in all kinds of mining. However, there is great variety when the figures are broken down by type of

Table 8.10 Accident frequency rates, seriousness and fatality rates by type of mining activity

	Large-scale copper mining	Small- and medium-scale copper mining	Non-copper metallic mining
Frequency rate:			
Average 1987–89	20.1	32.3	35.7
Average 1990–92	13.5	31.6	29.1
1993	10.0	20.8	24.1
1994	12.4	21.3	21.8
Seriousness rate:			
Average 1987–89	2,143	2,950	4,844
Average 1990–92	1,496	4,554	3,954
1993	1,352	2,357	3,208
1994	1,055	2,558	7,127
Fatality rate:			
Average 1987–89	0.25	0.39	0.69
Average 1990–92	0.16	0.64	0.57
1993	0.16	0.33	0.42
1994	0.11	0.36	1.11

Source: National Geology and Mining Service, *Year Book 1994*.

mining. In 1994 the accident rate in large-scale copper mining was 12.4, compared to 21.3 in medium and small-scale mining and 21.8 in non-copper metallic mining.

The seriousness rate has been falling in large-scale copper mining, but has remained more or less stable in the case of medium and small-scale operations. Serious accidents have increased significantly in non-copper metallic mining, owing to a rise in fatal accidents. This rate also varies widely when different types of mining are analyzed; non-copper metallic mining shows the highest rates in every year.

The fatality rate has come down in recent years in large-scale copper mining, remaining stable in medium- and small-scale copper mining and rising in non-copper metallic mining. Fatalities in large-scale copper mining can be compared with the rates for the USA: averages for the period 1987–89 are 0.25 and 0.13 respectively. In 1991, the fatality rate in US mining was 0.078, whereas large-scale copper mining in Chile had a fatality rate of 0.16 over the three-year period 1990–92.[56] Thus, the lowest fatality rates in Chilean mining are approximately double those in the United States.

An aspect that needs to be stressed is the difference in rates between mining companies and sub-contractors. According to data from the National Geology and Mining Service, while frequency rates are similar in each case, the seriousness and fatality rates are both significantly higher among sub-contractors: 4,588 as against 2,801 for serious accidents, and 0.71 compared to 0.37 for fatality rates. This could be a sign that sub-contractor firms are not complying with minimal standards for avoidance of workplace accidents – which would be worrying, given that their use is expanding in the mining sector. The higher rates among sub-contractors may also be due to their high labor turnover, which means they do not train their workers; it may also be the case that the more risky activities are the ones being sub-contracted.

Another source of information that permits a comparison of accident rates between mining companies and sub-contractors is provided by the Labor Department: the rate of fatal accidents in subcontractor firms is 1.8 accidents per 1,000 workers, as against 0.9 among mining companies. In large-scale copper mining, the frequency of accidents is 19.5 among subcontractors compared to 9.2 in mining companies.[57]

Finally, it is interesting to differentiate between workplace accidents caused by unsafe acts, such as the violation of some established safety procedure, and those caused by hazardous conditions, i.e. some physical condition or dangerous circumstance. Data from the National Geology and Mining Service for 1994 indicates that 72 per cent of mining accidents are caused by unsafe acts and 28 per cent by hazardous conditions.

The data obtained points to the conclusion that there is no general problem of non-compliance with labor legislation in the mining sector; however, measures need to be taken to improve accident indices, essentially among sub-contractor firms. Data on causes of accidents suggest that what is basically needed are training programs in labor health and safety, for sub-contractors and their workers.

(iv) Fruit growing for export and agribusiness. Labor conditions in export fruit-growing and agribusiness have been called into question at the international level, basically for two reasons: the possible effects of pesticide use on workers' health, and working conditions for seasonal workers (mostly women) where labor standards differ from those governing permanent workers.[58]

The international press, especially in Canada, has drawn attention to the dark side of the export fruit-growing boom in terms of scant regulation and poor working conditions. The most common allegations relate to the effects on workers of the use of pesticides that are prohibited in developed countries, a lack of protective material (masks and clothing), working days that are longer than the legislation allows, child labor, practices of sexual harassment, absence of bathrooms, abandonment of children by mothers who go to work, etc.[59] Some international press reports describe a situation of widespread abuse in this sector.

Although the sector does have labor problems, some of the allegations seem to relate to particular rather than general cases, while others are frankly untrue. For example, it is argued that the Chilean government tried to lengthen the summer holiday period to allow adolescents to work for a longer period in fruit growing.[60] Yet, the available information points in the opposite direction: the government in fact reduced the summer holiday period by one week and extended the length of the school day. Other allegations invoke standards that are not even met in developed countries, such as the requirement to provide crèche facilities for young children for all agricultural workers, as well as compensation for dismissal in this sector.[61]

While some of these criticisms seem to lack widespread support, or else they relate to specific problems, there are other situations which are well documented. For example, a comparative study of child malformation has been widely cited: the number of malformed children for every thousand live births in the city of Rancagua[62] is 3.6, as against 1.93 at the national level; 93 per cent of all cases of malformation correspond to mothers who are seasonal workers or fathers who are exposed to toxic agricultural substances (Medel and Riquelme 1994).[63]

The workforce employed in the forestry and agriculture and livestock sectors numbers approximately 830,000, or 18 per cent of the national labor force. Of this total, wage-earners account for about 500,000, 80 per cent of whom are seasonal (Echeñique 1993).[64] Seasonal workers also mostly work throughout the year, albeit in different firms and areas. Only one-third work exclusively in the spring–summer season; these are basically housewives and students. The number of women in casual work is 125,000, mostly linked to seasonal tasks in the fruit sector; they account for about 52 per cent of the total work force in the fruit-growing sector (Venegas 1992).

Legislation does not authorize collective bargaining for seasonal workers hired for transitory jobs; nor is there redundancy pay for workers hired for a fixed period (unless this is agreed voluntarily in collective bargaining). Joint Committees (Comités Paritarios) can only be made up from workers who have more than one year of service in the firm, unless half of the workers do not fulfill this requirement. Social security is also different for temporary workers: 240 months of pension contributions are needed to have the right to a minimum pension.

Figures presented by Echeñique (1993), based on surveys (of limited representativeness), indicate that the working day for seasonal workers, especially those hired through an intermediary, is likely to exceed 8 hours; labor safety and the provision of protective equipment at work (gloves, masks) generally has serious deficiencies, although the non-use of these elements is in some cases the worker's responsibility. An absence of social security and insurance against workplace accidents was also detected among temporary workers.

Apart from this, a survey of seasonal workers in the grape-growing sector reveals an extension of the working day beyond the legal limit, as well as health problems deriving from working conditions and the use of pesticides. However, despite all this, seasonal workers attach a positive value to having a job.[65] Among negative factors, the survey highlights bent posture, excessive heat and the overload of domestic chores. A set of general ailments affect nearly half of all female workers; these include varicose veins, impaired eyesight and lumbago, together with complaints arising from contact with toxic substances: skin ailments (23 per cent), eyesight problems (19 per cent), and respiratory complaints (10 per cent).[66]

Data on the length of the working day, presented in Table 8.11, show that a high percentage of female workers in the fruit-packing industry work more than 10 hours a day.[67] There are several pieces of information which draw attention to the fact that the working day extends beyond the legal limit at certain times of year (e.g. harvest); however, these are difficult situations to supervise as they often form part of voluntary agreements between employers and workers.[68]

Table 8.11 Normal working hours in orchard and packing (percentages; N=300)

	Orchard	Packing
Up to 8 hours	3.3	6.3
Between 8 and 10 hours	50.0	15.3
Between 10 and 12	24.0	24.7
Up 16 hours	–	27.3
More than 16	–	9.0
Did not work	22.7	17.4

Source: Medel and Riquelme (1994).

Table 8.12 Degree of non-compliance with preventive measures in high-risk firms

Preventive measure	Non-compliance among firms using highly toxic products (%)
Non-availability of drinking water	32
Non-existence of hygiene service	31
Non-existence of changing rooms	46
No standards for the washing of containers	34
Pesticide operators not trained	50
Improperly labeled products	19
Impermeable gloves not provided	17
Respiratory protection not provided	22
Impermeable suits not provided	11
Complete protection equipment not provided	63
Working week longer than 48 hours	65

Source: Labor Department. Survey of 213 agricultural estates. Regions V, VI, VII, and Metropolitan, 1993.

However, as mentioned above, they are pleased to have a job; moreover 74.3 per cent declare that their psychological state is mostly good when working, whereas the percentages falls to 54 per cent in situations of unemployment.

Probably the best documented issue, and the one that has given rise to most allegations internationally, is the health risk faced by workers from the use of highly toxic pesticides. Apart from the study by Medel and Riquelme for the city of Rancagua, mentioned above, a series of complaints have been filed with the Labor Department alleging lack of preventive measures when using such elements.

Table 8.12 shows the high degree of non-compliance with basic safety standards among firms using highly toxic pesticides.

The agricultural export sector clearly appears to have labor problems deriving from the working conditions themselves (physical effort), as well as from the employment conditions (temporary work) and the situation of female workers who also have to take care of home and children. Although conditions can be improved, they do not seem to be as dramatic as some international press reports suggest. The aspect that seems most serious relates to the use of highly toxic pesticides and their possible effects on workers' health.

5 Final comments

The experience of NAFTA regarding the inclusion of labor side-agreements in free trade treaties, points to a series of interesting conclusions for Chile and for any developing country interested in entering into this type of agreement with more developed nations.

A labor side-agreement can turn each member country's labor legislation into a "binding constraint", by acting as an additional pressure to ensure enforcement. Such pressure could turn out to be more important than that exerted by Labor Ministry inspection.

Moreover, the inclusion of side-agreements in free trade deals may help to get socially desirable labor standards adopted. With the backing of trade treaties, governments increase their bargaining power *vis-à-vis* powerful interest groups that might oppose the establishment of certain standards.

These complementary agreements also have the virtue of making it possible to analyze "marginal cases"; although these may not infringe the legislation, strictly speaking (or this is difficult to prove), they do act against its spirit. The existence of such agreements increases the political cost to a country of not enforcing its own labor laws.

Side-agreements and the institutional framework set up under their wing, have indirectly provided opportunities for international coordination between unions on issues such as the promotion of standards similar to those of developed countries, for the subsidiaries of multinational firms operating in developing countries.

In Chile's labor legislation, the greatest weaknesses seem to be concentrated in labor health and safety standards, and the working conditions in certain primary exporting sectors. Indeed, it is precisely on these issues that pressure from abroad has been focused, unlike in Mexico where disputes have related to freedom of union affiliation and collective bargaining.[69]

The cases analyzed in Chile confirm that although the legislation is complied with in general, there are problems in certain export sectors. These arise from legal loopholes, or differences between an export sector in particular and the general rule (for example, legislation for seasonal workers), enforcement problems in isolated areas (salmon farming and forestry) and the pushing of flexibility norms to the limit (e.g. special work periods in mining). Without condoning cases of non-compliance, which we believe need to be put right, we do not think these warrant the seriousness they are accorded abroad, especially in parts of the international press. Nevertheless, there is a real risk of these problems damaging the country's image and being used as an argument for restricting Chilean exports. They also have the potential to affect consumer behavior in foreign countries.

With respect to both labor and environmental standards, those who allege non-compliance try to influence consumer behavior. In the labor case, the effect on consumer behavior would come basically from press publications, whereas in environmental standards the pressure tends to be exerted through more precise instruments, such as eco-labeling.

A pertinent question, to which we made reference at the start of this chapter, is the extent to which accusations of social dumping confront firms with a situation of contingent protection that may cause them to alter their behavior. Although there are no detailed data, it would seem that in Chile the threat of trade restrictions has more impact on the government's attitude than on the firms themselves.

The information that has been gathered suggests that it is government attitudes that have shown most concern due to the possible effect of labor conditions on the export sector, in the framework of integration agreements. This is not only because it is obviously the government that is most directly involved in treaty negotiations, but it also seems to show the government's concern about effective external pressures in terms of country image and the political cost involved.

In this sense, the strategy of foreign pressure on Chilean firms is probably indirect, both through the government and through consumers in developed countries – a pressure which, when exerted through the international press, operates via "country image".

This concern among government and congress for issues that could give rise to dispute is reflected in a series of legislative amendments that are currently in process or being debated in congress, although these are not solely motivated by external pressure. For example, an amendment to the Labor Code has been passed making a Sunday rest day obligatory at least once a month; a bill presented by the Labor Commission of the Chamber of Deputies has been approved to end work by children under 15 years old; the creation of a night-time inspection brigade at the Labor Department is under study, as is a proposal to make "parent" companies responsible for their subcontractors' compliance with labor laws. As regards maternity protection, an employer may not make hiring a woman conditional on her not being pregnant (*Temas Laborales* 1995–96).

A study of the information presented here on legislative differences and the case studies of Chilean export sectors, leads us to reiterate aspects that have been stressed by trade theory. Wages, working conditions and, to some extent, labor standards, are endogenous to development processes and depend on the internal characteristics of markets. Countries should respect a certain set of minimum standards, but differences in factor endowments mean that firms use technologies that differ not only in their capital–labor ratios, but also in terms of working conditions and the level of risk associated with them. In this sense, differences in working conditions between countries are not exogenous or merely political phenomena, they also relate to different productive factor endowments and different preferences among the population.

Trade itself, and the negotiation of trade agreements, has raised the profile of labor issues, which had generally been confined to the domestic sphere of the countries involved. However, if this greater concern for labor standards, and hence their enforcement, leads to trade restrictions that slow down growth in developing countries, it would imply lower standards and worse living conditions of workers in those countries.

Appendix

Table 8.A1   Aspects of labor health and safety legislation in Chile

Workplace accidents	
Characteristics of the system	Obligatory social security against workplace accidents and professional illnesses.
Responsibility	Graded compensation
Benefits	*Temporary disability*: 100% of salary, maximum period 52 weeks.
	Permanent disability:
	Total disability:
	100% pension of the base wage.
	Partial invalidity:
	If disability is more than 15% but less than 40%, compensation is awarded between 1.5 and 15 base wages.
	If it is more than 40% but less than 70% a pension is awarded equal to 35% of the basic wage.
	If it is more than 70% a pension of 70% of the basic wage is awarded.
Protective standards for safety and hygiene	
Regulations and prohibitions	The employer will be obliged to take all necessary measures to effectively protect the life and health of workers. Health Services will fix minimum hygiene and safety measures (Regulation).

Table 8.A1   (cont.)

	Special cases are only defined for activities in ports, underground work, tunnels and exploitation of mines.
Maternity	*Rest period*: 6 weeks before and 12 weeks after giving birth. *Wages*: 100% of wages.

Source: Prepared by the authors on the basis of official information.

Table 8.A2   Endowment, budget and firms supervised by the Labor Department

Years	1988	1989	1990	1991	1992	1993	1994
Labor Department staff endowment	779	779	813	981	1,088	1,223	1,263
Labor Department budget (Ch$ million June 1993)	3,038	2,860	2,736	2,945	3,697	4,498	5,648
Total number of inspections		29,266	28,986	26,868	30.936	41,218	53,973	54,359

Source: Labor Department, Inspection Department Annual Report, various years.

Notes

1 These pressures have found concrete expression in the NAFTA side-agreement on labor cooperation. See North American Agreement on Labor Cooperation (1993).

2 For a complete discussion of these arguments see Bhagwati (1996).

3 These differences in adjustment times are significant even considering that changes in labor standards in most countries require legislative approval. However, when the problem is essentially one of compliance with already existing regulations, adjustment times are shorter.

4 The topic of labor standards in the context of trade agreements has had little discussion in Chile; however there is a study by Alburquerque (1994) which raises certain points relating to this issue which arise in the context of Chile's possible membership of NAFTA.

5 Nevertheless, other authors argue that these incentives to lower labor standards need not exist, as these are a potential determinant of economic efficiency in the sense that imposing minimum conditions for wages and job protection makes it possible to create stable relations and improve human capital and labor productivity. In this sense, it might even positively affect the country's capacity to compete internationally (Sengenberger 1991; Castro *et al.* 1992; Piore 1990). For example, De Castro (1995) cites a series of

studies relating to recently industrialized Asian countries, which show that their successful economic performance does not rest on the exploitation of cheap labor, but rather on the restructuring of their technologies from those intensive in cheap labor towards those intensive in skilled-labor.

6 In such situations, where the argument for linking trade to compliance with certain standards is related more to moral considerations, it is not correct to speak of social dumping.

7 The French President Jacques Chirac argued in the G7 meeting in April 1996, that differences in wage levels, labor legislation and social security should be tolerated less and less as international competition grows in intensity. In contrast, the UK Finance Minister argued that the social clause proposal might be turned into protection "through the back door".

8 In the limiting case, where the value workers place on the standard is equal to its cost to employers, imposing the standard has no effect at all on labor costs or employment.

9 This analysis is similar to that of tax incidence.

10 This analysis assumes competitive international markets in which labor standards are not used as a strategic tool to affect the terms of trade, and hence trade flows. The empirical evidence in this regard shows that most of the existing standards are policies aimed basically at the labor market; they are highly correlated with the countries' development level and do not involve strategic behavior on their part.

11 This might be the case of immigrant workers who obtain free public healthcare in the host country without paying for it.

12 A study carried out in OECD countries shows a clear relation between the labor conditions existing in these countries and their level of economic development (OECD 1994).

13 For example, between 1988 and 1991 Chile was suspended from the GSP for not respecting internationally recognized worker rights (union freedom, the right to organize, etc.).

14 It would also be justified to make trade conditional on the adoption of certain labor standards when there is a danger that a country might use them strategically to alter their terms of trade. But, as mentioned above, there is no empirical evidence that this occurs.

15 Most of the agreements signed by Chile have been with other Latin American countries of similar development level (e.g. Mexico and the MERCOSUR countries), for which reason in these cases one would not expect trade pressures relating to compliance with labor standards in Chile.

16 In 1994 the cooperation program included the following areas: labor health and safety, labor training, productivity and quality, labor legislation and workers' rights. In these areas seminars, forums and talks by experts were organized both in Mexico and in the USA.

17 For that reason the deal between Chile and Canada did not contemplate trade sanctions, but only the payment of fines.

18 The *Maquiladora* was operating under the name of *Magnéticos de Mexico* and employed 1,700 unionized workers, 80 per cent of whom were women.

19 The case covers aspects of freedom of association and the right to freely organize; the NAO rejected the argument relating to minimum employment standards.

20 The case is against a subsidiary of the Sprint Corporation, called "La Conexion Familiar" a company that sells long-distance telephone services in Spanish.

21 See Table 8.A1 of the Appendix.

22 However, the sectors of the economy bringing the highest percentage of complaints and actions before the Labor Department in relation to their labor force are: construction, commerce, transport and industry. See *Temas Laborales*, Labor Department, January 1996.

23 For example, labor-related infringements are distributed as follows: wages (non-compliance with legal provisions), 28 per cent; length of working day, 25 per cent; pension fund payments, work contract and others, 16 per cent; safety and hygiene at work, 13 per cent; child labor, 10 per cent; equal treatment between men and women, 8 per cent (*Source:* Labor Department, based on inspections carried out by 16 Workplace Inspections in 1992.) (Dirección del Trabajo 1993).

24 According to the 1990 National household survey, 64.2 per cent of the population declared themselves to be affiliated to a pension system: 33.6 per cent were not affiliated and for 2.2 per cent there was no data. It should be remembered that affiliation is voluntary for self-employed workers.

25 Social security against Work Place Accidents and Professional Illnesses aims to prevent such accidents and illnesses, provide medical attention and rehabilitation for injured workers and make economic provision in the case or work disability or death of the worker.

26 There are two other regimes covering public-sector employees and the Armed Forces and Police. Insurance can be managed by the following bodies: (i) The Instituto de Normalización Previsional (INP), which shares administration with the National Health Service System (SNSS); (ii) Private Employers' Mutual Associations; and (iii) large firms may self-insure.

27 Of this, 75 per cent were insured through mutual associations, 24 per cent by the INP, and about 2 per cent by systems administered by firms themselves.

28 It should be noted that a very low rate, especially in developing countries, might point to a lack of inspection and problems of under-declaring.

29 Likewise, days of work lost per accident have come down; the average number of days of subsidy per accident dropped from 15.4 in 1982 to 13.7 in 1992. The existing data shows that firms paying into the INP have not reduced the seriousness of accidents to the same extent, as in 1992 the average number of days' subsidy was 39.2.

30 Compliance with Labor Code is controlled by the Labor Department of the Ministry of Labor and Maritime Boards; the Sanitary Code is controlled by the National Health Service, Department of Environmental Health (Ministry of Health), and COMPIN; Insurance against Workplace Accidents and Professional Illnesses (Law 16.744) is supervised by the National Health Service, the Superintendency of Social Security, the Labor Department, the National Geology and Mining Service and Maritime Boards; the Health Regulation (369/85) (Law 18.469) is controlled by the National Health System and the Public Health Service; finally, rules on social security and labor disability subsidies come under the Superintendency of Social Security. (See Inspectors' Report *Informes Fiscalizadores*, p. 51).

31 See, "Seminario nacional para la formación de fiscalizadores de trabajo e inspectores de salud en la agricultura y en las industrias agroalimentarias", Labor Department, March 1993.

32 An example of this is the preventive work being carried out by the Chilean Insurance Association and entrepreneurs in forestry and salmon farming, by means of reports, seminars, courses and post-graduate diplomas aimed at detecting and preventing the job hazards that exist in the sector. See, for example, ACHS (1994), Labor Department (1993), Infante (1995).

33 For example, a Working Conditions and Environment Unit (Unidad de Condiciones y Medio Ambiente de Trabajo) has been set up in the Labor Department, and coordination improved between the Ministry of Labor and the Health Ministry.

34 Article 38 of the Labor Code establishes that the Labor Department can authorize firms to introduce special working hours.

35 These are legally established participatory bodies, in which workers and employers act jointly to prevent workplace hazards.

36 A rate expressed as the number of accidents per 1,000 workers.

37 Forestry activities include: thinning out, pruning, fencing, clearing, planting. Harvest activities include: felling, use of chainsaw, wood chopping.

38 Only 8.6 per cent of workers in large forestry firms have had training, according to a study by Apud and Valdés (1995). Fundación Chile, in the study mentioned above, reports that 42 per cent of firms surveyed did not provide any type of training for their workers, 16 per cent only provide them basic on-site instructions, 34 per cent only train those operating chain saws, and only 8 per cent train all their workers (Apud and Ilabaca 1991).

39 Inspection programs in the forestry sector cover the following aspects: job contracts, working hours, rest periods, wages, benefits (conditions of lodging and food hygiene, adequate infrastructure, and transport for workers).

40 Chile is divided into 13 administrative Regions. Forest activity is concentrated in Regions VII to IX, which correspond to distances of 400 to 1,000 km from Santiago.

41 An ILO report (1991) shows that the accident rate and the risk of fatal accident in forestry are very high compared with other sectors of the economy. Despite the problems involved in comparing data from different countries, this report concludes that rates in developing countries are several times higher than those in developed countries.

42 Measures implemented in Finland include: constructive cooperation between the interested parties at the national level and in workplaces; sustainable forestry ordinance and long-term planning; effective training which includes aspects relating to labor health and safety; training of specialists in labor safety, legislation which establishes minimum standards for safety, health and conditions of work; competent and effective administration of worker protection, with the emphasis on advice; research into working methods, technology, machinery and equipment that is effective and safe; and a continuous improvement in the design of machinery and equipment (Jokiluoma and Tapola 1993).

43 In the case of salmon farming in the sea, which is the case of most salmon farms, most firms' centers of activity, or concession areas, are located in small coves. Each center is composed of two or three sets of raft-cages, which in

turn are made up of 12 to 20 cages forming a compact or "train". Most of the work is carried out on the walkways of these raft-cages, and because of the requirements of the work the rafts do not have handrails on the outer edges. The sets of cages are located between 100 to 300 meters from the coast, and access to them is by small boats; accordingly, this is a working area that is in constant motion from the sea's waves (Labor Department).

44 The ACHS report states that there were three fatal accidents among salmon industry workers on the Island of Chiloé during the first half of 1994 alone.

45 According to Labor Department reports the accident rate in the fishing sector is 20 per cent. According to figures from the Mutual Safety Association, the accident rate among its salmon farming affiliates is about 13 per cent.

46 In 1991–93 , out of a total of 2,235 accidents, 1,140 occurred among workers with more than one year of service, 66.3 per cent of those suffering accidents were less than 30 years old; 83.6 per cent of those suffering accidents were hired permanently by the firm; only 47.6 per cent of those suffering accidents contacted the ACHS on the day of the accident; 83.3 per cent of accidents occurred between 8.00 and 18.00 hours, and 97 per cent of those suffering accidents had been working between one and eight hours at the time of the accident (ACHS).

47 The Labor Department carried out a program of inspections among salmon farms in the Xth Region in November and December 1995, specifically during the stage of salmon cultivation in raft-cages on the sea. Sixty-three workplaces were visited, belonging to 47 firms and representing more than 40 per cent of those existing in the Xth Region.

48 Concession areas were reported which had well-equipped locations with kitchen, dining-room, toilets and clothes lockers; safety conditions were adequate, with good-quality life-jackets, solid boats for transit to the rafts, protective handrails and thermal clothing of a suitable quality. However, in general, firms lack these characteristics.

49 Other problems have been detected by unions in this sector relating to the non-existence of radios in the rafts to communicate with land, and poor-quality life-jackets.

50 Another cause for concern in the salmon industry relates to the side-effects of this activity on the natural environment, due to the discharge of waste material and the effect of salmon feed on marine flora and fauna. However, these issues go beyond the strictly labor domain.

51 The main export market is Japan (34,019 tons), followed by USA (18,094 tons), EU (6,345 tons), Latin America (828 tons) and others (462 tons) (1993 figures). Pressure to improve environmental conditions generally comes from markets in the EU, USA and Canada.

52 Naturally, safer working conditions might mean using alternative technologies and employing less labor.

53 See, for example, the article "Golden Quest" that appeared in the Canadian newspaper *The Toronto Star,* dated May 28th, 1995.

54 The Mining Confederation is to carry out a pilot study to measure the degree of mercury contamination to which workers are exposed in the processing plant at the La Coipa mine belonging to the Compañia Minera Mantos de Oro, owned by Canadian investors.

55 *Frequency rate*: number of injuries involving time lost, plus those on light work, for every million man-hours worked.

Seriousness rate: measures the consequences of injuries suffered by a firm's workers for every million man-hours worked, in terms of the number of days lost to accidents during the treatment and recovery process.

Fatality rate: relates the number of accidents that have caused the death of a worker to the time of exposure to the risk, with a reference basis of one million man-hours worked.

56 See Annual Labor Statistics (*Anuario de Estadísticas del Trabajo*) 1995.

57 See *Temas Laborales*, no. 2, January 1996, Labor Department.

58 However, it should borne in mind that in most countries legislation on temporary or seasonal workers differs from that governing permanent workers, for example in the use of systems of unemployment insurance.

59 See for example, reports in *The Toronto Star*, May 27th to 29th, 1995; *The Financial Post*, April 22nd, 1996; *The Globe and Mail*, November 14th, 1995 and December 7th, 1995.

60 *The Toronto Star*, May 27th, 1995.

61 This sector is subject to the same legislation on children's crèches as nationally: it is the employer's responsibility to provide facilities for children under two years old in any firm hiring more than 20 female workers.

62 Rancagua is the main city in of the most important fruit producing areas.

63 Also quoted in the *Toronto Star*, May 27th, 1995.

64 Data from Echeñique (1993), based on INE figures, state that the number of wage-earners in 1992 was 263,000 in the winter period and 345,000 in summer, between Chilean Regions III and VII.

65 Survey of 300 female seasonal workers in the grape sector in the region of Valparaíso, carried out between May and June 1992. The absence of a control group makes it hard to interpret this data.

66 The workers claim not to suffer from the ailments when not working; however, the study does not use control groups.

67 In this sample of female workers, 85.7 per cent replied that they had a job contract and 82.3 per cent that they paid social security contributions. As regards the type of contract, 65 per cent were piece-work, 10.7 per cent indefinite, 7 per cent fixed-term, 3 per cent did not know and 14.3 per cent did not have a contract.

68 An example of this complex relationship is contained in a Labor Department report which states that it sanctioned a packing company for an excessively long working day. However, this led to complaints from existing workers, as the hiring of additional staff had caused their wages to be lowered (Labor Department, 1993).

69 A topic that has not surfaced in international discussion, but where there are also sharp differences between developed and developing countries, is gender discrimination. As mentioned earlier, the situation as regards employment and wage conditions *vis-à-vis* maternity protection varies from country to country.

References

Alburquerque, M. (1994). "Implicancias del factor laboral en un eventual Tratado de Libre Comercio con EE.UU", *Proyecto de Estudios Prospectivos*, Santiago, Chile.

Apud, E. and C. Ilabaca (1991). "Diagnóstico del estado actual de la mano de obra en algunas empresas de servicio", *Actas III Taller de Producción Forestal*, Concepción, Chile.

Apud, E. and S. Valdés (1995). *Ergonomics in Forestry. The Chilean Case*. ILO, Geneva.

Asociación Chilena de Seguridad (ACHS) (1989). "Normas Legales sobre Accidentes del Trabajo y Enfermedades Profesionales", ACHS.

Asociación Chilena de Seguridad (ACHS) (1994). "Prevención de Riesgos Profesionales en la Acuicultura", ACHS and Universidad de Los Lagos.

Bhagwati, J. (1994). "Free trade: old and new challenges", *The Economic Journal*, 104: 231–46, March.

Bhagwati, J. (1996). "The demand to reduce domestic diversity among trading nations", in Bhagwati and Hudec (eds).

Bhagwati, J. and R. Hudec (eds) (1996) *Fair Trade and Harmonization*. Cambridge, Mass: MIT Press.

Bhagwati, J. and T.N. Srinivasan (1996). "Trade and the environment: does environmental diversity detract from the case for free trade?", in Bhagwati and Hudec (eds).

Brown D., A. Deardorff and R. Stern (1996). "International labor standards and trade: a theoretical analysis", in Bhagwati and Hudec (eds).

Castro, A., P. Mehaut, and J. Rubery, (1992). *International Integration and Labor Market Organization*. London: Academic Press.

Charnovitz, S. (1987). "The influence of international labour standards on the world trading regime: a historical overview", *International Labour Review*, 126 (5), 565–83.

Charnovitz, S. (1992). "Environmental and labour standards in trade", *The World Economy*, 15(3), 335–56, May.

Charnovitz, S. (1994). "The World Trade Organization and social issues", *Journal of World Trade*, 28(5), 17–33, October.

Collingsworth, T., W. Goold and P. Harvey (1994). "Time for a Global New Deal", *Foreign Affairs*, January-Februrary, 813.

Cooper, R. N. (1994). *Natural Resources and Environmental Policies*. Washington DC: The Brookings Institution.

De Castro, J. (1995). *Trade and Labor Standards. Using the Wrong Instruments for the Right Cause*. UNCTAD, Document No. 99, May.

Dirección del Trabajo (1993). "Informe de Seminario Nacional para la Formación de Fiscalizadores de trabajo e Inspectores de salud en la Agricultura y en las Industrias Agroalimentarias", Dirección del Trabajo, mimeo.

Dirección del Trabajo. *Temas Laborales*, various issues, Ministry of Labor, Chile.

Echeñique, J. (1993). "La modalidad de contratistas de trabajadores en la fruticultura chilena", mimeo, ILO, July.

Edgren, G. (1979). "Fair labour standards and trade liberalization", *International Labour Review*, 118 (5), 523–35.

Ehrenberg, R. (1994). *Labor Markets and Integrating National Economies*. Washington DC: The Brookings Institution.

Fields, G. (1990). "Labor standards, economic development and international trade", in Herzenberg and Perez-Lopez (eds), pp. 19–34.

Herzenberg, S. and J. Perez-Lopez (eds) (1990). *Labor Standards and Development in the Global Economy*. Washington, DC: US Department of Labour.

ILO (1991). *La seguridad y la salud en el trabajo en la silvicultura*, 3rd Report of the Forestry and Timber Industry Commission. Geneva.

ILO (1994). "La justicia social en el desarrollo rural chileno: Aspectos laborales en el libre comercio", ILO, mimeo, October.

Infante R. (1995). "La vida en las balsas", Hatfield International S.A., mimeo, paper presented at ACHS seminar.

Jokiluoma, H. and H. Tapola (1993). "Seguridad y salud de los trabajadores forestales en Finlandia", *Unasylva*, 175 (44).

Klerovic, A. (1996). "Reflections on the race to the bottom", in Bhagwati and Hudec (eds).

Lawrence, R. Z. (1995). "Comercio Internacional y Empleo", ILO Lecture, mimeo, Center for Applied Economics, DII, U. Chile.

Medel, Julia and V. Riquelme (1994). *La Salud Ignorada: temporeras de la fruticultura*. CEM. North American Agreement on Labor Cooperation, 1993.

OECD (1994). *Employment Outlook*. OECD, Paris.

Park, Y. (1993). "Industrial relations and labor law developments in the Republic of Korea", *International Labour Review*, 132 (5–6), 581–92.

Parra, M. (1996). "Condiciones de trabajo y salud en la mineria", mimeo.

Piore, M. (1990). "Labor standards and business strategies", in Herzenberg and Perez-Lopez (eds).

Raga, F. (1993). "Planteamientos corporativos sobre la productividad y bienestar laboral", mimeo, Forestal Mininco S.A.

Sengenberger, W. (1991). "The role of labor market regulation in industrial restructuring", in Standing, G. and V. Tokman (eds), *Towards Social Adjustment*. Geneva: ILO.

Servicio Nacional de Geologia y Mineria. *Anuario 1994*.

Steil, B. (1994). "Social correctness is the new protectionism", *Foreign Affairs*, January–February, 14–20.

Torres, E. (1991). *El desarrollo forestal chileno y su impacto sobre la accidentabilidad laboral del sector*, Minutes of 3rd Workshop on Forestry Production, Concepción, Chile, November.

Unda, A. and A. Stuardo (1996). "Chile: Expansión forestal en la Novena Region y desarrollo sustentable", *Working Paper No. 29*, Multidisciplinary Technical Team, ILO.

Venegas, S. (1992). *Mujer rural: Campesinas y temporeras*. Ministry of Agriculture, FAO, INDAP, SERNAM, Santiago.

Walwei, V. and H.Werner (1993). "Employment and social dimensions of the single European market", *Institute of Employment Research No. 1*.

9
Investment Risk and Latin American Multinationals

Jorge Friedman

1   Introduction

Foreign investment has always been a sensitive issue – both in host countries as well as in source countries. Even developed countries that have a long history of foreign investment have shown a deep distrust of foreign investment. In the United States, for example, the detractors of the North American Free Trade Agreement (NAFTA) claimed that North American manufacturers would relocate their plants and supply the US market from Mexico. In some countries, nationalism augmented by political and social tensions directed against foreign investors adds to this distrust.

Although at present there are no major discriminatory measures against foreign investors in Latin America, the liberalization of foreign direct investment (FDI) still faces a major obstacle in that host countries always have the potential to adopt protectionist measures in response to future tensions. In this situation, a multinational risks its revenue flows and its investment, so it is extremely sensitive to the risks to future income flows associated with foreign ventures. Protectionist measures available to host countries include the sudden introduction of restrictions on foreign firms' activities, unfair treatment compared to domestic investors, or even more stringent measures such as new taxes, which by covert means may effectively expropriate the firm's profits. Although seldom actually implemented, the mere possibility that such measures could be applied in the future sets up effective entry barriers to foreign firms and distorts present foreign investment flows.

This chapter studies the effect of potential future measures on current foreign investment flows, through case studies of Chilean investment in other Latin American countries. Multinationals are at least as important in the Chilean economy as they are in countries with an extensive foreign investment record. The degree of internationalization of the Chilean economy was estimated at approximately 11 per cent of private-sector GDP in 1998, a high percentage even by the standards of other countries with a tradition of investing abroad.

Chilean investment abroad has grown significantly since 1990. During the period 1990–98, detected FDI by Chilean firms amounted to approximately US$ 23.7 billion, with an additional US$ 17.6 billion corresponding to capital injections made by local investors or by firms from third countries associated with these investment projects.[1]

The forces driving these investment flows seem to stem from the know-how acquired by Chilean firms in successfully undertaking activities of a similar type and scope in Chile over the last two decades. As these firms have a proven record of overcoming management problems in a similar environment, they tend to be singled out by authorities or firms in other Latin American countries when awarding contracts or concessions or setting up joint ventures. Moreover, the favorable rating given to Chile's firms and banks on international financial markets in the early 1990s, enabled them to obtain financing on more favorable terms than their counterparts in other developing countries.

This expansion of Chilean investment abroad is occurring at a time when most Latin American countries have liberalized their policies towards FDI. However, despite strong government support in host countries, these investments are subject to risk stemming from the fact that FDI may be discriminated against in the future.

This chapter addresses the effects of risk and uncertainty on FDI, focusing on the Chilean case. We identify a set of situations that represent potential protectionist threats, and show how they have eventually become barriers that increase the cost of foreign investment, restrict and obstruct its development and may even eliminate it on occasion. We also compare the approaches and procedures of different companies that have invested abroad; different perceptions of future risk lead to differences in behavior in their host countries. We discuss how this risk is increased by the sensitive nationalist issues that historically divide bordering countries, and also by regulatory shortcomings governing capital flows in certain countries. Finally, we attempt to identify the consequences for foreign investment that arise when countries arbitrarily interpret the treaties and contracts regulating multinational companies.

The rest of this chapter is organized as follows. Section 2 gives an overview of Chilean FDI, and Section 3 presents a standard and widely accepted theoretical framework for analyzing the behavior of multinationals. Section 4 makes a detailed analysis of a set of cases where the potential threat of future protectionism has actually affected transnational firms' behavior. These cases relate specifically to Chilean investments in four other Latin American countries, but the conclusions drawn in Section 5, on how protectionist threats become real barriers to foreign investment, can be extended to investment undertaken by any country.

2   Characteristics of Chilean investment abroad[2]

Chilean multinationals invest directly by acquiring a majority interest in the equity of a local firm, or by setting up a subsidiary in another country. These multinationals belong mainly to the services sector, so the focus of their interest is on horizontal investment, i.e. producing the same goods or services in the host country as they produce in Chile, rather than vertical investments where the firm breaks up the different stages of the productive process geographically.[3] In this context, Chilean investment patterns are consistent with those seen among multinationals in developed countries, for a considerable part of FDI by these countries is also horizontal. As evidence, note that only 13 per cent of the production of North American multinationals is exported back to the United States (Brainard 1993).

Chilean investment abroad grew significantly in the period 1990–98, reaching US$ 23.7 billion by the end of that period. New investment in 1991 amounted to US$ 300 million, while investment accumulated in 1987–91 came to slightly less than US$ 1.2 billion. The amounts invested in each of the ensuing years are shown in Table 9. 1.

Table 9.1   Chilean investment abroad, 1991–98

Year	Amount invested (US$ billion)
1991	0.3
1992	1.1
1993	1.6
1994	2.0
1995	1.2
1996	6.5
1997	7.0
1998	3.5

Source: See notes 1 and 2.

The trend is clearly rising, except for 1995 (when investment fell back by 40 per cent in relation to 1994) and 1998 (55 per cent down from the 1997 figure).

The total value of projects in which Chilean firms are currently participating amounts to US$ 41.4 billion, including capital contributions made by local and other foreign firms in partnership with Chilean ones. More than 200 Chilean companies have invested in over 1,100 projects abroad, generally involving amounts smaller than US$ 100 million.

Much of Chilean FDI is concentrated in neighboring countries, and this also replicates patterns seen in other parts of the world, where Japan is the main foreign investor in Asia, other European countries are the main investors in Europe, and the United States is the main investor in Latin America.[4] About 80 per cent of Chilean investment has been channeled towards four neighboring countries (see Table 9.2).

Although Chilean investment in Bolivia only amounts to US$ 400 million, it accounts for a major share of that country's inward foreign investment, making Chile one of the largest investors in Bolivia.

Chilean investment in these five countries is concentrated in services, and within this sector, the area that most attracts investors is electricity generation and distribution. In 1998, just 23 per cent of total FDI was assigned to the industrial sector, while services took 77 per cent, as follows: energy, 60 per cent; banking and finance, 5.5 per cent; other services (mainly commerce), 11.5 per cent.

Most Chilean multinationals are medium-sized firms with total annual sales of between US$ 75 million and US$ 150 million. This is not surprising: companies invoicing US$ 50 million or less are unlikely to become multinationals, but once a company has reached a certain size, total sales cease to be a determining factor in the internationalization of firms. Companies that invoice US$ 100 million, US$ 1 billion or US$ 5 billion are equally likely to be transnational (Markusen 1995).

Table 9.2   Chilean FDI in neighboring countries

Country	% of total Chilean FDI	Value (US$ billion)
Argentina	38.3	9.1
Colombia	18.6	4.4
Brazil	11.7	2.8
Peru	10.8	2.6

Source: See notes 1 and 2.

3   The OLI framework[5]

3.1   Understanding OLI

What leads companies to invest abroad? If foreign firms were identical to their local counterparts, entering foreign markets would not be profitable, since investing abroad involves different and higher costs, including those associated to communications, transport, cultural differences and lack of local contacts. Thus, as Dunning (1977, 1981) proposed in his well-known OLI[6] framework, multinationals must have countervailing advantages in order to set up business abroad. Dunning suggests that the comparative advantages for a multinational firm are based in three areas: ownership (O), localization (L) and internalization (I).

Ownership advantages may arise from proprietary patents, formulas or secret productive processes, famous brand names or the commercial prestige of the firm. The advantages of localization are associated with the existence of tariffs, transport costs or cheaper inputs in the foreign location, which make direct investment more profitable than exporting. Finally, internalization advantages are associated with the exploitation of comparative advantages that are internal to the firm, instead of participating in looser associations over which the firm does not have full or sufficient control.

In recent theoretical models the main determinant of FDI is the last of these three characteristics: the need to internalize a relationship with a foreign firm. The public-goods nature of the information being handled, together with its complexity and large volume, probably explains the need to internalize. If, instead of internationalization, the company establishes an association with a foreign partner, it has to face all the problems implied in the exchange of information between agents. The most common of these include the following: (i) in order to enable the counterparty to decide whether or not to participate in an agreement, it must be provided with information prior to signing; this is a complex high-stakes transaction where valuable strategic information is handed over before an agreement is reached; (ii) the associate firm in the host country has incentives to restrict information, by minimizing profit projections, for example, so as to avoid rents being extracted; (iii) the parent company can neither control nor adequately evaluate the economic benefits derived from the use of the information it has provided; (iv) moral-hazard problems may lead the associate firm to develop new relationships with rivals and reduce its sales effort in favor of these new associations; (v) the need to prevent the partner from using acquired knowledge to compete in future investments, because a firm that transfers its know-how is nurturing its own competitors; and finally, (vi) there are aspects that cannot be transferred to other firms, even though both parties may wish to do so, such as organizational culture.

If the information flows exchanged were small and simple, contracts could probably be devised to cover most possible contingencies. However, when information flows are large and decision-making is complex, the parent company needs to control its subsidiaries if it wants them to comply with its directives.

Even if the foreign investor is able to deal adequately with the issues mentioned above, the firm in the host country also faces serious problems in handling the association. It cannot control the research and development effort of its foreign partner nor determine whether it alone is providing the available information, for it is in the foreign company's interest to limit the transfer of know-how. Given these limitations, the junior partner may try to break the association as soon as possible and acquire a dominant role. Thus, a major obstacle in trying to set up an association relates to the *ex post* incentives to break away.

On the other hand, the reasons that lead a firm to seek internalization relate to fact that a central firm is more efficient in coordinating the work of a series of plants than if each plant acquired the necessary inputs and factors independently. For instance, the parent company provides all foreign subsidiaries with not only the results of its research and development, but also its management, publicity, marketing and know-how. Practically all the reasons that can be adduced to explain direct foreign investment arise from the possibility of transferring the capital embodied in accumulated knowledge and other inputs to several plants simultaneously. A parent company is needed in order to provide inputs and factors to its subsidiaries regardless of the location of the productive process.

3.2 Applying the OLI framework

OLI analysis enables us to understand what leads Chilean firms to invest abroad. Location advantages are obvious: a large percentage of their investments have been made in the service sector, where the provision of the product must be done on site, and exporting is not a viable alternative. Chilean multinationals possess no proprietary brand names, patents or formulas that would provide an advantage to subsidiaries, so the other advantages must stem from internalization.

Studies of developed country multinationals have noted that internalization advantages tend to be most significant in the following situations: (i) the industry has high levels of research and development expenditure in relation to sales, (ii) production includes recently developed and technically complex goods, (iii) the work force includes a high proportion of technicians and professionals, (iv) there is a high degree of product differentiation, and (v) large amounts are invested in publicity.

To some extent, these features do apply to Chilean multinationals. Between the mid-1970s and the mid-1980s, these firms achieved a huge turnaround in productivity and efficiency. This feat required changing, developing and improving management and production structures in order to turn firms with a track-record of losses into efficient and profitable organizations. Converting backward state-owned monopolies into efficient and profitable companies took years of trial and error before successful processes were identified and developed. As a result, these firms possess a large stock of accumulated knowledge that can potentially be transferred to several plants simultaneously. On the other hand, competitors that have not gone through similar changes have to start from scratch, and may need to experiment for years before understanding what needs to be changed and how to proceed in these situations.

Until recently these advantages did not have much importance beyond Chile's borders. However, since the early 1990s, many Latin American countries have decided to establish efficient service sectors and have implemented policies that would have been unthinkable a few years ago: namely, allowing transnational corporations to enter sectors such as telecommunications, electricity and transport, as well as the financial sector including insurance and pensions.

Chilean firms possess experience and know-how in restructuring, modernizing and in enhancing factor productivity in obsolete state-owned enterprises. They also have the experience and knowledge to move into monopoly markets which are not consumer-oriented and increase quality, variety and product supply, leading to improved profitability. Thirdly, they have developed strategies for dealing with and negotiating with workers with lengthy union tradition. Finally, they have a broad knowledge and understanding of the political, social and economic climate of the countries in which they invest.

4 Foreign investment and protectionism

Explicit restrictions on foreign investment in Latin America are few (Deloitte Touche Tohmatsu International 1996),[7] yet most countries resort to one or more of the following to greater or lesser extent: (i) restrictions on the entry of foreign firms or on their activities; and (ii) denial of even-handed treatment compared to national investors, by providing subsidies for national producers, and through the use of regulations and restrictions affecting the subsidiaries of foreign companies. Typically these might include the following: (i) higher reserve requirements for foreign banks; (ii) restrictions on product types in banking, insurance and other activities; (iii) limits on the geographical distribution of certain investments; (iv) a bias in government procurement in favor of national firms; (v) more demanding tax treatment than what national firms are subject to (so-called national treatment); (vi) restrictions on the nationality or residency of directors, managers and employees of foreign investor companies; (vii) upper limits on the percentages of local firms that can be owned by foreign investors; and (viii) other informal restrictions.[8]

The case studies described later in this chapter all relate to the services sector, which accounts for a major share of Chilean investment abroad. Investment in this sector requires special attention, firstly because many service activities have traditionally been provided under monopoly conditions, so the question arises as to the degree of intervention that the government should or should not exert. In the second place, services have traditionally had negative connotations for external accounts, as they were seen as net imports negatively affecting the balance of payments.

For these reasons, in the past, investment in the services sector was subject to many restrictions. Nowadays, most Latin American governments understand that there are no good economic reasons justifying special barriers or protection for investments in services. Nevertheless, the liberalization of international trade in the services sector means lifting a major set of legal constraints, plus the need to develop a regulatory framework on a sector-by-sector basis. This creates a new problem, namely a trade-off between gradual liberalization and the high social costs of rushing into an unsuitable legal framework.

Once a foreign investor achieves market access, it faces the problem of integrating into the new market in an operational sense and reducing future discrimination compared to local competitors. In the services sector there is a high risk of future discrimination against investments already undertaken, as services tend to be closely regulated; not only is the service provider regulated, but so is the product and its distribution.

The degree of regulation in services makes it easy to impose discriminatory measures *ex-post* against foreign investment in place. For example, the regulatory body for public utility monopolies may decide to fix prices or establish price bands that could lead to losses; the ground rules for future tenders may rule out participation by firms already installed and so limit their expansion plans. There also is the possibility of quality standards on services being changed, firms may have to pay commissions, and their actions may be obstructed by state regulatory agencies.

5 Case studies: multinationals and risk

Even though a large number of restrictions and controls have disappeared, multinationals continue to face a complicated network of rules. Multinationals perceive that they face unstable and high-risk conditions. Given that multinationals risk not only their revenue flows, but also their capital, their sensitivity to risks associated with future income flows is likely to be extremely high. This is the greatest barrier facing foreign investment.

In this context, reducing risk is one of the key determinants of the behavior of transnational companies. Firms may abstain from participating in projects if the risk is perceived to be excessive, and they may pull out of projects in which they are already participating, if the risk turns out to be greater than anticipated. Firms may also raise the return they require from a project to offset the greater uncertainty, and they may make large-scale and costly administrative efforts to maintain good relations with their workers and with the social environments in which they operate. Finally, they may simply abandon an area or sector of business if they decide it is too risky. Depending on the specific country, projects face different levels of risk and uncertainty.

The rest of this section discusses case studies involving Chilean investments in four South American countries: Argentina, Bolivia, Brazil and Peru. The cases presented were carefully chosen. Firstly, press reports between 1992 and 1995 were searched for examples where risk and protectionism in the future led to changes in the operations of Chilean firms abroad. Secondly, we interviewed executives from these firms. Finally, we selected the examples that best illustrates the behavior of firms when faced with the possibility of new barriers and restrictions in their foreign ventures.

The cases selected for detailed investigation display a variety of characteristics. We consider first the electricity sector in Argentina, where it is possible to compare different approaches and procedures of foreign investors; these differences seem to be specially motivated by different perceptions of the future risk to their investments. The second case, involving the privatization of Bolivian railroads, illustrates the effects of nationalism on foreign investment, and how the associated high risk discourages investors. The third case taken from the Brazilian electrical sector, considers the effects of regulatory uncertainty. In this case, the potential investors decided to abstain from participating in the bidding for state-owned electricity companies. The importance of these auctions to the companies is revealed by the sharp fall in the companies' share price after their decision. The example from Peru, which is of a different nature, involves the financial sector. It shows the negative effects of an ambiguous interpretation of regulations and agreements. In extreme cases such as the one examined here, they can bring the flow of investment in a given sector to an end. In the following pages we review these cases.

5.1 Future risk and current management

In Argentina, local governments have warmly welcomed investment from Chile. Despite being a neighboring country, Chilean companies do not face serious obstacles when investing in Argentina. Many firms considered the mid-1990's to be the best moment for Chilean firms to invest in Argentina, in order to exploit the relative advantages their entrepreneurs had in financing their operations – an advantage that in time was bound to become less exclusive.

Notwithstanding the generally favorable climate, barriers remain. Political and social tensions directed against capital in sensitive sectors can play a very significant role. To analyze this, we consider the strategies of two electrical firms, Edesur and Central Puerto, the first with an investment of well over US$ 350 million, and Central Puerto[9] with an investment of more than US$ 150 million. Different perceptions of risk affecting their investments have led these firms to act differently, even though they operate in the same sector.

The strategy followed by Central Puerto tries to minimize risks by handling relations with the local milieu particularly carefully, whether these be labor relations, dealings with unions, with the authorities or with the community at large. The company tries to maximize probable future profit flows by minimizing the chances of social conflict, even at the cost of lowering current profitability. In contrast, Edesur does not allow political or social issues to alter their administrative approach or affect their current return.

Since it was acquired by three Chilean firms,[10] Edesur, which handles 21 per cent of electricity distribution in Argentina, has had to deal with several outbreaks of conflict. One major problem involved human resource management, where massive lay-offs provoked an immediate reaction from the unions. The need to reduce staffing was obvious given the company's low productivity, disproportionate wages relative to hours effectively worked and the poor control by supervisors. The crisis was triggered by the severity of the measures, which were adopted without consultations or reaching an agreement with local or national unions, and by the fact that they were introduced sequentially, rather than simultaneously. A further aggravating factor was the hiring of a number of Chilean technicians and engineers. Tensions mounted, with local and national unions threatening to strike and challenge the privatization of Edesur. Given that foreign ownership of electrical companies is a highly sensitive issue in Argentina, mounting public pressure could have caused general problems for future privatizations. Without the solid backing and mediation provided by the Argentine government, we believe Edesur would have been unable to overcome the crisis. This would have meant serious losses for the Chilean investors in Edesur, and the Argentine government would have faced the consequences in future privatizations.

Another serious problem at Edesur was the company's decision to eliminate losses arising from electricity that was provided but not charged, and from illegal connections (energy theft). In implementing this policy, Edesur adopted a confrontational approach. It cut supplies to a large number of consumers, including homes, business and even government offices. The policy was effective, both by putting electricity provision on a sound footing and by quickly reversing operational losses. The policy angered many people, and Edesur found itself fighting a large sector of the population. The company then found itself up against a political power barrier that it was unable to neutralize, and the impasse, which could have lasted a very long time, was only resolved after the central government repeatedly voiced strong support for Edesur.[11]

In its policies, Edesur ignored the social and political dangers that arise from: (i) being a transnational, (ii) coming from a neighboring country, and (iii) located in what many see as a vital or strategic sector. Whatever the pressures for rapid solutions, most multinationals follow a different course of action, negotiating and reaching agreements with the parties involved in an effort to avoid confrontation. This was the strategy followed by Chilgener in our next example.

This second case relates to Central Puerto, in which the Chilean electricity generator Chilgener is the major shareholder. Although Central Puerto was not free from the problems that arose in the Edesur case, the strategy for overcoming them was different. On the one hand, any public appearance that might cause a negative image was avoided, and extreme care was taken in handling staff, with special consideration for factors that in one way or another might cause discontent among the union movement.

A central feature of the strategy was that most jobs in the organization should be occupied by Argentines, with a very small number of Chileans. Argentine employees are sent for training and experience exchanges to Chile about as often as their Chilean counterparts are sent to Argentina.

Traditional sensitivities (characteristic of neighboring countries) were calmed when a former member of the Argentine Armed Forces was appointed to the post of security chief. As this is a key sector for the military, the appointment reassured the Argentine army.

When the need for downsizing became apparent, at least a minimum understanding was achieved with unions. To deal with the problem of low productivity, an agreement was reached on voluntary retirement with the opportunity to take up a redundancy compensation plan. Layoffs were programmed, informed, negotiated and carried out immediately; and after the initial adjustments, further redundancies were avoided as far as possible.

The approach followed by Edesur surely maximized current profits, while that followed by Central Puerto minimized the risk of measures being applied in the future in response to political and social tensions directed against foreign investors. Perceptions of future risk affected the behavior and profits of these foreign investors.

5.2 Social and political tensions

In Bolivia, privatization is associated with nationalism and social tension; foreign investors know and fear the risks involved. Railroads were one of the early candidates for privatization, and an international bidding process which involved over 100 foreign railroad companies. There were 15 interested companies, of which seven were selected: five North American and two Chilean firms. However, soon only the Chilean firms remained in competition since strikes and union mobilization frightened off the North American companies, which were very sensitive to social instability. Of the two Chilean firms interested in buying, Cruz Blanca and Antofagasta Holdings, the latter was ruled out as it presented more than one bid for the same network. By reaching the final stage unchallenged, Cruz Blanca ended up as the only contender for the two lines to be privatized – Oriental (1,424 km.) and Andina (2,274 km.) – and it paid a combined total of US$ 39.1 million for a 50 per cent stake.

Privatization of the Andina railroad, which connects Southern Cone countries, included neither track nor stations, as these continue to belong to the Bolivian state. Nevertheless, the US$ 13.2 million offered for the network was way below book value, and it was sold for less than what the Bolivian authorities had hoped for.

After acquiring the two companies, Cruz Blanca announced a plan to seek strategic partners. Eventually, it joined forces with Antofagasta Holdings, whereupon it sought participation in the Belgrano railroad in Argentina which belonged to Antofagasta Holdings. In the end, Cruz Blanca ended up with 76 per cent of the Oriental network, while Antofagasta Holdings kept 24 per cent. On the Andina network, Antofagasta Holdings took control of 63 per cent of the ownership, while Cruz Blanca owned the remaining 37 per cent. This association made it possible to consolidate a bi-oceanic corridor, starting in Sao Paulo, crossing Brazil and passing through Bolivia and then Argentina at Salta before finally arriving in Chile. The first steps taken by Cruz Blanca in its management of the railroad network were cautious, in keeping with Chilean investment trends in Bolivia, as the country is sensitive to Chilean presence and has a historical aversion to foreign capital. The aim was to appoint very few Chileans to management posts (three or four) and limit staff redundancies to retirement plans promoted by the Bolivian government itself.

Since Bolivian society is quite reluctant to acknowledge the benefits of foreign investment, the mere announcement of the privatization of a state oil company (IPFB), met with protests and strikes against the possibility that it would be acquired by foreign companies. Sentiments turned violent in March 1996, when mobs burnt vehicles belonging to Chilean executives of the railroad company, and stoned the offices of the Chilean airline LAN Chile, burning Chilean flags. Feelings were running high, and following the disturbances even the president of the Bolivian supreme court announced that he would petition the government to annul the Cruz Blanca franchise to prevent a further worsening of social tension.

After these violent incidents, there were several additional problems. The newspapers in La Paz identified the Bolivian Army as one of the main opponents of railroad privatization, and in some circles there was even talk of Cruz Blanca handing back the Andina network – something that never actually happened.

However, the incidents continued. In one case, the Bolivian army complained about a cut in water supply to the Chihuahua frontier post, which was a responsibility of the railroad company. It took intervention by the authorities to resolve this situation, as apparently Cruz Blanca was unaware that every fortnight the railroads sent a cistern of water to this military outpost.

It was not only the army that showed its disapproval; many other institutions and social organizations also demonstrated against the sale of the railroad network. An important business association in Santa Cruz, the second largest Bolivian department, claimed that the contract was a burden on the national economy and that the procedures had harmed Bolivian interests. They argued that other measures should have been taken to allow Bolivians to participate in the process. Another focus of nationalist sentiment was the powerful Bolivian Workers Union (Central Obrera Boliviana). According to one of their leaders, the handing of a strategic company like railroads to a Chilean firm involved sovereign risks in the event of military conflict. Arguments of this kind, as well as the attitude of the army, gave foreign investment a geopolitical dimension.

Despite these hostile reactions, the Bolivian government decided to bear the political cost of its decisions and continued to support foreign investment in the country. Thus the Sánchez de Lozada administration guaranteed the protection of Chilean investments. In meetings with the Bolivian military high command, the government stressed that in the event of foreign or domestic emergency, the railroad, like any other company regardless of ownership, would be subject to the laws and dictates of the Bolivian state.

The government in La Paz reiterated its intention to proceed with this and other privatizations. As the President of the Bolivian government stated, "It would have been very easy for me to say that we will not accept Chilean capital, and people would have applauded me...[but] we must break free from the shackles of 19th century when we are about to enter the 21st."

The Bolivian government's backing for Chilean investments can be seen in the fact that it approved a rise in train fares once the management of the railroad company had been taken over by Cruz Blanca. This aroused sensitivities, and the president of the Chamber of Exporters (Gamex) threatened to call for a review of the sale to Cruz Blanca. The Bolivian government had to intervene, and the Under-secretary for Transport announced that the state would compensate Cruz Blanca for the next seven years to prevent fare hikes on certain sections of the network.

5.3 Inadequate regulatory frameworks

Some of the most relevant forms of protectionism against foreign investment involve restrictions on the firm's activities, or the imposition of excessive tax burdens, as these measures are analogous to regulatory takings. Foreign investment statutes that are clear and subject to few amendments help to reduce uncertainties. The cases concerning Brazil relate to uncertainty caused by the fact that the laws to regulate the privatized sectors had not yet been approved. The authorities called for tenders on the basis of provisional legislation, requiring franchisees to accept unspecified future permanent regulations whenever these might be enacted.

In 1995, the Brazilian government set out to privatize 14 petrochemical industries and two electrical companies, with others to be handed over in concession. The intention was to privatize all state-owned firms except (initially) telecommunications, and the process was seen as part of a broader liberalization of economic activity. To this end, Congress first had to approve the abolition of Constitutional restrictions on foreign investment in sectors like infrastructure, communications, mining, energy, transport, gas and petroleum. In addition, the program included privatizing provincial banks and allowing the entry of foreign capital.

The privatization of Escelsa, a franchise company involved in the generation, transmission and distribution of electrical energy, controlled (with 72.34 per cent of the shares) by the state-owned Electrobrás, as well as the auctioning of Eléctrica Light of Río de Janeiro, raised a series of questions regarding the risks facing foreign investment in Brazil. Notwithstanding Brazil's interest in foreign firms participating in the privatization process, its inadequate regulatory framework raised significant barriers.

The regulations in the electricity sector at the time of privatization imposed operating constraints that do nothing to help improve the efficiency of the firm. According to these regulations, any change in costs can trigger a rates review, with no certainty that the new rates will reflect the new costs. The rules are also unclear about fines for poor service quality, compensation for termination of the contract and security regarding its maintenance. Moreover, restrictions require authorizations for all expansions of the area covered by the distribution company.

In the electricity sector, an investment earns an adequate return either by improving operations, which is bound to reduce costs, or by increasing sales and gaining new customers. Investment is impeded if rates can be changed arbitrarily when costs are reduced and if permission to expand the service to neighboring areas is uncertain. It is unclear whether the firm can keep even a fraction of the profits generated by improved efficiency, or whether it will face restrictions that arbitrarily limit its initiatives.

The Brazilian authorities acknowledged that regulations in the electricity sector were weak and inadequate, and are drawing up a new and improved framework. However, they refused to give companies a choice between operating under the new electricity law, once decreed, or continuing under the existing contract. This means that when the concession is awarded the franchise-holder must not only abide by existing legislation – which would be the normal case – but they must also abide by future rules – which is a display of discretionary power.

The Brazilian government understands the problem arising from the opaqueness in the legal and regulatory framework. A spokesman from the Brazilian Federal Budget and Planning Ministry stated, "there can be no doubt that our aim is a rapid opening up – drastic, massive", and then immediately added that, "in the electrical sector there is some complexity in the franchise regulations, but it is only a matter of time".

However, these were not the only problems. An 8–2 ruling by the Federal Supreme Court upheld a motion allowing full use of privatization bonds by Brazilian firms – mainly the Transcom-Amurad consortium – but not in the case of foreign firms. At that time the bonds were being quoted at 50 per cent of their par value, and the fact that Brazilian companies could use a higher percentage of these bonds in their bids (at par value) than foreign firms put the latter at a disadvantage. In the opinion of a top executive from the Chilean multinational, Enersis, this constituted open discrimination against foreign investors; Enersis and the other interested foreign companies could only use only 30 per cent of these debt instruments at par value.

In the end, Chilean firms, like many other foreign companies, decided not to participate, as the technical details were unclear and because of the possibility of future discrimination. The complexities arising from regulatory shortcomings, together with discretion in the operation of contracts, substantially raised the risks facing foreign investors.

5.4 Discretionary power and regulatory framework

When gathering information on Chilean foreign investment in the 1990s, one's attention is drawn to a case involving the Central Banks of Chile and Peru. The case also involved a Peruvian finance house and three banks with offices in Chile (a Chilean bank and two Chilean subsidiaries of foreign banks). The three banks made loans from Chile to Peru, and claimed protection under the auspices of a trade convention (the Latin American Integration Association, LAIA) which in the end was overruled. The results led the Central Bank of Chile to rethink a policy that it had been nurturing for some time: namely, to turn Chile into a Latin American financial center.

The Peruvian finance house Financiera Nacional owed US$ 32.3 million to the three Chilean banks through debts contracted between 1992 and 1993: US$ 1.9 million to the Chilean subsidiary of the North American Chemical Bank, US$ 14.6 million to the Chilean subsidiary of the Dutch ING Bank and US$ 15.8 million to the Chilean Banco O'Higgins. These loans were granted under the assumption that they were covered by the LAIA convention, which implied a dual guarantee from the Central Banks of both Chile and Peru. During the first half of 1993, Financiera Nacional of Peru ceased payments and defaulted on the US$ 32.3 million lent by the three Chilean banks.

However, the Central Bank guarantees did not come into effect because although the Financiera Nacional had made use of the money, in March 1993 the Central Banks claimed that the operations involved did not comply with the rules and procedures of the LAIA Convention on Reciprocal Payments and Loans. They further argued that they could not be considered foreign trade operations, since they involved pre-shipment rather than post-shipment financing and hence were credits granted prior to the export of goods. This meant the operation was not covered by LAIA.

The Chilean banks argued that in no part of the convention, and still less in the corresponding regulations, was it established that pre-shipment credits were not covered by LAIA. In their view the rationale that applied in this case was straightforward: "no one can be fined for disregarding a red light on a corner where there are no traffic lights".

The banks also argued that as the loans were approved by the two Central Banks, they should bear the full responsibility. They cited Article 2 of the LAIA convention which states that within the framework of the system, payments can be made for direct operations of any kind between member countries. The convention did not require the operation to be carried out after shipment for payment to be approved.

The Central Bank of Chile claimed that over US$ 20 million corresponded to discounts on promissory notes made by the three banks, and perhaps through negligence, they did not clearly state a specific shipment date. Accordingly, and in line with the position taken by the Central Bank of Peru, the Central Bank of Chile refused to accept responsibility for those loans within the established LAIA framework.

Under the terms of the LAIA convention, responsibility should rest with Financiera Nacional. From the standpoint of the banks providing the loans, the Central Bank guarantee is sufficient to ensure repayment of the funds. However, nowadays this argument seems unacceptable, since most of the trade operations that gave rise to the loans took place.

The Chilean banks argued that the Central Banks were trying to shirk their responsibilities, having arbitrarily decided that the operations were not covered under the LAIA convention so that they would not have to pay. A similar example involves a credit from ING Bank for US$ 2.8 million granted to a Peruvian firm, for the export of mango from Peru to Ecuador. Investigations showed that this operation did not take place, and the Central Banks failed to provide the corresponding information to ING Bank.

In Chile, investigations have not led to the possibility of legal action, but in Peru litigation is under way against the Financiera Nacional executives. In both countries, insiders have expressed surprise at the volume of loans provided to such a small finance house. The Chilean banks' explanation was that they were protected under the LAIA convention; in fact, the word LAIA even appears on the covers of the document folders, and for that reason the operation ought to have been guaranteed. The Peruvian finance house has been semi-intervened to prevent it from falling into insolvency.

In Chile, it has been suggested that responsibility should rest with the Central Bank of Peru, because it channeled the operations, granted the approval, and failed to raise the alarm, despite having been aware of the problem for several months. Although it is accepted that these operations did not meet all the requirements to be included under the LAIA framework, the Central Bank of Peru approved the loans, yet now advises that it does not qualify for protection on the grounds that it was a pre-shipment loan.

In Peru, on the other hand, the authorities do not understand how the Banco O'Higgins could have paid US$ 7 million into Financiera's account in New York, where the money turned up in an account associated with real estate projects and not with foreign trade. The operation was supposed to have financed the export of building materials from Chile to Peru. It was not reported to the Financiera board of directors. The Peruvian authorities do not see how they can be held responsible for financial transfers outside their jurisdiction.

After an investigation, the Central Bank of Peru concluded that the operations were fraudulent, claiming that: "the loans not only were in breach of the LAIA framework, but had probably been planned deliberately by executives of the Chilean Banks and Financiera Nacional in order to breach the framework".

The recommendation that emerges from this dispute is that banks should be very cautious when operating under the LAIA convention. It is the convention itself that stands to suffer most from this incident. If

Central Banks do not assume responsibility for the entities they supervise, nor verify their operations, the convention loses its value. At that time, LAIA covered promissory notes for around US$ 220 million from Chilean banks and US$ 37 million from those in Peru.

6 Conclusions

At present there are few restrictions on foreign direct investment in Latin America. However, investment risk involves the possibility of future regulatory changes that could harm investments. The regulations enable discriminatory measures to be taken *ex-post* against foreign investment that is already established in the country. For example, prices may be set below cost, or the ground-rules of future bidding processes might exclude participation by multinationals with local presence and so restrict their expansion plans. There is also the possibility that new standards or demands are imposed by state regulatory agencies.

This chapter has illustrated the above through case-studies involving Chilean firms. Chilean firms mobilize important resources through its foreign subsidiaries, and indicators put the degree of internationalization of the Chilean economy on the order of 10 per cent of private GDP. The advantages of Chilean firms are concentrated in know-how, i.e. a stock of knowledge on how to restructure outdated state-owned enterprises and improve the quality, variety and provision of its services. Until a few years ago these advantages did not have much importance beyond Chile's borders. Many Latin American countries have decided to develop an efficient services sector, causing Chilean investment to flow to neighboring countries.

This study provides evidence to support the idea that an adequate regulatory framework in the host country plays a fundamental role in the decision to invest abroad. This is illustrated by the decision of Chilean firms not to enter the Brazilian electricity sector, because the law regulating the sector had not been approved, and the concession would be governed by provisional statutes committing successful bidders to accept the future regulations. The problem is that future regulations are unknown in the present, so the regulatory framework is subject to regulatory discretion.

In general, a high percentage of foreign investments takes place in neighboring countries, so it tends to arouse sensitivities and provoke nationalistic sentiments. Nationalism and the associated political and social tensions directed against foreign investors may force the closure, cession or sale of the foreign investment. This chapter discussed the outbreak of violence in the case of railroad privatization in Bolivia. There was a possibility of revoking the concession awarded to Chilean multinationals, and the Chilean firms also considered abandoning the project. The support provided by the Bolivian government to the investors proved to be the key to resolving the dispute.

When a solid regulatory framework is in place, investment protection schemes and bilateral and multilateral agreements help to reduce the perception of risk. However, regulations lose their purpose if firms doubt whether the protection schemes will be effective. This was illustrated by the case of loans granted by Chilean banks to Peruvian exporters, with the approval of the Central Banks in both countries. The Chilean banks operated (or claimed they did) under the assumption that they were protected by a convention (LAIA). The Central Banks of both countries declared the convention inapplicable in this particular instance, thus making the commercial banks absorb the losses. This led to a decrease in credit flows mobilized under the auspices of the convention, and set back a proposal to turn Chile into a financial center for the whole region.

The behavior of foreign investors may also be influenced by political and social tensions. When these forces are aimed against capital in highly sensitive sectors, they may force the host government to take measures against the foreign investors. The awareness of this risk conditions both the decision to invest and the way in which investments proceed. This is illustrated by the different approaches of two Chilean companies investing in the electric sector in Argentina. One group (most of Chilean foreign investors) handles its relations with the local community with special care – whether these be labor relations, or dealing with unions, authorities or the community in general. The underlying goal, even at the cost of lower current profits, is to maximize expected future returns. To this end, these companies take care to avoid social conflict. The second group of firms ignores these considerations and refuses to let political or social issues change their management approach; the investors ignore the impact of their project on local sensitivities and concentrate on achieving adequate results within a reasonable period of time. The huge fines imposed on Edesur for leaving consumers without electricity seem to indicate that the future costs of the second strategy can be large.

This chapter has analyzed a number of case-studies of the effects of uncertainty on foreign investment in Latin American countries. The cases selected involve sectors and projects that are important both for the recipient countries and for the investors, and we believe they show that present uncertainty about future conditions acts as a barrier to foreign investment. Clearly there are numerous elements of protectionism which, in one way or another, hinder the activities of multinational firms and thus discourage foreign investment from taking place.

Notes

1   The figures on detected investment are collected by the Chilean Foreign Investment Committee, the agency in charge of monitoring foreign investment. Data is obtained from financial statements or reports filed by firms that generate or benefit from investment projects. Investments with maturities longer than one year are assigned to the period in which they are detected, so the figures for investments detected do not necessarily correspond to actual capital disbursements. This explains discrepancies with the investment figures recorded by the Central Bank of Chile, based solely on investment reported under Chapter XII of the Compendium of International Exchange Rules.

2   Figures on Chilean foreign investment come from *La Inversión de Capitales Chilenos en el Mundo ("Chilean Capital Investment throughout the World"), Foreign Investment Committee, Chile 1998.*

3   The shipment of electronic equipment parts for assembly in Mexico, for subsequent re-export to the USA, is a typical example of vertical foreign investment, whereas producing American cars in Mexico for sale there is an example of horizontal foreign investment.

4   FDI flows are also larger between countries having similar relative factor endowments and similar per-capita income levels. Thus, per cent of the investment coming from developed countries is carried out in other developed countries; in fact the G-5 group of countries absorb 70 per cent of all foreign investment generated by those nations (matching investment). In the Chilean case also, most of the investment goes to countries with similar income levels and factor endowments.

5   Much of the discussion in this section draws on Markusen (1995).

6   Where O stands for ownership, L for localization and I for internalization

7   This only refers to barriers affecting FDI. Barriers to trade in goods and services also have an effect on investment flows: on the one hand, they raise the advantages of location and cause substitution towards foreign direct investment; but this is more than offset by the lower levels of trade and investment associated with countries that impose trade restrictions (Balasubramanyam, Salisu and Sapsford 1996).

8   The sectors most affected by these conditions include basic services, insurance, banking and retail trade, which coincides with behavior observed elsewhere (Duncan and Sauvant 1994). The main restrictions on foreign companies compared to national firms are detailed below. In the first place, there are absolute entry barriers to local (national) air and sea transport services. Secondly, a limited number vacancies are available to firms operating international air and sea transport services. There are also additional or

alternative restrictions such as a percentage of coastal shipping reserved for national ships, or access only to a percentage of the total cost in foreign currency. Finally, there are also limited places for foreign firms operating services in the financial and insurance sector.

9 Both Edesur and Central Puerto are among the earliest Argentine privatizations.

10 Chilectra, Enersis and Endesa.

11 This behavior would come back to haunt EDESUR in 1999, when an electric distribution plant failed, leaving more than one hundred and fifty thousand consumers without access to electricity for a long period. The penalty of US$90MM depressed the earnings of the Chilean owners.

References

Balasubramanyam, V., M. Salisu, and D. Sapsford (1996). "Foreign Direct Investment and SI countries", *The Economic Journal*. 106, 92–105.

Brainard, S. Lael (1993). "A simple theory of multinational corporations and trade with a trade-off between proximity and concentration", *NBER Working Paper*, No. 4269.

Deloitte Touche Tohmatsu International (1996). "Normas sobre Inversión Extranjera en Argentina, Brasil, Colombia, México, Perú y Venezuela", Mimeo, Preliminary report.

Duncan, R. and K. Sauvant (1994). *Liberalizing International Transactions in Services: A Handbook*. United Nations Publications.

Dunning, J. (1977). "Trade, location of economic activity and MNE: A search for an eclectic approach", in B. Ohlin, P. Hesselborn and P. Wijkman (eds), *The International Allocation of Economic Activity*, London: Macmillan. 395–418.

Dunning, J. (1981). *International Production and the International Enterprise*. George Allen & Unwin.

Markusen, J. (1995). "The boundaries of multinational enterprises and the theory of international trade", *Journal of Economic Perspectives*, 9 (2).

Index